International Trade and Labor Standards

International Trade and Labor Standards

A PROPOSAL FOR LINKAGE

Christian Barry and Sanjay G. Reddy

Columbia University Press New York

Columbia University Press
Publishers Since 1893
New York   Chichester, West Sussex
Copyright © 2008 Columbia University Press
All rights reserved

Library of Congress Cataloging-in-Publication Data
Barry, Christian.
International trade and labor standards : a proposal for linkage /
Christian Barry and Sanjay G. Reddy.
p.   cm.
Includes bibliographical references and index.
ISBN 978-0-231-14048-5 (cloth : alk. paper)
ISBN 978-0-231-51296-1 (e-book)
1. International trade. 2. Labor laws and legislation, International.
3. Labor—Standards.   I. Reddy, Sanjay. II. Title.

HF1379.B375   2008
331.202′18—dc22   2007053051

This book is printed on paper with recycled content.
Designed by Audrey Smith

Printed in the United States of America
c 10 9 8 7 6 5 4 3 2 1

CONTENTS

TABLES

This book is a contribution to the fervent current debate about whether the evolving global economic order is ethically defensible and whether it can be improved. This debate is often framed in terms of whether we need more or less "globalization," which is understood as the expansion of international trade in goods, capital, ideas, and (to a much lesser extent) people within a private property–entrenching market-oriented framework. Some participants in this debate have argued that globalization may have "gone too far," while others have maintained that "the failure of our world is not that there is too much globalization, but that there is too little."[1] However, conceiving of the task of evaluating ethically the global economic order in such terms is deeply misleading. It assumes that globalization (or a global economic order that "deglobalizes" economic relations, for that matter) can only take *one* form and that we must therefore choose either to be in favor of or against "it." In fact, a globalizing economy can take many forms, some of which will be more likely to secure valuable opportunities for the mass of the world's people than others. Our aim in this book is to develop and defend one family of proposals for the reform of the emerging global economic order that would enable and encourage countries to adopt policies that would benefit the mass of their people, and particularly their less advantaged members, without causing undue harm to others. In doing so, we hope both to illuminate the problem we address and to offer an example of a method that can be applied to other such problems.

Rational argument about whether the present global economic order is ethically defensible and whether it can be improved can be of three primary kinds. It can concern the ends—the goals, values, and ideals—that global institutional arrangements ought to embody or be designed to achieve. It can be about the specific institutional arrangements that would best realize these ends under present circumstances. Finally, it can relate to the allocation of prerogatives and responsibilities to bring about and sustain the institutional arrangements that would best realize these ends under present circumstances.

We do not take on the tasks of evaluating *all* of the institutional arrangements that compose the global economic order, of defending a comprehensive theory of the ends that global institutional arrangements should embody or be designed to achieve, or of providing a detailed recipe for their reform along with an account of the allocation of prerogatives and responsibilities to reform them. Any book setting for itself such an ambitious set of tasks would be very unlikely to perform any of them adequately, let alone well. Instead, we attempt to address in detail one public policy issue: the governance of international trade, specifically, the concern over whether rights to engage in international trade should in any way be made conditional on the promotion of labor standards. This issue—commonly referred to as the debate over whether there ought to be "linkage" between trade and labor standards—has been the focus of much heated debate among activists, politicians, scholars, and policy-makers in recent years, and it has been especially heated since the advent of the World Trade Organization (WTO) in 1995. Indeed, fundamental disagreement about linkage is widely thought to have been a major contributing factor to the breakdown of the WTO talks in Seattle in the fall of 1999, and it has since been a continuing source of tension in multilateral and bilateral trade talks outside the auspices of the WTO.

We argue that some rights to engage in international trade should indeed be made conditional on efforts to promote *basic* labor standards—specified levels of attainment of wages and working conditions that are deemed minimally adequate in each country—provided that the system of rules for international trade implementing such linkage meets appropriate requirements. We argue that the system of linkage must be unimposed, transparent, and rule-based, applied in a manner that reflects a country's level of development, that it must involve adequate international burden-sharing, and that it must incorporate measures ensuring that appropriate account is taken of different viewpoints within each country. We argue that such a linkage system can substantially reduce the costs incurred by exporting countries that attempt to promote the interests of workers and that by enabling and encouraging countries to promote labor standards, an appropriate form of linkage can serve as a cornerstone of a worker-oriented world trading system while showing adequate respect for national sovereignty.

Both those arguing for and against making some rights to trade conditional upon promoting basic labor standards seem to share the view that one very important end that global institutional arrangements should be designed to achieve is the broadening of opportunities of less advantaged persons throughout the world. We argue that linkage of an appropriate form should be adopted because it can powerfully aid the interests of less advantaged persons in poorer countries by creating incentives for governments to implement policies that further their interests without imposing unreasonable burdens. We try in addition to indicate how responsibility for bringing about and maintaining such a system of linkage might plausibly be allocated both across and within countries.

If successful, our arguments are of more than academic interest: our proposal would offer a means of potentially moving beyond the existing conceptual and political deadlock concerning a matter that will partly determine the working conditions and living standards of persons throughout the world. Still, its aims are also limited. Our proposal for linkage between trade and labor standards is only one of many possible means of increasing the extent to which the global economic order can better serve the interests of the mass of the world's people. There are other competing priorities for action for those who share this aim, the choice among which ought to depend upon the probable long-term effects of pursuing them. We do not therefore claim that bringing about the reforms defended here should take precedence over other concerns. We do hope to show, however, that the possible benefits of these reforms are sufficient to warrant further intellectual and practical exploration—explorations that have been unduly foreclosed in the recent world debate.

Although we focus on the particular issue of trade and labor standards, we hope that our approach to addressing it can serve as an instance of how to make headway in the larger ethical and practical debate about the evolving global economic order. The approach that we adopt is *interdisciplinary*, *practical*, and *realistically utopian*.

It is *interdisciplinary*, drawing on philosophy for moral orientation; development studies, microeconomic theory, labor economics, and international trade economics for a theoretical and empirical understanding of the relation between labor standards and trade; the social and political sciences more generally for insight considering the feasibility of establishing such a system and sustaining it over time; and on legal theory to identify institutional forms for linkage that are compatible with existing norms and practices.

Since ours is fundamentally a work of public policy analysis, however, we go only as far as is necessary into questions particular to specific domains—economic theory, theories of how the global economic order should be ethically assessed, or the available evidence on the possible effects of alternative institutional arrangements—to develop and sustain the arguments presented in defense of our reform proposal. In some cases, however, this has required that we go rather deeply into questions particular to these fields. We believe that our argument contributes to a better understanding of the practical applicability and theoretical limits of certain economic arguments (which have often been misapplied in the recent literature on international institutions and in particular on linkage) and to the clarification and partial resolution of thorny philosophical questions (which have often been sidestepped in the recent literature on international justice).

The heterogeneity of our arguments and sources makes this book rather unlike most works focusing on public policy, but we do not consider this an embarrassment. Indeed, we believe that public policy analysis, correctly done, requires drawing upon different ways of interpreting the world and their respective insights and that the integration of disciplines such as philosophy and economics can lead to the practical and theoretical enrichment of each and to the overcoming of the impoverished empirical and theoretical conceptions that often handicap them individually. This principle is applicable to all public policy analysis, and our present effort is only a single illustration of it.

Our approach is *practical* in two senses. First, it focuses on concrete questions of institutional design. We begin with the present circumstances, in which rights to trade are not made in any significant way conditional upon the promotion of basic labor standards, and we examine whether imaginable proposals for changing these arrangements would be desirable and feasible to bring about and maintain—drawing upon all of the social-scientific and normative arguments relevant to apply, irrespective of their disciplinary origin. Second, our approach to justification is practical. We address our arguments to those who disagree with us, and begin our arguments from premises that we believe we share with those who disagree with us. In particular, we identify a shared premise through an inductive survey of the arguments that have been made: that a very important factor in determining whether one institutional arrangement for the governance of the global economy should be viewed as superior to another is whether it enhances the opportunities of less advantaged persons in the world to a greater extent. Our inductive approach is appropriate given our main aim, which is to develop and defend a practical proposal for global institutional reform that can be widely accepted. We do not set out to present a comprehensive account of desirable arrangements but rather to present a compelling argument for one particular kind of institutional reform.

Our approach is *realistically utopian*, in John Rawls' sense. It "extends what are ordinarily thought to be the limits of practical political possibility."[2] It is utopian in that we do not argue that our proposed reform could be adopted or implemented easily under current political conditions. Indeed, it may well turn out that a proposal of the kind defended in this book will be infeasible (for example, because certain influential agents remain implacably opposed to it—perhaps for no other reason than that it would somewhat erode the privileges they enjoy at present). It is realistic, however, in that we identify conditions under which our proposed reform could be brought about through the actions of existing agents, and we attempt not to make obviously unreasonable assumptions about these agents or the context in which they interact.

As with many other debates about the global economic order, the debate on linkage, due to a lack of institutional imagination, has been overly narrow. Our method is to be attentive to constraints of feasibility but imaginative in identifying what is feasible. In this way, we hope to free the intellect and the practical imagination, changing the form of the debate and opening the door of shared possibility.

ACKNOWLEDGMENTS

This book has been in the making for a long time. It began with a meeting that seemed to be the product of chance a little more than seven years ago. Our first discussion on the topic of the role of labor standards concerns in the international trading system came soon after our first meeting. We began this project in earnest, in the form of weekly discussions on related issues, within months, and we have worked on it since then, independently or together, in places as different as Bangalore, Brasilia, Cambridge (Massachusetts), Dublin, Geneva, Montauk, London, Oslo, Princeton, and São Paulo, although the bulk of our work was undertaken together in New York. We have each learned how much more we could achieve through collaboration than we could independently. Each of us complemented and corrected the thoughts of the other, and over time, our ways of thinking have become similar in many respects. Our collaboration is one between disciplines and across nationalities and perspectives, but it is also between like minds and has been intellectually and personally enriching. The majority of the sentences in the book have been written and rewritten by both of us and it is often difficult to identify who is responsible for them.

This project could not have been completed without the support, contributions, and involvement of many others, whom we would like gratefully to acknowledge, without implicating them in any way in the imperfections of our work. We are very grateful to Tanweer Akram, Kyle Bagwell, Allen Buchanan, Steve Charnovitz, Stephen Gardiner, Andrew Glyn, Robert Hockett, Raghbendra Jha, Kamal Malhotra, Thomas Pogge, Michael Pollak, Kate Raworth, Robert Staiger, Leif Wenar, and three anonymous reviewers for Columbia University Press for their (in some cases quite extensive) written comments. Many others offered invaluable suggestions, criticism, encouragement, or assistance. These include Paige Arthur, Jairus Banaji, Kaushik Basu, Patrick Belser, Akeel Bilgrami, Andre Burgstaller, Vivek Chibber, Álvaro da Vita, Kabir Dandona, Arindrajit Dube, Gerald Epstein, Raghav Gaiha, Dario Gil, Carol Gould, David Grewal, Julia Harrington, Rolph van der Hoeven, Attracta Ingram, Inge Kaul, Aaron James, Arjun Jayadev, Prem Shankar Jha, Inge Kaul, Jomo K. S., Stephan Klasen, Kevin Kolben, David Kucera, Andrew Kuper, Eddy Lee, Mark Levinson, Tienmu Ma, Stephen Macedo, Daniel Markovits, Babu Mathew, Perry Mehrling, Camelia Minoiu, Gautam Mody, Tanni Mukhopadhyay, Mary O'Sullivan, Ludmila Palazzo, Robert Pollin, Jedediah Purdy, Nadia Rasheed, Francisco Rodriguez, Dani Rodrik, Joel Rosenthal, Don Ross, Rathin Roy, Sanjay Ruparelia, Ari Selman, Prakash Sethi, Peter Spiegler, Devin Stewart, Ashwini Sukthankar, Todd Tucker, Eric Verhoogen, Robert Wade, Tamar Weber, and participants at seminars or conferences of the American Philosophical Association, the American Society of International Law, the Carnegie Council for Ethics in International Affairs, Cornell University (School of Industrial and Labor Relations and Law School), Columbia University, the Green Group of the European Parliament, the International Labour Organisation, the University of Massachusetts at Amherst, Princeton University, and the World Bank.

We would like to thank Mark Levinson, in his previous capacity as chief economist of the UNITE HERE labor union, for facilitating our field research with garment manufacturers and buyers. We are also most grateful to Catherine Choi, Prabhjot Kaur, and Lydia Tomitova for their excellent research assistance. We are indebted to Matthew Peterson and Lydia Tomitova for valuable editorial assistance on various parts of this book.

We are deeply grateful to our editor at Columbia University Press, Peter Dimock, for his moral sense and intellectual encouragement and for skillfully shepherding us through the publication process. Kabir Dandona of the press also offered us good-humored and invaluable assistance at various points.

We are thankful to Barnard College of Columbia University, the Carnegie Council for Ethics in International Affairs, the Edmond J. Safra Foundation Center for Ethics at Harvard University, and the University Center for Human Values at Princeton University for providing valuable financial support for this work.

We would like to express our sincere thanks to Kyle Bagwell, Robert Goodin, Rohini Hensman, and Roberto Mangabeira Unger for their willingness to contribute thoughtful comments on the main argument of this book.

Finally, we would like to thank our respective families and friends for their extraordinary and good-natured forbearance as we have traveled this road. Due to them, it has been long but not lonely.

International Trade and Labor Standards

Introduction

Whether rights to trade ought to be made in any way conditional on the promotion of labor standards is an issue that currently engenders a great deal of heated disagreement.

This essay presents a proposal for linking trade and labor standards.[1] We develop a proposal for linking rights to participate in international trade with the promotion of basic labor standards.[2] We argue that implementing our proposal would improve working conditions and living standards in poor countries without imposing undue burdens and would therefore be *one* means of advancing valued ends, including the ends of justice.[3] We identify the arguments that have been offered (or could plausibly be offered) against linkage in order to show that, although these arguments articulate legitimate concerns, they rest on unwarranted assumptions concerning the practicability and likely effects of linkage, and the appropriate framework for it.[4]

Our argument consists of five steps. First, we identify a proposition that proponents of linkage accept—and its opponents reject—as well as an objective that both groups seek to promote. Second, we identify the arguments that can be offered against linkage thus defined. Third, we show why proposals for linkage that do not possess certain features should be rejected on the basis of these arguments. Fourth, we identify additional features of a proposal for linkage that would suffice in order for it to be immune to these arguments. This enables us to identify a class of proposals for linkage that withstand all of the previously identified objections. We argue that such proposals are superior to nonlinkage proposals in promoting the common objective of the groups on both sides of the linkage debate. Fifth, to provide a concrete starting point for discussion, we describe one such proposal.

Although we will take as our premise that gains from trade can exist, nothing in our argument relies on a specific view regarding the trade policy that maximizes these gains.[5]

CHAPTER ONE

What Is Linkage? Two Propositions

Proposals to promote labor standards can be divided into two types: those that involve linkage and those that do not. Further, all proposals to promote labor standards, whether or not they involve linkage, can be characterized according to how they answer the following two questions:

(Q1) What are the labor standards to be promoted?
(Q2) How should labor standards be promoted?

Disagreements between opponents and proponents of linkage either concern the objectives that should be promoted or the means of promoting them. Both opponents and proponents of linkage seem to affirm the following proposition:[1]

Proposition O: *A very important factor in determining whether an institutional arrangement for the governance of the global economy should be viewed as superior to another is whether it improves the level of advantage of less advantaged persons in the world to a greater extent.*

Those who affirm this proposition are committed to the view that improving the level of advantage of less advantaged persons in the world is a very important objective, which we therefore refer to henceforth as "the objective." Advantage can be understood in various ways.[2] We leave it unspecified other than presuming that for members of the labor force advantage is generally enhanced by higher employment, higher real wages, and improved working conditions. We define "labor standards" as the level of real wages and the quality of working conditions. Together with higher employment, the improvement of labor standards is an important way of increasing the level of advantage of less advantaged persons.

We understand *basic* labor standards to refer to a specified level of attainment of labor standards that is deemed *minimally adequate*. In order to fix these ideas and render this notion more concrete, the basic labor standards may be thought of in terms of the "core" labor standards promoted by the ILO. The ILO's core labor standards consist of "freedom of association and the effective recognition of the right to collective bargaining; the elimination of all forms of forced or compulsory labor; the effective abolition of child labor; and the elimination of discrimination in respect of employment and occupation."[3] Although we leave the exact content of the basic labor standards deliberately unspecified (since the argument we present below does not depend on any highly specific conception of them), we think it implausible that an account of basic labor standards would not include some reference, even if minimal, to standards of each of these kinds. We think that any plausible account of basic labor standards will also additionally make reference to a level of real wages that may be deemed minimally adequate in each context, although we do not take a position here as to what that level should be.[4]

Similarly, our argument assumes the value of the objective identified without relying on any specific interpretation of it (within some reasonable range of variation). We understand an institutional arrangement to be a set of norms or rules (whether formal or informal) that govern the interaction of the participants of a social system (e.g., countries engaged in international trade). Proponents of linkage adhere to the following proposition and opponents of linkage reject it (in relation to the organization of the international economy):

Proposition L: *It is desirable to bring about an institutional arrangement in which rights to trade are made conditional upon the promotion of labor standards, and there is reason to believe that such an arrangement can be brought about and sustained.*

Proponents of linkage must answer Q2 (at least) in a manner that reflects their adherence to proposition L.[5] Opponents of linkage must claim either that it is undesirable to bring about an institutional arrangement in which rights to trade are made conditional upon the promotion of labor standards or that the institutional arrangements of this kind that would be desirable are infeasible.

It is often presumed in discussions of linkage that linkage proponents necessarily favor the application of trade sanctions to countries that fail adequately to promote labor standards. In fact, this is in no way entailed by proposition L, since a system that *offers*[6] countries additional trading opportunities if they promote labor standards adequately—without sanctioning them when they do not—is a form of linkage as defined by proposition L.[7] Indeed, we argue below that extending additional opportunities to countries that adequately further labor standards will play an important role in a feasible and effective system of linkage.

CHAPTER TWO

Three Types of Linkage, and What Linkage Proponents Must Show

What is linkage, and what are the conditions under which it is desirable to "link" things? At least three distinct types of linkage can be relevant in designing institutional arrangements.

The first type of linkage arises as a result of the interdependence of different attainments (in health, education, security, and so on) in the process of evaluation. The assessment of an outcome may depend on the extent to which distinct objectives are each attained. When attainments of more than one kind necessarily enter jointly into the evaluative process, we may refer to this as "evaluation linkage." Evaluation linkage influences the design of institutions, since the desirability of each outcome depends on the extent of all of the attainments that define that outcome. Each institutional arrangement may give rise to different combinations of desirable and undesirable attainments. Moreover, it may sometimes be impossible to assess the desirability of specific attainments without taking due account of other attainments. The choice among different institutional arrangements must be made on the basis of the extent to which the combinations of attainments to which they give rise contribute to some "master-goal."[1]

A second type of linkage is that in which the promotion of distinct attainments is taken to be the objective of some agent.[2] For example, it might be required that a government agency discharge more than one function, such as the prevention and curing of illness or the health and educational achievements of young children. We may refer to this type of linkage, in which distinct ends are assigned to single agents, as "agency linkage."

A third type of linkage is that in which the rights of agents are made conditional on their conducting themselves in a specific way. For example, the right to receive certain social benefits may be made conditional on having paid (or on having promised to pay) taxes. We refer to this type of linkage as "rights linkage."[3]

Those who affirm proposition L and those who deny it disagree about whether there ought to be rights linkage between trade and labor standards. They need not disagree about either evaluation linkage or agency linkage as defined above. In particular, both proponents and opponents of proposition L appear to accept evaluation linkage between trade and labor standards. However, they disagree about rights linkage between these domains since they differ over whether rights to trade ought to be made conditional on adequately promoting some labor standards.

It is important to note that opponents of rights linkage (in which rights to trade are made conditional upon the promotion of labor standards) need not oppose agency linkage (in which single agents[4] are charged with the goals of promoting trade and labor standards). They may find it desirable that some agency aim both to promote trade and the observance of basic labor standards, while opposing the conferral of power to any agency to limit other agents' rights to trade on the basis of whether or not they have adequately promoted basic labor standards. On the other hand, those who affirm rights linkage must affirm some kind of agency linkage, as they must affirm that some agent(s) ought to be charged with making authoritative determinations regarding whether or not other agents have or have not adequately promoted basic labor standards and how their conduct in this area should affect their rights to participate fully in international trade.

What reasons might there be to affirm or reject evaluation, agency, or rights linkage as defined above? Reasons to affirm or reject evaluation linkage seem perhaps most obvious. Attainments of more than one kind ought necessarily to enter jointly into the evaluative process whenever each type of attainment is deemed important in evaluating outcomes. For example, health and educational achievements ought to be "evaluation linked" for social institutions, because both are important in assessing the outcomes generated by such institutions.

Whether different attainments should be agency linked depends largely on how effectively alternative assignments of aims to agents would promote the desired ends. In some contexts, charging a single agent with promoting more than one attainment may be an effective way to promote the desired attainments, whereas in other contexts they may be better promoted by a more functionally differentiated system in which distinct agents are charged with promoting distinct attainments. The judgment as to whether such functional differentiation is desirable will depend heavily on empirical considerations.

Whether rights linkage is desirable depends on considerations of two kinds. The first consideration, *effectiveness*, is empirical. Whether rights linkage is effective depends on whether two or more attainments (such as enhanced levels of trade and the attainment of basic labor standards) are achieved more or less by linking rights to participate in trade with the promotion of basic labor standards. The second consideration, *appropriateness*, concerns additional moral considerations that may be relevant to justifying rights linkage. For example, while some may argue that making the right to vote conditional on not having been found guilty of serious criminal offences is *morally* appropriate (whether or not such conditionality contributes to desired ends such as voter participation or reductions in crime), others may deny this. Rights confer benefits on agents, and it may or may not be held that an agent should be conferred such benefits if they have failed to abide by specific normative standards. *Throughout the rest of this paper, when we refer to proponents and opponents of "linkage" we mean proponents and opponents of proposition L, and therefore of rights linkage only.*

It is possible to favor only specific linkage proposals (and then only under specific conditions). For example, certain linkage proponents argue that linking trade and labor standards through the WTO is undesirable because the WTO by its very nature is hostile to labor standards. However, such persons may endorse linkage under an alternative institutional order of world trade. Similarly, those who object to a form of linkage that allows developed countries unilaterally to bring trade sanctions against those countries they deem to have neglected labor standards may not object to a form of linkage that precludes potentially opportunistic misuse of this kind. Furthermore, those who reject the idea that the rights of countries to trade internationally may be made conditional on the extent to which they adequately promote basic labor standards can endorse the idea that those countries that make marked improvements in their promotion of such standards ought to acquire further rights to trade. Our goal in this paper is not merely to defend proposition L but to develop criteria for distinguishing plausible from implausible linkage proposals.

We shall argue that any system for guaranteeing mutual access to markets (a rule-based system of international trade) can potentially be enhanced by making rights to trade conditional on the promotion of those standards in an appropriate way (i.e., through linkage). In doing so, we do not presuppose that the system for guaranteeing mutual market access (in relation to which linkage is being considered) is the WTO, although, for simplicity, we shall often assume in our discussion here that the trading system that we are considering is the WTO. The case that we make here for linkage, therefore, potentially applies to all multilateral trading agreements.

Proponents of linkage hold that there exists at least one proposal for linkage that, all things considered, is desirable to bring about under current conditions. Opponents of linkage contend that there is *not even one* proposal for linkage that, all things considered, is desirable to bring about (at least under current conditions). To reject this view, it would be sufficient for advocates of linkage to show that there is at least *one* proposal for linkage that, all things considered, is desirable to bring about (under current conditions). The central task of this paper is to demonstrate this. We do so by showing that there is a class of proposals for linkage that meets *all* of the objections commonly advanced (and widely held to be plausible) against proposals for linkage and that, moreover, linkage proposals belonging to this class would perform better than nonlinkage proposals in promoting the objective (as defined in proposition O above) we presume is shared by both proponents and opponents of linkage. In doing so, we meet a much stronger test than is strictly necessary in order to sustain proposition L, which depends on the existence of *a* proposal for linkage that it is desirable to bring about, all things considered.[5]

CHAPTER THREE

What Linkage Opponents Must Show

Principles commonly espoused with respect to the organization of the domestic economy can be invoked in favor of linkage. Regulations protecting labor standards in the domestic economy effectively condition the right to produce and trade goods and services on the adherence to some standards. Failure to abide by labor regulations protecting basic labor standards breaks fundamental rules governing membership in a cooperative economic union whose members are provided certain economic privileges (e.g., to produce and to trade with one another) as a condition of their full membership in the union. Those who reject proposition L in the context of international trade[1] must provide a compelling account of why the provision of economic privileges (in particular trade) should be made conditional on adherence to labor standards–related requirements in the domestic context but not in the international context.[2]

One reason why some may reject proposition L with respect to international trade is that they believe that international cooperation in this area will be unsuccessful even though it is in principle desirable. However, those who believe this must explain why international cooperation with respect to the promotion of labor standards should be expected to be less successful than international cooperation to promote other goals. In particular, the WTO, which is favored by many fierce opponents of linkage, is itself a system of international cooperation intended to promote a goal (greater world trade and its potentially resulting benefits). Although existing forms of international cooperation in various diverse areas may be flawed, they are widely thought to improve upon alternatives in which there is no such cooperation. Indeed, the WTO system is itself often cited by opponents of linkage as being a cooperative system for the governance of international trade that significantly improves upon its predecessors by offering countries more reliable access to one another's markets and a fairer system of resolving trade disputes that may arise among its members. Those who reject linkage as a means of achieving its stated aims must explain why international cooperation is likely to be much less successful in this area than in other areas in which they affirm that international cooperation has been successful.

The arguments we offer below will be especially relevant to those who believe linkage to be appropriate in the domestic economy but inappropriate in the international economy and who accept that multilateral institutions enabling international cooperation can be effective in at least some contexts. We do not attempt to address all of the arguments of those who object in principle to all labor market interventions or to all multilateral institutions. Few prominent critics of linkage hold either view. If they did, they would be critics of labor market interventions or of multilateral institutions more generally rather than of linkage as such.[3]

CHAPTER FOUR

Arguments Against Linkage

We identify below five partially overlapping objections to linkage. We believe that this classification of arguments is exhaustive of the arguments that can plausibly be advanced against linkage.

STANDARD OBJECTION 1: LINKAGE IS SELF-DEFEATING OR INCONSEQUENTIAL

This type of argument claims that linkage will either be inconsequential or that it will backfire and have the opposite of its intended effect of improving the level of advantage of less advantaged persons in the world. It is therefore often claimed that while perhaps well intentioned, linkage will "hurt those it is meant to help."

It is widely alleged that countries will opportunistically misuse the possibilities for restricting imports provided by linkage in order to protect their domestic producers and harm those elsewhere.[1] The trade opportunities available to poor countries will diminish. The world trading system will gradually become subordinated to powerful interests, and gains from trade will contract.[2] Linkage will be used as an excuse to limit the access of developing-country exporters to developed-country markets through the imposition of tariffs or quotas, or it will impose cost-raising improvements to labor standards on developing countries that will diminish the income of those countries, since it will reduce their gains from trade by interfering with the basis of those gains—the reallocation of production according to comparative advantage.[3]

Moreover, it is argued that linkage will have a negligible or perverse effect on the living standards and working conditions of most workers because of its limited reach. First, it is contended that linkage will only affect export-producing sectors, which may account for only a small fraction of the labor force in most developing countries.[4] Second, it is held that linkage is likely to have a negligible or perverse effect on the working conditions, employment, and wages even of many workers in export production.[5] It will thus allegedly most likely drive bad practices in export-oriented production out of sight rather than out of existence. By raising the cost of hiring workers, the imposition of labor standards will therefore cause a reduction of employment.[6] The living conditions of displaced workers may even worsen, since they will either become unemployed or will be employed in sectors with employment conditions no better (and possibly worse) than those they formerly enjoyed. Third, linkage will increase relative inequalities in working conditions or in command over resources, creating a "labor aristocracy."[7] This may be undesirable under certain interpretations of the objective.[8]

Finally, it has been argued that introducing labor standards through linkage reduces the advantages of individuals by impeding them from entering into contracts through which they expect to enhance their well-being. For example, T. N. Srinivasan argued that

> parents would allow their children to be employed in their own economic enterprise or as wage workers only if, given their market and non-market constraints, family welfare is enhanced by the use of children's time in such employment rather than in other activities (including being in school). Thus proscription of such labor, if strictly enforced without compensation, would lower family welfare of those who are already desperately poor.[9]

STANDARD OBJECTION 2: LINKAGE IS AN INFERIOR
MEANS OF PROMOTING THE GOALS IT IS INTENDED
TO PROMOTE

It is sometimes argued that there are superior means of achieving the goals of linkage.[10] Such arguments do not entail a denial that linkage may achieve its objectives but rather involve an insistence that there are other better means of achieving them.[11] In particular, opponents of linkage claim that alternative approaches perform at least as well as linkage at promoting the ultimate ends of improved labor standards and improved levels of advantage for the globally less advantaged. Examples of alternative approaches include moral suasion to bring about voluntary compliance with ILO standards,[12] market pressure facilitated by social labeling (e.g., "ratcheting"[13] labor standards, "rugmark"[14] style social product labels), and international and intranational resource transfers, perhaps conditioned on adequately promoting basic labor standards.[15] It could be argued with respect to international resource transfers, for example, that linkage is unnecessary as a means of promoting labor standards improvements in poorer countries because the incentives that could be provided to these countries by a linkage scheme could equally well, or indeed better, be provided by such transfers. Additional resource transfers could be offered to those countries that undertake specified measures to improve labor standards. Since trade preferences granted to specific countries are likely to lead to distortions in the pattern of trade (i.e., shifts in production away from their lowest cost locations), global income will be higher when such preferences are not present. It can be argued that (so long as there are efficient international tax and transfer instruments available with which to redistribute the higher global income in the manner desired) a system providing financial incentives alone for the promotion of labor standards is always superior to one that includes trade incentives. Indeed, it may be held that even *unconditional* financial transfers to poorer countries could have the effect of leading to improvements in labor standards, if they influence the interest and capacity of countries to enhance labor standards (e.g., because labor standards are a "luxury good").

Linkage is also often deemed to be inferior to nonlinkage alternatives because it is said to be in contravention of the conclusions that may be drawn from economic theory concerning sound institutional design.

There are two primary versions of this claim. The first is that linkage allegedly violates a principle sometimes referred to as the "two birds" principle, according to which it is always best to employ as many instruments as there are objectives. Employing fewer instruments than there are objectives is said generally to lead to an inferior attainment of the objectives.[16] The principle is interpreted by critics of linkage as implying that at least as many independent institutions are required as there are objectives, and that entrusting the promotion of two or more objectives to one institution will lead to an inferior attainment of each.[17] Critics of linkage claim that they and linkage opponents are concerned with promoting two distinct objectives—maximizing the gains from trade and reducing disadvantage (by promoting improved labor standards and higher employment), and that the best approach for achieving these goals would be to dedicate an independent institution to achieving each. They argue that the two birds principle implies that at the international level the concerns of workers are best served by promoting them through an independent agency, such as the ILO, rather than by confusing the mandate of the existing institution (the WTO) presently charged with fostering the growth of world output through trade by charging it additionally with promoting labor standards.[18]

The second version of the claim is that a well-known theorem of international trade (which demands that "domestic distortions" be "corrected at the source" in order for a first-best optimum to be attained) demonstrates that linkage is inferior to other means of obtaining its goals. The content of the theorem and the attempt to apply it to the analysis of linkage will be discussed further below.

The third version of the claim is that linkage is not needed to achieve its aims, since an appropriate system of international trading rules can be designed that does not incorporate linkage and that leaves countries free to choose the level of labor standards appropriate to them while fully reaping the gains from international trade.[19] Kyle Bagwell and Robert Staiger offer an ingenious economic argument to suggest that linkage is not necessary in order to achieve its aims. In particular, they propose the addition of a new rule to the multilateral trading system (which will be defined and discussed further below).[20] The authors presume that there is a social value to be attached to higher labor standards and an economic value that derives from greater gains from trade, and that these are to be added (or more generally aggregated) in defining the maximand (which they refer to as "the domestic surplus") that is pursued by the government in each country. They point out (see their observation 2) that "international negotiations over tariffs alone will lead to a globally inefficient outcome described by partial tariff liberalization and a weakening of labor standards in import competing industries." In other words, the outcome resulting from an international trading system designed without consideration for labor standards will be one in which both the degree of tariff liberalization and the extent of labor standards will be suboptimal, in the sense that the domestic surplus objective will not be met to the maximum extent feasible in all countries. The underlying reason for this has to do with (a) the fact that lowering labor standards in import-competing industries is a means of strengthening the market access of domestic, import-competing industries and diminishing that of foreign industries producing the imported good; and (b) if labor standards are set independently by each country without regard to the "external effect" this decision has on the gains from trade experienced by other countries, then labor standards and tariffs will be jointly set at levels that are not optimal.

They also point out (see their observation 3) that this problem can be overcome in one of at least three ways. The first proposed method is for labor standards to be introduced directly into trade negotiations as objects of interest. This amounts to a form of linkage, since the failure of a country to meet its labor standards commitments under such agreements would presumably entail consequences in the form of the failure by other countries to meet their commitments (whether regarding trade or labor standards), thereby leading the system to satisfy proposition L. The second and the third proposed methods incorporate a rule that can in principle eliminate the incentive of individual countries to use labor standards as a means of increasing market access and thereby permit the optimal level of labor standards as well as trade liberalization to arise. The rule requires countries to engage in "Kemp-Wan adjustments." Adjustments of this kind demand that if a country raises (or lowers) its labor standards, then it must correspondingly raise (or lower) its import tariffs so as to maintain the foreign export price (i.e., the price received by foreign producers that export their goods to the country) at an unchanged level.[21] Rule systems for international trade that demand such adjustments eliminate the incentive to lower labor standards in order to enhance the market access of domestic producers. Such rule systems enable countries to put in place labor standards at the level that *they* deem "optimal" as long as they undertake to revise their import tariffs so as to maintain an unchanged level of market access for foreign producers. This general approach is advertised by the authors as enabling national sovereignty to be respected while helping to protect labor standards attainments.

Along the same lines, it has also been argued that a linkage scheme is likely to reflect the preconceptions and priorities of external actors (perhaps arising from their greater wealth or cultural specificity) and thus to demand that developing countries put in place inappropriately high labor standards. The present level of labor standards in poorer countries may be inadequate, and action on the part of domestic actors to increase this level may indeed improve the condition of the least advantaged. A linkage scheme, however, may require that the level of labor standards demanded be so high that it leads to outcomes inferior to those that would have been achieved through domestic activism (and perhaps even relative to the status quo).

STANDARD OBJECTION 3: LINKAGE CREATES AN UNFAIR DISTRIBUTION OF BURDENS

First, as noted above, it is argued that the loss of jobs caused by the imposition of labor standards is likely to harm most those persons who are most in need, such as poor children, women, and men.[22] It is perverse that less advantaged persons throughout the world—those that linkage is intended to help—will disproportionately bear the burdens imposed by linkage.[23] The imposition of labor standards is likely to create a loss of livelihood (and perhaps even of lives, it is claimed) in developing countries, while consumers in developed countries will likely experience only a relatively small increase in prices.

Second, it is argued that linkage arbitrarily and unfairly targets only some of the sectors and firms in developing countries that practice poor labor standards. In particular, only export-producing firms belonging to the formal sector (and therefore effectively subject to state regulation) will be directly targeted, despite others being equally guilty or more guilty of seriously objectionable labor practices.[24]

Third, it is argued that so-called violations of labor standards may occur for morally justified reasons, in which case penalizing violators of labor standards is unfair. In particular, employers who "violate labor standards" are in fact offering "exploited" workers the opportunity to improve their life circumstances.[25] Given the difficult background conditions faced by these workers, it is alleged that employers act well by offering them work and deserve credit rather than punishment.[26] It has been suggested in this vein that neglect of labor standards may be morally justified because it may enable some agent involved in their neglect to fulfill distinct moral obligations to other agents, or that it may help her further other ends she has reason to value. For example, by being inattentive to labor standards an employer may be able to hire more employees than otherwise, or realize profits that ultimately generate benefits for poorer persons (by enabling voluntary transfers to such persons to be increased or by augmenting the demand for domestic goods and services produced by employing such persons). Disregard for labor standards can enable an employer to increase the amount of good that she does. Finally, she may be able to pursue other ends she has reason to value, such as providing her children with a sound education. It may be argued that an employer can plead some justification for her indifference to labor standards if the good produced by that indifference is significant. In practice, the regrettable necessity to "do bad in order to do good" may arise due to competitive pressures. A factory owner in a developing country, for example, may be compelled to disregard labor standards in order to compete effectively with other firms that do the same. Moral dilemmas of this kind are prevalent in the contemporary world and frequently unavoidable.

Fourth, it is argued that linkage makes the citizens of one country bear the costs of satisfying the preferences of citizens of another country.[27] If a country chooses to outlaw child labor in its own territory, the costs of this sovereign choice are borne in the first instance by the citizens of that country. It is argued that this is as it should be. People ought not to impose the costs of achieving the values they hold dear on others who may not attach the same priorities to these values, at least in their present circumstances. In contrast, linkage requires that the countries (e.g., those in the developing world) that bear the cost (in particular, the direct cost of achieving labor standards and the indirect cost of lost output) are different from those that gain the benefit (e.g., the satisfaction of the preferences of many in developed countries that certain labor standards be attained).

Fifth, it is argued that linkage represents an *illegitimate* abridgement of fundamental freedoms.[28] To use Robert Nozick's memorable phrase, linkage prohibits "capitalist acts between consenting adults."[29] It is frequently argued, moreover, that if restricting rights to trade are unavoidable, then fundamental fairness requires that such restrictions should apply to products of particular *kinds* rather than ones produced in particular places or by particular *processes*, unless a compelling reason (such as maintaining national security) can be provided to depart from this principle. The extension of "most favored nation" trading status (which requires that each country be treated no worse than others) to a wider range of countries has made the world trading system fairer. This is a major achievement that must be protected.[30]

STANDARD OBJECTION 4: LINKAGE IS CONTEXT BLIND AND POLITICALLY IMPERIALISTIC

There are two senses in which it is widely argued that linkage is context blind. First, linkage ostensibly prevents a country from choosing policies that appropriately reflect its level of development. The urgency of improving the living standards of people in poor countries requires that priority be given to rapid development, even though this may lead to the nonfulfillment of labor standards.[31] Although regrettable, such nonfulfillment must be viewed as a necessary evil. There are two distinct reasons that may be offered for prioritizing development over promotion of labor standards. First, the premature imposition of labor standards can act as an obstacle to the development process. It may even be that development can only take place *through* the nonfulfillment of labor standards. It is well known that even so-called basic labor standards were widely violated in factories during the European industrial revolution. Second, the importance attached by the citizens of a country to labor standards may change as their country develops.[32] Fulfillment of labor standards may be a "luxury good" for which the intensity of the preference increases with income.[33] It is asserted that to fail to respect the preferences individuals have for themselves is to act paternalistically, imposing the preferences of the currently rich on those who are currently poor.

It is claimed that endorsing universal human rights is wholly compatible with insisting that the weight attached to the improvement of labor standards relative to other goals (such as the fulfillment of other rights or the improvement of aggregate welfare) should vary with context. Such critics claim that whereas opponents of linkage are context-sensitive proponents of human rights, proponents of linkage are (at best) context-insensitive proponents of human rights and (at worst) context-insensitive proponents of satisfying the preferences of the rich.[34]

A second sense in which linkage is said to be context insensitive is that it is a form of cultural imperialism. It is alleged to unfairly impose a moral vision specific to a single cultural sphere. It is asserted that even when stated at a high level of generality, any set of purportedly "basic" labor standards (such as the "core" labor standards defined by the ILO) is culturally specific. This objection challenges the very idea that there is a universally binding set of standards, since by definition such standards are not culturally specific.

It is argued that these standards are influential merely because great importance is attached to them in the developed countries, many of which happen to share a specific cultural tradition. Such critics claim that there is no universally acceptable rationale that can be provided for any given set of basic labor standards, nor is it possible to develop an "overlapping consensus" among different parties (who might be imagined to have distinct rationales for accepting these standards) in favor of accepting such standards.[35] Even if it is agreed that there are some basic standards (stated in an adequately general way) that are universally relevant, these must be defined further in order to be practically applied.[36] But this further step cannot be taken, it is therefore maintained, without appealing to the preconceptions and priorities of a specific culture. Detailed interpretations of standards are thus likely to conflict. Indeed, it is sometimes asserted that the practices constituting so-called violations of labor standards are in fact sometimes an integral part of traditional family and work life in certain societies. It is suggested, for example, that "child labor" can offer a humane and effective form of teaching and apprenticeship.[37] The imposition of "basic labor standards" in such a situation is alleged therefore to amount to nothing less than cultural imperialism.

Lastly, it is argued that linkage is a form of *political* imperialism. State sovereignty guarantees the right of the citizens of a country to choose their domestic institutions and policies, including the organization of work and production. It is argued that linkage significantly limits such rights and is therefore a violation of state sovereignty.

STANDARD OBJECTION 5: LINKAGE IS INFEASIBLE

Critics of linkage often claim that it is infeasible. What do they mean by this? One sense in which a proposal may be deemed infeasible is that it is judged *impossible* to bring about or maintain. Another sense in which a proposal may be deemed infeasible is that it is believed that efforts to bring it about and maintain it are "likely to fail," where this phrase refers to some threshold of likelihood (call it P) deemed relevant to the choice of policies (in the sense that any proposal unlikely to succeed with likelihood P is not worth pursuing for this reason). It might thus be argued that a morally legitimate system of linkage will be exceedingly difficult or indeed impossible to implement and maintain (i.e., that it will fail with a likelihood of at least P). Many empirical claims are presented in support of the idea that linkage is infeasible. It is sometimes argued, for example, that a linkage scheme would be infeasible because it would violate the existing rules of the international trading system. In particular, it is claimed that the rules of the WTO system preclude linkage. For example, it is suggested that a central principle undergirding the WTO (and previous to it the GATT) is the "most favored nation principle," which requires that all exporting countries' goods be treated identically by an importing country, and that this principle precludes linkage since linkage potentially requires discrimination among countries. Many empirical claims are presented in support of the idea that linkage is infeasible. It is alleged, for instance, that developing countries will "simply not accept" the incorporation of labor standards into the discussion of trade issues.[38] If linkage is established, it is said, it will be because it is imposed by powerful and rich countries, in which case it will be unduly coercive and therefore morally illegitimate. There are also groups in developed countries, such as users of imported intermediate inputs and consumption goods, that will be implacably opposed to linkage. Those who are in favor of linkage, on the other hand, are numerous and disorganized, and are very likely to remain so. Furthermore, there is little agreement among proponents of linkage regarding the appropriate form and content of the linkage proposal. For all these reasons, it is argued, the "political will" to establish linkage does not exist.[39]

One reason the political will to establish linkage allegedly does not exist is that *all* countries are vulnerable to charges of having violated basic labor standards.[40] It is argued that, recognizing their own vulnerability, states will tend to forego opportunities to establish linkage, or, if it is established, they will fail to bring charges against other countries, in which case the system of linkage will fail to emerge. It is also sometimes suggested that the informational requirements of implementing and sustaining a system of linkage are daunting. Linkage requires that authorities be able to monitor millions of small firms, many of which are in the informal sector, in every region of the world. This requires the cooperation of governments, which may believe that linkage will only diminish their gains from trade and thus be reluctant to provide such cooperation. Critics of linkage argue that it is highly unlikely that these difficulties can be overcome.[41]

CHAPTER FIVE

Ruling Out Linkage Proposals

To justify proposition L, we will identify a class of linkage proposals that withstands the five standard objections raised by linkage critics identified in chapter 4. Some linkage systems very obviously fail to do so because they straightforwardly fail to meet a number of the objections. In this chapter we argue that those institutions that fail to be rule-based and impartial, to arise through a process of fair negotiation, or to incorporate adequate burden sharing between countries will not meet some of these objections.

First, note that systems of linkage can be of two types: those that are imposed on one or more of the parties and those that are not imposed on any of the parties. The latter type of scheme can be called an unimposed scheme. An important class of unimposed schemes are those arising through a process of fair negotiation. We understand a process of fair negotiation as one in which the conclusion of the negotiation is defined by agreement of all of the parties to the negotiation, and in which the procedures leading to a conclusion of the negotiation are equitable and uncoercive. It may be seen from this definition that a process of fair negotiation minimally involves the absence of imposition, although it involves other features as well. We take as our premise that a morally legitimate system of linkage must be unimposed.[1] We further note that those originating in a process of fair negotiation are especially attractive from a normative standpoint. Because all systems arising from a process of fair negotiation are unimposed, it is sufficient (although not necessary) to assume that a linkage scheme originates in such a process in order to safeguard it from the objections applicable to an imposed scheme. We choose therefore to focus on linkage schemes arising from a process of fair negotiation in what follows.

An imposed system would be more likely to harm developing countries and unfairly distribute the burdens of adequately promoting labor standards and would therefore be perceived as (and would indeed be) morally illegitimate. Moreover, a scheme that is widely perceived to be morally illegitimate is much less likely to be successful in securing compliance.[2] For both of these reasons, imposed systems of linkage should be rejected.[3]

Second, as noted above, a potential risk of linking trade and labor standards is that rich countries may opportunistically use linkage as a means of unfairly protecting their markets from low-cost, developing-country exports. If linkage can easily be used as a disguised instrument of protectionism, it may well be self-defeating because it will reduce income and employment in developing countries. Allowing countries unilaterally to determine whether the requirements to adequately promote labor standards have been met, and what actions should be taken when they have not been met, clearly invites misuse.[4] The importance of establishing a transparent and rule-based system that protects against such misuse is therefore evident. For a system of linkage to promote labor standards effectively, an adequate number of countries must find it in their interest to participate. It will otherwise have to be imposed, in which case it will be illegitimate. A system open to opportunistic misuse is indeed likely to eliminate incentives for uncoerced participation on the part of developing countries.

Third, forms of linkage that lack adequate burden sharing should be rejected. Any form of linkage is likely to impose costs on certain groups. We refer to these direct and indirect costs as the "burdens" generated by linkage.[5] A scheme for burden sharing is one that changes the distribution of these costs by reducing the burdens of those who would otherwise bear them and increasing the burdens of those who would otherwise not. For example, it is often supposed that establishing basic labor standards in poor countries will cause a decrease in employment. If this does indeed occur, burden sharing might reduce these costs through various domestic policy instruments (such as social insurance, credit, employment generation, and job retraining programs), which reduce the costs of adjustment suffered by individuals, as well as through various international policy instruments (such as resource transfers from North to South) that reduce the costs of adjustment suffered by countries (and in particular the cost of their implementing domestic policies such as those mentioned above).[6] Alternatively, the feared reduction in employment may be averted in a different way, such as by offering the countries that undertake such reforms more favorable access to markets for their exports through additional trade liberalization.[7]

Our concern in this paper is to explore possible institutions governing international trade that would not merely be feasible but also morally legitimate. For an institutional reform to be morally legitimate it must not only serve morally valuable objectives. The costs of implementing the reform must also be distributed fairly. For example, it is widely held that the costs engendered by an institutional reform should be allocated in a way sensitive to the capacity of agents to bear them.[8] Indeed, many critics of linkage not only accept this view but also criticize linkage by pointing to it, arguing that the burdens imposed by linkage will be unfair because they will be borne by those who are least able to bear them: poor persons in poor countries. There are other principles relevant to determining the appropriate distribution of burdens. The fact that some agent has or is contributing to the problems that an institutional reform is meant to address, for example, is widely held to strengthen that agent's responsibility to bear the burdens of implementing it.[9] Although it is difficult to determine with great precision whether and to what extents different agents have contributed to shortfalls in basic labor standards, it seems likely that agents in both the North and South have made substantial contributions to such shortfalls. Indeed, in cases in which there is evidential uncertainty concerning whether an agent has contributed to deprivations, the agent may nevertheless be plausibly viewed as having compelling reasons to help alleviate the deprivations in order to avoid the possibility that they have failed to remedy deprivations to which they had in fact contributed.[10] A linkage system that does not include adequate burden sharing should therefore be rejected.

A system that imposes burdens on poor countries but does not require rich countries to share these burdens will also be infeasible. It will not provide adequate incentives for developing countries to join it without coercion, since they will bear the preponderance of costs generated by the linkage system in the absence of burden sharing.[11] The alternative, an imposed system of linkage, would be illegitimate.[12]

A negotiated system will be feasible only if countries judge that a trading system involving linkage will further their interests in comparison with the status quo (in which they may trade even without complying with labor standards). Without such incentives, the transition to a negotiated linkage system will be infeasible. The willingness of countries to comply will be influenced by the incentives offered to them. Without assurance that the costs that a linkage system imposes will be diminished, countries are unlikely to participate or fully comply with its demands. An important determinant of whether a country's participation and compliance with linkage can be made feasible will be the domestic pressures faced by its government. An adequate coalition of agents (individuals, firms, and interest groups) within countries must find it in their interest to endorse the participation of their country in a linkage system and the country's compliance with the rules of such a system if it is to be effective. Whether or not they possess such an interest will be influenced by the size of the burdens and benefits they expect to experience as a result of linkage.[13] Without assurance that the costs that linkage imposes on individual and groups will be diminished or eliminated, they are unlikely to have such an interest.[14] Moreover, agents in developing countries will be more likely to support linkage if they believe that burdens are being shared fairly across and within countries. The perception that the system of linkage is fair is likely to be important in determining whether it is feasible to implement and sustain.[15] Moreover, the extent to which producers find that there is profit in evading labor standards will influence the extent to which a country can readily comply with them. Incentives to comply with these standards are required. Financial resources may be required in order to provide such incentives. Countries are unlikely to have an interest in establishing incentives for producers to enhance labor standards, and may even lack the ability to do so, if they are not themselves offered incentives to adopt the desired policies and the necessary means to do so.

It has been argued that *plausible systems of linkage must at a minimum be unimposed, transparent, and rule-based, and involve adequate burden sharing.* In addition to these three central characteristics, it may be necessary that linkage systems have *additional* features, as we shall see below, if they are to withstand all of the standard objections.

CHAPTER SIX

A Constructive Procedure—Identifying Linkage Proposals That Meet the Standard Objections

Proponents of linkage must identify an institutional arrangement that is both feasible and desirable to bring about. Such an arrangement must possess the three features identified above, and perhaps more. At a minimum, they must be transparent and rule-based, incorporate adequate international burden sharing, and arise through a process of fair negotiation among states. In this chapter, we will attempt to show that it is possible to identify such institutional arrangements. Throughout this chapter, we employ what we refer to as a "constructive procedure" to clarify and emphasize the role that the requirements already identified play in making a linkage proposal immune to the standard objections, as well as to identify *additional* requirements of a proposal for linkage that, when combined with those requirements already identified, will permit the proposal to withstand the standard objections.[1]

The constructive procedure that we employ takes the following form. We consider the first of the standard objections and identify whether additional conditions are required to enable the proposal to withstand this objection. We then consider the second of the standard objections, and similarly identify whether still more conditions will be required to enable the proposal to rebut this objection. We continue this procedure, adding additional requirements that are necessary to overcome the standard objections cumulatively considered to that point, until we have exhausted them. As the standard objections identify reasons that proposals for linkage are ostensibly inferior to nonlinkage proposals, we will thus have identified a class of proposals for linkage that may not be deemed inferior to nonlinkage proposals on the basis of these particular objections and that may indeed improve upon such nonlinkage proposals. Addressing the standard objections in this way serves also to further clarify the content of the requirements already identified above.

It is important to note, however, that even if no linkage proposals withstand all the standard objections, it would not follow that proposition L cannot be sustained. Showing this would require a demonstration that some nonlinkage proposal was superior on balance to all linkage proposals. Our constructive procedure for identifying a desirable class of linkage proposals requires that members of this class satisfy all of the standard objections. However, this is not required for some linkage proposals to be superior on balance to all nonlinkage proposals, even if they perform worse than nonlinkage proposals in one or another respect. We therefore set a more stringent task for ourselves than is required to justify proposition L.

If proposition L is true, then there exists a specific institutional arrangement for which it is true. We assume that any such institutional arrangement will have the following features:

(1) A *Complaints Function* that is defined by who (e.g., countries, persons, nongovernmental organizations, public institutions) can make a complaint about labor standards noncompliance, how they can register their complaint, against whom such complaints can be lodged (e.g., countries or firms), and under what conditions (e.g., failure to adhere to or adequately promote labor standards on the territory of a country or by firms owned, managed, or registered in a country).

(2) A *Fact-Finding Function* that is defined by who (international organizations, governments, nongovernmental organizations, individuals, etc.) is charged with determining whether there has been compliance with a standard, and the procedures that must be followed in investigating complaints—for instance, rules of evidence-gathering and presentation (as may be found in a domestic court or existing dispute resolution bodies of international organizations).

(3) An *Adjudication Function* that is defined by how the validity of the complaint is to be determined on the basis of the evidence provided (in-

cluding the rules of adjudication, etc.) and by the steps to be taken in the event of failure to adhere to labor standards.

(4) *A Promotion Function* that is defined by how compliance with labor standards is to be brought about, including the actions that should be undertaken to promote compliance with labor standards and by whom. These actions might take the form of resource transfers, technical assistance, the withdrawal of enhanced trading rights offered to countries under the linkage system, or the further limitation of rights to trade in the case of repeated and egregious failure to abide by the requirements of the system. Such actions may or may not be triggered by a formal complaint.

The four functions can be combined in a single institution or distributed across different agents and institutions.[2]

The *sine qua non* of a system of linkage is that it must include at least some incentives related to trade among the incentives it offers to agents to foster improved labor standards. Incentive schemes related to trade, whether or not related to labor standards, may vary in three ways. First, they may vary in terms of the subjects (e.g., countries or firms) whose rights to trade are broadened or limited, the deciders (e.g., a duly authorized adjudicative body or individual countries), and the executors (e.g., sets of countries or firms) required to enforce such broadened or limited rights to trade. Second, they may vary in terms of the circumstances under which they allow or demand that an agent's rights to trade be broadened or limited. Third, they may vary in terms of the manner in which an agent's rights to trade may themselves be broadened or limited. For example, the existing Dispute Settlement Body of the WTO can be characterized in these terms as follows: First, the subjects of the system are individual countries, the decider is the Dispute Settlement Body itself, and the executors are the complainants who come before the Dispute Settlement Body. Second, a country's rights to trade may be limited by the Dispute Settlement Body only if it has judged that the country has violated its existing obligations under the WTO. Third, a limitation on a country's right to trade under the system takes the form of tariffs the Dispute Settlement Body authorizes the complaining countries to introduce against the country found to be in violation.

Proponents of proposition L favor an institutional arrangement in which rights to trade are made conditional upon the promotion of labor standards. There are many different ways of understanding the requirement of promoting labor standards. For example, a state might be said to have failed to promote a labor standard adequately if it (a) actively engages in practices that diminish the attainment of the standard, (b) fails to require of agents falling under its jurisdiction that they refrain from practices that diminish the attainment of the standard, (c) fails to engage in practices that promote the attainment of the standard, (d) fails to encourage agents falling under its jurisdiction to engage in practices that promote the attainment of the standard, and/or (e) fails to require agents falling under its jurisdiction to engage in practices that promote the attainment of the standard. Although the specific conception of the requirement that states promote labor standards is deliberately left open here, we do indicate some features that it must have below.

We now proceed to implement the constructive procedure, by considering in turn each standard objection.

RESPONSE TO OBJECTION 1: LINKAGE IS SELF-DEFEATING OR INCONSEQUENTIAL

What would be required to show that linkage will hurt those it is meant to help? To identify whether the statement is true, it is necessary to do three things. First, we must identify what might be called the focal group (all of those who are the intended beneficiaries of the reform) and determine whether or not they would benefit from it.[3] For the purposes of this argument, we assume that the intended beneficiaries include all members of the group that we refer to roughly as "less-advantaged persons across the globe." Second, we must identify the focal variables— those features of the members of the focal group that are deemed relevant to assessing the level of their advantage or disadvantage. We assume here that we are concerned with labor standards, employment, real wages, and other factors that contribute to advantage, broadly understood. Third, insofar as the focal group ("those whom it is meant to help") is made up of more than one person, we must invoke some principle that can be used to identify the overall level of advantage experienced by this group. This is important, since it is very easy to imagine that some members of the less advantaged as a group may be made worse off by a reform even while it makes most of the members of that group much better off. While we do not endorse here any particular principle specifying how the advantages of different members of the focal group should be aggregated for the purposes of assessing a reform, we do reject the view that showing that some members of this group (however few) are harmed by a reform is in itself sufficient to show that it has "harmed those it is meant to help."[4]

In what follows, we shall argue that a well-designed system of linkage will not in fact "hurt those it is meant to help" and indeed can help them. This does not necessarily mean that every single member of the less advantaged as a group would be made better off were such a system brought into being. Indeed, this is true of few if any reforms, including many advocated by fierce opponents of linkage. Take, for instance, key institutional reforms associated with worldwide trade liberalization, such as the ending of the Multi-Fiber Arrangement (MFA) in 2005. There are many exporters and countries who benefited from this agreement who have likely been made worse off by its abolition, even though more countries (and poor persons) may have benefited from its abolition. It does not immediately follow from the fact that the abolition of the MFA has hurt some that this reform hurts those it is meant to help.

Robert Staiger has presented a powerful economic argument as to why linkage is unlikely to hurt those it is meant to help, and indeed may help them.[5] He points out that the rationale of the WTO has been to provide reliable conditions of mutual market access to countries engaged in international trade. The binding of tariff rates (i.e., the placement of ceilings on tariffs) by the WTO has had as its premise that, left to themselves, countries will engage in a damaging competition to maximize access to markets of their own producers, which will result in a collectively self-defeating outcome. Hence, a rule-based multilateral trading system in which countries' freedom to raise tariffs unilaterally is eliminated is in the interests of all. Staiger points out that this very argument suggests that a floor on labor standards is also in the interests of all. The reason for this is that once tariffs are bound, countries have available to them only one major instrument for increasing their own producers' access to markets: labor standards. In particular, by lowering (or failing to raise) their own labor standards, countries can reduce the costs of their producers and increase these producers' competitive advantage. As a result, incentives for a self-defeating "regulatory chill" that puts downward pressure on labor standards are created by the prohibition on a self-defeating "beggar-thy-neighbor" policy of competitive inflation of tariffs. As a result, the gains generated through a rule-based system of international trade in the form of the WTO may only be achievable alongside minimal labor standards by extending the scope of the system to incorporate labor standards, for example, by requiring the promotion of labor standards as a condition for participating fully in the world trading system—in short, linkage.[6] The force of this argument will depend on the strength of the incentives actually present for countries to engage in a race to the bottom, an empirical matter about which we do not express a view here. However, Staiger does present incentive-based reasons to believe that a regulatory chill of this kind may exist. If it does indeed exist, then a convincing case would arise for linkage as a means of both enhancing the gains from trade and improving social outcomes.[7]

It has often been assumed that linkage will likely be used as a fig leaf for protectionism in the North and will diminish the effective access of Southern exporters of goods produced in a labor-intensive manner to Northern markets. However, this assumption is unwarranted. Indeed, there are reasons to believe that exactly the *opposite* may be true.

In particular, linkage is strongly desired by at least some influential constituencies in the North, and further trade liberalization in the North is desired by at least some constituencies in the South. As a result, a "trade" between South and North in which the South accepts linkage and the North liberalizes access to its markets can potentially benefit each. A system of linkage could offer entrants to the system liberalized access to Northern markets as an initial benefit of membership, along with progressively increased access to the same markets as a reward for meeting their further obligations under the system.[8] In this way, a linkage system could mitigate or even entirely neutralize the adverse effects on the competitive position of Southern countries that may result from the improvements in labor standards they undertake. Indeed, even those developing countries failing to promote labor standards may be made better off as a result of a linkage scheme. Strikingly, this can be true *even* if limitations on their rights to trade are imposed! The reason is that such countries will experience increased demand for their relatively lower-cost exports if their competitors' costs increase due to labor standards improvements. The net effect of an increase in tariffs faced by the country in Northern markets and this increase in demand for the exports produced by such a country is therefore difficult to gauge.

Discussions of linkage have been dominated by the presumption that they must entail sanctions against developing countries, but this seems an unduly narrow view of the form linkage must take. A system of linkage need not in any way involve sanctions, since it may operate purely by offering benefits to developing countries that are *additional* to those they are presently guaranteed under the rules of the WTO system. While it is likely that a plausible system of linkage will allow for the possibility of limiting rights to trade in extreme cases, it is by no means necessary that it must rely solely on such negative inducements to achieve its aims. It is on the contrary entirely likely that a plausible system of linkage will need to incorporate significant positive incentives in the form of granting developing countries enhanced access to the markets of developed countries.

This type of liberalized access to markets will bring gains from trade in the North and in the South. However, since it leads to a lessening of the burdens experienced in the South as a result of improvements in labor standards, it qualifies as a form of burden sharing under the definition we have outlined above.

There are reasons to believe that a "policy trade" of the kind we have outlined, in which developed countries ensure greater access to their markets by developing countries in return for acceptance of linkage by the latter, may well succeed.[9] The resistance of workers in developed countries to the liberalization of trade will likely lessen if they believe that liberalization will be accompanied by improvements in labor standards in developing countries, since this will marginally reduce the competitive pressure that they will face in a liberalized environment. As noted above, these workers also have a stated moral interest in the material advancement of workers elsewhere. Workers in developing countries are likely to welcome a policy trade of this kind, as it ensures them the ability to improve labor standards (with all its attendant benefits) and will provide the additional employment that is created as a result of liberalization of trade in developed countries.

Owners of fixed capital in import-competing industries in the North are likely, on the basis of their material interests, to most prefer the policy combination of linkage without additional trade liberalization. The worst policy combination from the standpoint of their material interests is likely to be additional trade liberalization without linkage. The two other policy combinations (additional trade liberalization with linkage, and no additional trade liberalization and no linkage) are of intermediate value and are ambiguously ranked from the standpoint of their material interests. It is clear, however, that these owners of capital are likely to oppose liberalization less if it is accompanied by linkage. Owners of fixed capital in export-producing industries in the South may, on the basis of their material interests, most prefer the policy combination of liberalization in the North without linkage. The worst policy combination from the stand-point of their material interests is likely to be linkage without additional trade liberalization. The two other policy combinations (additional trade liberalization with linkage, and no additional trade liberalization and no linkage) are of intermediate value and are ambiguously ranked from the standpoint of their material interests. It is clear, however, that these own-ers of capital are likely to oppose linkage less if it is accompanied by lib-eralization. The pattern of interests outlined above gives some reason to believe that additional liberalization with linkage is a policy "trade" that could realistically be proposed and sought in international negotiations.

The fear that linkage can become a disguised instrument of protection-ism takes two specific forms, which we now consider in more detail. The first is that if individual countries (or groups of countries) have discretion over whether the labor practices in other countries constitute sufficient grounds for limiting rights to trade, this will enable them to use that dis-cretion opportunistically.

This fear is well founded with respect to any form of linkage in which those countries that complain about labor standards noncompliance are also charged both with determining whether there has been compliance with these standards and with deciding whether it is justified to impose a specific sanction. However, the fear is not well founded if the linkage system prevents individual countries from making unilateral determina-tions of this kind. In that case, such opportunistic use would not be as readily possible.[10]

A rule-based and impartial system of linkage can incorporate fact-find-ing and adjudication mechanisms that would prevent such opportunism. For example, it might be required that countries present their complaints to a transparently constituted and functioning representative body. Such a body would interpret, assess, and act on the claims presented to it with reference to a system of rules. Requirements of various kinds, such as that the findings and reasoning of the body be presented for public scrutiny, can help to ensure that it functions in the desired manner. Approaches to fact-finding and adjudication of this kind are familiar, even if sometimes difficult to implement fully in practice. They may be found in both do-mestic and international settings.[11]

Institutions of this kind are intended to function in a transparent, rule-based, and impartial way. Although they may fall short of these goals, the existence of such shortfalls would not be a sufficient reason to reject the existence of the institutions if they improve upon the outcomes that would arise in their absence.[12]

A related fear is that even a rule-based and transparent system of fact-finding and adjudication may indirectly act as a fig leaf for protectionism. In particular, the system of rules may function in such a way as to privilege the protectionist interests of rich countries. The interests of rich countries may be privileged both in the content of the rules and in their implementation. For example, only countries in whose territory basic labor violations occur may be made liable for them, attaching no responsibility to countries whose firms directly or indirectly participate in practices that lead to such violations.[13] Alternatively, the decision-making body may be inappropriately influenced by the interests of rich countries, either due to its composition or to the incentives offered to its members.

The legitimate concerns raised by these objections can be allayed though an appropriate institutional design. Specifically, a transparent, participatory, and consensual procedure for *establishing* the linkage system can significantly diminish the possibility of undue influence being exercised by the rich countries. It is unlikely that such a process would lead to a system that systematically favors the interests of rich countries in the manner feared.[14] A transparent, participatory, and consensual process of negotiation is likely to lead to a system of rules more acceptable to developing countries. For example, it may be required of developed countries that they take responsibility for ensuring that their firms do not participate in labor standards violations. Moreover, demonstration of a very high likelihood that a country has egregiously and systematically failed to comply with the requirements of the linkage system may be required before a country's trading opportunities are in any way diminished.[15] In such a system, the determination that there are isolated instances of failures to adequately promote labor standards in a poor country would be insufficient to trigger limitations on its rights to trade. It is notable that existing adjudication systems, such as domestic courts and international dispute resolution mechanisms (such as the Dispute Settlement Body of the WTO), often establish stringent standards of proof in order to meet such concerns.[16] Moreover, the threshold for triggering limitations on rights to trade may be made context sensitive and, in particular, dependent on a country's level of development. We see no reason why a system of linkage could not also be made context sensitive in this way.

There are two main responses to the objection that the imposition of labor standards will diminish the income of developing countries by reducing their gains from trade through interfering with the basis of those gains—the reallocation of production according to comparative advantage. First, the basis for the gains from trade is the difference in the costs of production for particular goods across countries. For instance, goods that are produced in a labor-intensive way are likely to be produced most cheaply in countries that have a relative abundance of labor. The objection is grounded in the premise that the cost advantages of developing countries that presently exist would be substantially undermined if not eliminated by the introduction of labor standards. Although it is true that the basis of gains from trade would be reduced by increases in the costs of labor in developing countries that may arise from the imposition of labor standards, there is in fact no reason to believe that this impact would be substantial, especially if labor standards were to be adopted simultaneously in a large number of developing countries. The price elasticity of demand for the exports of an individual developing country may be relatively large in magnitude due to the presence of alternative sources from which the exports produced by developing countries can be procured. However, the price elasticity of product demand for the exports of developing countries taken as a whole is likely to be relatively small in magnitude, as the decisive cost advantage enjoyed by developing countries in the production of labor intensive items will not disappear as a result of the cost increases likely to be generated by the adoption of labor standards (see appendix).[17] In the presence of large North-South cost differentials, the level of cost increase needed to make uneconomical Southern production of commodities that employ labor intensively in their production (i.e., to displace production from the South to the North rather than from one developing country to another) would have to be massive indeed, making implausible the notion that linkage could offer an effective fig leaf for Northern protectionism.[18]

Even in the absence of coordination among developing countries, however, there are other ways in which individual developing countries can enhance labor standards while continuing to reap the gains from trade. For example, a country can implement a wage subsidy simultaneously with the imposition of labor standards, so as to maintain the costs to employers of hiring workers at exactly the same level as prior to the introduction of labor standards. A policy combination of this kind would allow a country to fully reap the gains from trade, as ingeniously shown in the classic argument of Bhagwati and Ramaswami.[19] In fact, whether or not developing countries coordinate among themselves when imposing labor standards, it can be ensured that there is *no loss* in the gains from trade by implementing a policy combination of this kind. In an accompanying technical paper,[20] it is shown that the implementation of such wage subsidies can lead to improvements in labor standards without a change in any country's pattern of production and trade (thereby furthering the interest of all countries).

One possible objection is that implementing such a "first-best" policy combination would be infeasible for many developing countries due to limitations on their ability to tax and transfer efficiently. However, developing countries would not necessarily need to raise all of the relevant resources internally. Rather, international burden sharing can enable developing countries *wholly* to avoid the perceived tradeoff between improving labor standards and maximizing the gains from trade. Indeed, we have insisted from the outset that any plausible linkage proposal must incorporate adequate burden sharing.

Further, wage subsidies aimed at neutralizing the cost-raising effect of labor standards improvements need not necessarily be provided by the developing country's government. In principle, other agents, including buyers and developed country governments, could provide such wage subsidies to the producers in developing countries that improve labor standards. For example, a large multinational corporation could identify the extent to which labor standards improvements have caused increases in labor costs in the factories that supply it, and directly provide countervailing wage subsidies to these suppliers. The cost of such wage subsidies could be borne entirely by the firm or shared by other stakeholders and the entities representing them, such as governments. Alternatively, the government of a developed country that imports goods produced in a developing country that has improved labor standards could in principle pay wage subsidies directly to the firms in the developing country that produce these products for export. The objection that the low administrative capacity of developing countries stands in the way of the provision of countervailing wage subsidies in these countries is irrelevant if the wage subsidies are provided in these ways.

Of course, the inherent difficulties of collecting adequate information concerning the extent of the cost increases that result from labor standards improvements at individual production sites and of administering the provision of wage subsidies will be present in the implementation of any of these schemes. However, the mere existence of such difficulties is not reason alone to dismiss such schemes as infeasible. In what follows, we shall assume for expository simplicity that the entity administering the wage subsidy is the government of the developing country in which production occurs.

If it is not possible to neutralize fully the cost-raising impact of labor standards improvements through the provision of an appropriate wage subsidy, it may still be possible partially to neutralize this impact through other second-best policies. For example, developed countries that import goods whose cost of production is increased by the labor standards improvement can reduce tariffs or implement import subsidies so as to ensure that the cost of these goods to importers is unchanged. A measure of this kind would not require that any international resource transfers be made and would not depend on the limited administrative capacities of developing countries. However, such a policy can only partially neutralize the cost-raising impact of labor standards improvements, because (1) it cannot reverse the change in relative prices of different factors of production and the resulting change in the combination of inputs (e.g., capital and labor) used in the production process—which takes place in the developing country as a result of the labor standards improvement, and because (2) it makes exporting a good to a country in which there is such a subsidy more attractive than exporting the good to a country without an equivalent subsidy or selling it at home. In assessing a proposed import subsidy, the distortions introduced by it must be weighed against its possible benefits.

In principle, the first-best policy combination for a country to adopt if it wishes to reap the gains from trade and raise labor standards is simultaneously to introduce enhanced labor standards, wage subsidies that neutralize the labor cost-raising effects of the introduction of enhanced labor standards, and the optimal trade policy (e.g., free trade) so as to maximize the gains from trade. This first-best policy combination can in principle be adopted unilaterally. Why do countries fail to do so? The reasons are varied and complex. They likely relate to the incentives faced by governments and the limitations on their ability to undertake efficient taxation and transfers.[21] By requiring the provision of additional international transfers and conditioning rights to trade on the adequate promotion of labor standards, linkage can create powerful incentives for countries to adopt the first-best policy combination that fosters labor standards and allows countries to reap gains from trade.

It is important to note that, from this perspective, proponents and opponents of linkage can agree fully on the benefit of undistorted free trade, and indeed both can favor institutional arrangements that give rise to identical patterns of production and net exports. They need disagree only on the best international instruments with which to promote appropriate domestic policy choices that further the interests of workers.

The argument that the imposition of labor standards through linkage will have negligible or perverse consequences because of the limited reach of those standards takes several forms.

The first "negligible or perverse effect because of limited reach" argument of linkage opponents is that the imposition of labor standards through linkage will only affect export-producing sectors. There are three ways to respond to this claim. First and most importantly, a system of linkage need not and should not restrict itself to requiring that efforts to promote basic labor standards take place in export-producing sectors.[22] Indeed, the system that we envision would require that basic labor standards be promoted throughout a country and would provide the same set of inducements (whether positive or negative) for governments to ensure that such efforts are undertaken regardless of the type of production involved.[23] Second, even a linkage system that targets only export-producing sectors can benefit indirectly workers in other sectors. For example, improvements in wages and working conditions in export production will require employers in other sectors to compete for workers by also offering improved wages and working conditions.[24] If linkage results in an increase in workers' collective representation through labor unions, this may indirectly benefit workers who are not unionized. For example, unions may help to represent the interests of workers as a whole in the political process. Moreover, unions may also gain resources with which to organize workers elsewhere in the economy.[25] Third, it may be argued that the effect of linkage on working conditions in export sectors is in itself important and provides adequate reason to pursue linkage.

The second "negligible or perverse effect because of limited reach" argument of linkage opponents is that even workers in the export sectors will be benefited negligibly or indeed harmed. There are three responses to this claim. First, as Bhagwati and Ramaswami have shown in their classic paper, there exists a combination of "first-best" policies that will wholly eliminate the negative impact of labor standards on employment.[26] The provision of an appropriate wage subsidy to firms can fully counteract any increase in labor costs they may face as a result of linkage. This implies that the country's national income in the presence of this (linkage-cum-wage-subsidy) policy combination will be identical to that which would prevail in the absence of all of the elements of the policy combination (i.e., neither linkage nor wage subsidy). It follows that a country can afford to implement such a policy combination so long as it has access to appropriate fiscal (tax and transfer) instruments. If a country does not have access to appropriate fiscal instruments, then assistance from international institutions or donors (as presumed will be present in all plausible approaches to linkage) may still ensure that it has adequate resources with which to implement the first-best policy combination. Second, even if the first-best policy combination is unavailable, linkage will not necessarily reduce employment significantly. In order for a reduction in employment to occur, increases in labor costs must cause a displacement of production to other countries (developing or developed) or a substitution from a more labor-intensive to a less labor-intensive production technique. We have suggested above that increases in labor costs alone are unlikely to eliminate the substantial cost advantage of developing countries over developed countries in labor-intensive production. We have also noted that the simultaneous enhancement of labor standards by many developing countries will greatly reduce the potentially deleterious effect of linkage on employment. Finally, the decisive advantage of labor-intensive production techniques in developing countries is unlikely to be eliminated by the increase in wages entailed by linkage. An analysis of the likely impact of increases in unit costs based on the existing data on the share of labor costs in the unit costs of exports from developing countries suggests this.[27] Third, even if the employment losses from linkage are unavoidable and non-negligible, that may not be a sufficient reason to reject linkage. One reason is that linkage may result in improvements in the wages and working conditions of those who continue to be employed. As a result, improvements in the welfare of families and workers considered as a group may well occur even in the presence of employment losses.[28]

The third "negligible or perverse effect" argument is that linkage will cause an increase in relative inequality. There are four responses to this claim. First, it is far from clear that the net effect of linkage, even if it benefits only some workers, will be to increase inequality. It is clear that improvements in wages of some workers will increase the gap between these workers and those who are worse off, but it will also decrease the gap between these workers and those who are better off. The net effect on "inequality" is ambiguous. Second, the empowerment of some workers (even a "labor aristocracy") may benefit others, insofar as this empowerment strengthens the voice of workers' representatives in the political process. Third, even if the net effect of linkage is to increase relative inequality it may still be desirable, insofar as it improves the absolute condition of many individuals.[29] Fourth, the state may implement additional policies to shape the final distribution of advantages as desired.

Finally, it is sometimes alleged that linkage will reduce the well-being of individuals by impeding them from entering into contracts that enhance their well-being. There are a number of reasons to reject this argument. First, it does not follow from the fact that each household is better off by undertaking a particular action that a general restriction on the ability to undertake the action makes it worse off. The effect of an action on a household's welfare depends on the actions of other households. A general prohibition on such actions by all households may transform an action that increases the welfare of a particular household into one that decreases its welfare. For example, any particular family's material welfare may be enhanced by child labor because the child's earnings are necessary to meet the family's basic needs. In that case, the family might prefer to send a child to work rather than to school. However, if child labor was proscribed in general, adult wages might rise due to the resulting constriction of the labor supply.[30] If the household's income were to rise sufficiently as a result of this increase in adult wages, then the basic needs of the household might be met without a contribution from child labor, in which case the family might now prefer to send children to school rather than to work. In cases of this kind, a prohibition on child labor will *increase* the welfare of households.[31] Second, even if households are made initially worse off as a result of the restriction, they may be made better off by being compensated. A policy consisting of combining the restriction and a compensation scheme for those adversely affected by the restriction may lead to superior outcomes for all concerned.[32] Indeed, public policies combining restrictions and compensation in this way are increasingly being implemented in developing countries.[33] Third, the decision maker within the household may not adequately take account of the interests of other members of the household. For example, the decision to send a child to work may be made by an adult who does not adequately take note of the impact of this decision on the child's present and future well-being. In such a case, public policies may enhance the well-being of some individuals although they harm the interests of other existing and future persons. Distributional judgments are therefore required in order to assess them. Fourth, an agent's decisions may not always promote her ultimate best interests, due to inadequate information, myopia, or questionable subjective preferences.[34]

RESPONSE TO OBJECTION 2: LINKAGE IS AN INFERIOR MEANS OF PROMOTING THE GOALS IT IS INTENDED TO PROMOTE

We focus here on arguments that claim there are means other than linkage of achieving the goals of linkage and that they can promote these goals more effectively than linkage. As noted above, such arguments do not entail a denial that linkage may promote the goals it is intended to promote. Rather, they insist that there are other better means of promoting the same goals. Proposed alternatives either rely solely on moral suasion or seek to bring about voluntary decentralized action on the part of countries, consumers, and firms. In either case they are unlikely to be very effective. Schemes relying on moral suasion are generally ineffectual primarily because they do not provide adequate incentives to raise labor standards. Schemes relying on voluntary decentralized action are inferior to other schemes because they appeal to only some agents and are therefore likely to be relatively ineffectual.

It is sometimes suggested that the ILO should play the leading role in fostering the improvement of labor standards.[35] The ILO has indeed contributed immeasurably and in many important ways to the cause of improved labor standards. In particular, the ILO has been instrumental in helping to bring about consensus on the labor standards to be promoted and in offering technical assistance to countries wishing to design policies that have this effect. Regrettably, however, the promise of improved labor standards remains significantly unfulfilled. One important reason may be that incentives or disincentives available to the ILO to apply to countries in order to encourage them to promote labor standards that these countries have endorsed are limited in their effectiveness.[36]

Some opponents of linkage have argued for strengthening the machinery of the ILO as an alternative to linkage. It is clear that there is significant room for such strengthening. However, it is interesting to note that efforts to strengthen the supervisory machinery of the ILO in regard to basic labor standards have typically been resisted.[37] Even if significant strengthening of the ILO's supervisory machinery were to be achieved, there is reason to doubt that there would be a marked effect on the outcomes realized in the absence of a substantial enhancement of the incentives that the ILO can offer to countries (in return for their promotion of basic labor standards). We do not argue that linkage is the only means of providing such incentives, but we do argue both that it is one such means and that it is not obvious that there are other means superior to it in this respect. It should be noted in this regard that linkage is a form of strengthening the ILO and not an alternative to doing so. Indeed, in the proposal for a system of linkage sketched below, we envision an important role for the ILO.

It is widely recognized that arrangements for international cooperation must include adequate incentives and disincentives if they are to be successful in promoting the behavior they seek to promote. It is commonly held, for instance, that it is not feasible to reduce and eliminate national control over weapons of mass destruction through a program that depends solely upon the voluntary cooperation of each and every national government, due to quite familiar problems of collective action. Without enforcement through unilateral action or multilateral treaties containing binding mechanisms of monitoring and enforcement, countries may lack assurance that reductions in their military power are being matched by those of their competitors, and each may believe that they benefit by "defecting" from the system. Indeed, the WTO system is widely viewed as an advance over its predecessors because it provides disincentives to its members to violate or infringe one another's rights to trade. This is a feature of the WTO system that has been a central reason for the praise bestowed on it by many prominent critics of linkage.

A major reason why linkage is desirable is that it can create strong incentives for governments and employers to take steps to enhance labor standards. We have claimed that although they *could* take such steps even in the absence of linkage (especially if international burden-sharing measures are present), they are less likely to do so in the absence of linkage than in the presence of an appropriate form of linkage.

As we recognize, a world with a system of linkage may be one in which limitations on rights to trade are never actually enacted but in which the prospect that such limitations may occur is sufficient to induce govern- ments and employers to improve labor standards. This suggests, however, that there may be superior means of achieving the goals of linkage that do not involve linkage. In particular, a system of nontrade incentives to enhance labor standards (such as international financial transfers con- ditional on improving labor standards) may be superior. Alternative schemes for providing incentives to improve labor standards are unlikely to prove superior to a well-designed system of linkage. A system that in- volves nontrade (in particular, financial) incentives alone will likely be unattractive for four reasons.

First, as pointed out by Chang,[38] any scheme that involves positive in- ducements alone may produce perverse effects insofar as it encourages countries initially to weaken the standards that it seeks to promote or to exaggerate the costs of improving standards in anticipation of ultimately receiving financial inducements to make such improvements. Of course, both trade and nontrade measures can take the form of either positive or negative inducements (as judged against an expected status quo). This does not therefore provide a reason to favor a linkage or over a nonlinkage scheme as such. However, trade measures are likely to provide for greater flexibility in this regard, since there is a limited range of nontrade incen- tives that can be applied. Even when such incentives are potentially appli- cable, their scope of application may be restricted (for example, countries that are not already recipients of net financial transfers can only be pre- sented with positive financial inducements).

Second, to achieve the same incentive to promote labor standards that would arise under a system offering both trade and nontrade incentives (which we shall refer to as a "mixed regime"), the nontrade incentives that would have to be offered to poor countries would be necessarily greater.[39] In particular, the budgetary cost of these inducements to the governments of rich countries would be higher than under a mixed regime. As a result, implementing and sustaining a system to promote labor standards involv- ing nontrade (in particular, financial) inducements alone would be less likely to be feasible.

Third, significant and sustainable improvements in labor standards will likely require action on the part of countries in both the North and the South, those that are the sites of ownership, registration, and management of firms, and those that are the sites of production. Adequate action by Northern countries is unlikely to result from the nontrade incentives that would be offered by any scheme to promote labor standards, since those countries would themselves have to finance such a scheme.

Fourth, trade incentives can be used to express appropriate moral attitudes more flexibly than nontrade (in particular, financial) incentives can do. For example, it would be unfair to require Northern countries that do not actively participate in conduct that undermines labor standards to make net transfers to those that do for the purpose of providing the latter with incentives to desist from such conduct. Northern countries that do promote labor standards may quite reasonably ask why they should not receive *rewards* for their actions rather than being "punished" by being required to provide resources to other Northern countries that actively engage in conduct that undermines labor standards. A system that requires such net transfers from "good citizens" to "bad citizens," whether they are located in the North or in the South, seems therefore both unfair and likely to be infeasible. We would, for example, find it disturbing if a government were to offer monetary rewards to ex-criminals guilty of violent crimes for each year that they desisted from committing further violent crimes, even if this were a very effective system indeed. The analogy is far from exact, but does starkly capture the contrasting responses that may be appropriate to expressing moral opprobrium and disopprobrium.[40]

If the arguments above—to the effect that all feasible and morally legitimate schemes involve a mixed incentive regime—are valid, then a new question arises: what form should be taken by the disincentives that the system includes? In principle, these disincentives could take many forms. However, there are relatively few practical instruments available with which to create effective disincentives for countries without resorting to the use of force, which seems quite generally inappropriate for the purpose of promoting labor standards. The ability to impose limitations on rights to trade is one of the most powerful instruments of this kind. Indeed, it has been widely employed toward this end in the past. There is also evidence of its past value in encouraging countries to undertake specific actions.[41]

We may conclude: a well-designed system of linkage is likely to be more effective in providing incentives to countries to improve labor standards than alternatives that do not involve linkage.

There also exist a number of proposals to promote labor standards through voluntary decentralized action on the part of consumers and firms. These include voluntary codes of corporate conduct and product labeling ("fair trade" initiatives) and consumer boycotts.[42] There is reason to believe that some of these proposals can be helpful in promoting labor standards. However, they are unlikely to achieve as much as systemic policies such as linkage. One reason to believe this is that voluntary measures on the part of consumers and firms are unlikely to be universally adopted, leading to a patchwork of solutions containing holes in protection (possibly many and large) that permit poor labor standards to continue to exist.[43] Another reason is that private agents may adopt standards that impose undue costs upon the affected parties in developing countries without adequate consultation with them. For example, a group of consumers may unilaterally define and impose a set of labor standards that are insensitive to the context faced by the producers. The burden of fulfilling labor standards may in a real sense fall disproportionately upon producers. Moreover, agents in developing countries (firms and workers) may be unduly coerced into participating in such schemes in order to gain access to markets. Boycotts and other forceful measures may be as coercive as the types of linkage rightly rejected by linkage opponents.

These are strong reasons to doubt the claim that the promotion of a decentralized patchwork alone is the best policy for promoting labor standards. Indeed, it has been pointed out by Rodrik that this is one reason why "we routinely object to labeling as [the sole] solution to similar concerns in the domestic setting."[44] The comparison with domestic policy strongly suggests that it is possible that labor standards will be better promoted by a systematic policy solution than by a decentralized patchwork of voluntary initiatives. If such a decentralized patchwork is preferred, it must be for at least one of three reasons. The first reason is that it is more efficacious in promoting the goal of improving labor standards. The second reason is that it is preferable on procedural grounds. The third is that it is feasible whereas alternative approaches are not. In the previous section and immediately above, we presented arguments against the view that linkage was consequentially inefficacious compared to its alternatives. In subsequent sections, we will present arguments against the view that linkage should be ruled out on procedural grounds or because it is infeasible. In this way, we will demonstrate that the promotion of a decentralized patchwork of solutions alone does not constitute the first-best policy for promoting labor standards.

It has been claimed by some critics of linkage that a principle of institutional design first advanced by Jan Tinbergen (which they refer to as the "two birds principle," although that was not the name given to it by Tinbergen) rules out linkage. Does this claim have merit? To examine this question, it is useful to understand Tinbergen's original argument for this principle in detail. As recognized by Tinbergen, it is impossible to discuss the problem of policy choice coherently without making reference to an overall social preference relation, the greater satisfaction of which we may refer to as the "master goal."[45] The appropriate conception of the master goal will depend upon the normative perspective of the evaluator.[46] Different social states will be associated with different levels of achievement of the master goal.

In practice, many desirable characteristics of social states—for example, a higher aggregate income or a more even income distribution—can be promoted only indirectly through the adoption of appropriate policies that influence these characteristics. For example, higher aggregate income or a more even income distribution may be achieved through an appropriate choice of relevant "policy levers" such as trade, tax, and expenditure policies. Tinbergen refers to the available policy levers as "instruments" and to the characteristics of the social state the policymaker seeks to promote (in order to enhance the master goal) as the "targets."

The two birds principle can be understood as holding that achieving the desired levels of two distinct targets would in general require at least two distinct instruments. Where it is true, this is a consequence of the elementary logic of maximization. Suppose that there were only one instrument, the setting of which influences the attainment of each of the targets. For example, tariffs on imported goods may influence both the level of aggregate income and income distribution. In general, the setting of the instrument that gives rise to the optimal attainment of one of the targets will not be the setting that gives rise to the optimal attainment of the other target. Therefore, suboptimal attainment of at least one of the targets will have to be accepted. In contrast, if each of the targets had been advanced by its own independent instrument, then no such problem need have arisen; each of the targets could simultaneously have been optimally attained. For example, if the tariff rate is set to maximize aggregate income and an adequately efficient system of tax and transfer can be used to achieve the desired income distribution, then the theoretical impossibility of simultaneously achieving the desired aggregate income and the desired income distribution disappears.

This reasoning is not particular to the case of two targets but rather applies to an arbitrary number. In general, at least as many instruments as targets are required in order for it not to be impossible simultaneously to attain the desired levels of all of the targets. However, strictly speaking, this condition is neither necessary nor sufficient. Rare instances may arise in which the desired levels of two targets can be attained simultaneously by using a single instrument appropriately. But a fluke of this type cannot be relied upon.[47] Similarly, the availability of as many instruments as targets does not guarantee that the desired levels of all of the targets can simultaneously be attained. There may be factors that prevent this. If a single policy instrument plays a role in determining the level of attainment of more than one target, then both targets are very unlikely to be maximized simultaneously. For example, if the effects on income distribution of the choice of tariff rate can only be imperfectly neutralized (for example, because efficient tax and transfer instruments are unavailable), then a single instrument (the tariff rate) can have an unavoidable effect on more than one target (namely, the aggregate income and the income distribution). As a result, it will not generally be possible to attain the desired level of aggregate income *and* the desired income distribution.[48] In that case, it will be necessary to sacrifice the attainment of one of the targets to some degree.

Those who rely on the "two birds principle" to criticize linkage do not make clear what targets they have in mind (although they refer vaguely to "the freeing of trade" and to "moral and social agendas"). For the principle to come into play, we must be faced with a situation in which there are two or more distinct goals that we are trying to promote. Are the "freeing of trade" and "moral and social agendas" really distinct goals? At a superficial level they certainly appear to be, since promoting free trade does not itself entail anything with respect to the improvement of labor standards. At a deeper level, however, it is not obvious that they are truly distinct. This is because proponents of free trade typically defend the promotion of free trade not as an end in itself, but on the grounds that maximizing world output through trade can serve a master goal, such as improving the level of advantage of persons, understood in some way (for example, by bringing about increases in employment and real wages for workers and increases in consumption generally).

Advocates of free trade correctly view it as a possibly important instrument in furthering the master goal, through its potentially beneficial effect on material well-being. Those who are concerned with improving labor standards do so because they too are concerned with such a master goal. Indeed, they hold that the raising of labor standards is a target that should be pursued because it should enter constitutively into the master goal—i.e., that it ought directly to influence the ordering of alternative social states of affairs. It can thus be argued that the contrast between the promotion of trade and the "moral and social agenda" is not between two goals but between one *means* of promoting a single goal and another means of doing so. In that case, the case of trade and labor standards is not one in which the principle has any application, and so it cannot in itself be adduced as a reason against linkage.

Despite this vagueness in linkage critics' characterization of the targets being promoted, we shall make an assumption as to what these critics have in mind in order to assess further their arguments. We shall, for purposes of exposition, suppose that the two targets with which they are concerned are the maximization of world output and the promotion of labor standards (as we have expansively defined them here). The critics of linkage argue that these two targets must be promoted through at least two distinct instruments, and therefore that linkage (which on their account charges a single institution with promoting the two distinct targets) cannot be optimal.

The two birds principle implies that at least two distinct instruments are generally required to achieve maximally two distinct targets. Critics of linkage who claim that this principle gives us reason to reject linkage presume that there exist at least two distinct targets that advocates of linkage and nonlinkage alike wish to achieve but that proponents of linkage intend to adopt fewer than this number of instruments in order to do so. This is false. Proponents of linkage can recognize that it is desirable to wield as many instruments as targets but nevertheless call for the use of the distinct instruments to be coordinated appropriately.

The implicit assumption made by critics of linkage that multiple instruments cannot be wielded by a single institution is unwarranted. The optimal configuration of instruments may in principle be achieved in many different ways, and therefore the relationship between the optimal number of instruments and the optimal number of institutions can in principle vary. For example, the optimal configuration of instruments might be implemented by a central planner who has the ability to wield each of the instruments. Alternatively, the optimal configuration of instruments might be implemented by decentralized decision makers (independent institutions) acting in coordination with one another. A final possibility is that the optimal configuration of instruments might be implemented by decentralized decision makers (independent institutions) acting without coordination in pursuit of individually assigned targets. If there exists an optimal configuration of instruments, then *in principle* it is possible to attain it through *any* one of these three arrangements. If the optimal configuration of instruments cannot be achieved through any of these three arrangements, this must be for *empirical reasons* related, for instance, to the incentive structures and informational flows that affect the ability of different arrangements to promote the targets effectively.

Critics of linkage seem to believe that the targets to be promoted can best be promoted by the third option: decentralized decision makers independently acting in pursuit of individually assigned targets (in particular, the maximization of world output through free trade and the raising of labor standards). Specifically, they argue that the best outcomes will be achieved if the responsibility for the promotion of world trade is left to a single institution (the WTO) and the responsibility for the promotion of labor standards is similarly left to a single institution (the ILO). Proponents of linkage argue that targets such as high employment and real wages, decent working conditions, and high world output may best be promoted by a system involving coordination between decision makers involved in conferring rights to trade and those concerned with promoting labor standards. Although it has widely been presumed that linkage requires a single institution to take responsibility for promoting world trade and labor standards, this need not be so. Linkage can also be achieved through appropriate forms of coordination between distinct institutions. The alternative options for promoting the attainment of targets must necessarily be compared on *empirical* grounds.[49]

The preceding discussion has shown that a linkage system need not violate the two birds principle (at least as understood by Tinbergen). Distinct instruments may be distributed across institutions in different ways, and the institutions may or may not coordinate the use of these instruments. The best distribution of rights to use instruments across institutions and the appropriate form and degree of coordination in the use of these instruments must necessarily depend on empirical judgments. It may be thought that it is better to assign the right to use specific instruments to institutions that possess special expertise or capabilities. For example, it has often been argued that the ILO ought to be responsible for defining, monitoring, and promoting labor standards because of its special expertise and institutional capabilities in the area of labor rights. On the other hand, it may be thought that coordination in the use of distinct instruments can enhance effectiveness. For example, it has sometimes been suggested that the ILO is "toothless."[50] One reason to imagine that linkage may help to advance labor standards is that the prospect that rights to trade may be conditioned on the adequate promotion of labor standards may help to give teeth to this otherwise toothless institution. Empirical considerations of this kind must necessarily play a determining role in assigning instruments to institutions and in establishing the appropriate type of coordination between institutions.

Recent game-theoretic literature on "issue linkage" sheds light on the detailed empirical considerations that play a role in determining whether linkage is desirable. Agents are typically concerned with outcomes ("issue areas") of diverse kinds. Moreover, each outcome with which an agent is concerned can be influenced by diverse actions that this agent and others undertake. When the outcomes realized by each agent are the joint consequence of her conduct and the conduct of others, then it is possible that decentralized and uncoordinated choices of conduct by agents will lead to suboptimal outcomes (in the sense that a negotiated agreement to undertake different conduct could lead to an improved outcome for all). Often, the same agents face one another in such strategic interactions (in which negotiated agreements could bring about improvements) in connection to multiple outcomes. For example, governments may have an interest in the level of national income they possess as well as in the level of pollution their populations experience, and outcomes in each of these dimensions may be influenced by others' choices as well as their own. In this example, there are two distinct outcome dimensions, and in each of them governments may act in isolation or in conjunction with other governments (for example, on the basis of negotiated agreements concerning ceilings on tariffs or on CFC emissions).

Is it possible to identify conditions under which unified negotiation over multiple issue areas (aimed at producing a single agreement covering the different issue areas together) is superior to disaggregated negotiations over multiple issue areas (aimed at producing individual agreements over the different issue areas)? One way to assess whether a specific approach to negotiation is superior is to ask whether the outcomes produced by the agreement to which these negotiations would give rise would be superior from the standpoint of all agents. Of course, the outcomes arising when all agents obey their obligations under a negotiated agreement may differ from those that arise when agents fail to obey these obligations. It may therefore be important to assess a negotiated agreement not only in relation to the outcomes that would arise if all agents were to abide by their obligations under the agreement but those that may be likely to arise given the incentives that agents may possess to deviate from these obligations. Whether an agreement is self-enforcing (in the sense that agents have an interest in abiding by their obligations under it when other agents do the same) is of special interest in the analysis of international agreements, since there is no supranational enforcement authority.

Recent game-theoretic literature has included attempts to address this question. Spagnolo,[51] for example, points out that—from the point of view of enforceability—unified and disaggregated negotiations can be compared with each other in relation to two considerations. The first concerns how the unification of negotiations can improve the allocation of enforcement power across dimensions (in a sense to be defined below). The second concerns how the unification of negotiations influences the valuation placed by each agent on the threat of the withdrawal of future cooperation (which is the sole basis for securing cooperation in self-enforcing agreements) relative to the valuation placed on present noncooperation.

How can the unification of negotiations improve the application of enforcement powers across dimensions? The unification of negotiations can enable a superior allocation of enforcement powers across issue areas by permitting unused enforcement power to be redistributed from one issue area to another. In particular, the enforcement power available in one issue area may be in surplus in the sense that the punishment for deviation presented by the threat of withdrawal of future cooperation in that area may be greater than necessary to secure cooperation with the agreement in that area alone (specifically, the value of the benefits of foregone future cooperation may be greater than the value of the benefits of immediate noncooperation).[52] On the other hand, the enforcement power available in another issue area may be inadequate in the sense that the threat of withdrawal of future cooperation in that area may be insufficient to secure the desired level of cooperation in that area (specifically, the value of the benefits of foregone future cooperation may be less than the value of the benefits of immediate noncooperation). When this is the case, linking issue areas can increase cooperation in the area in which enforcement power is inadequate without decreasing cooperation in the area in which enforcement power is in surplus. Linking issue areas can enable unused (or "slack") enforcement powers to be used by reallocating them among issue areas. From this perspective, issue linkage can never diminish the enforceability of agreements and can often enhance it.

How does the unification of negotiations influence the valuation placed by each agent on the threat of withdrawal of future cooperation relative to the valuation placed on the benefit of present noncooperation? Let us assume that when there is issue linkage and cooperation is withdrawn as a punishment for noncooperation, it is withdrawn in all issue areas simultaneously, and when cooperation takes place it takes place in all issue areas simultaneously. Let us further assume that when issues are not linked and cooperation is withdrawn as a punishment for noncooperation in a given issue area, it is withdrawn in that issue area alone. The central question then becomes that of whether the relative benefits of future cooperation and present noncooperation change when issue linkage takes place. It can be shown that this depends on how the agents value different combinations of attainments in the distinct issue areas and on the specific causal interconnections between issue areas.[53]

It has been suggested that economic theory precludes linkage for another reason. Panagariya, for example, has argued that

the targeting literature, pioneered by Bhagwati and Ramaswami (1963) and Bhagwati (1971), tells us that when an economy is in a suboptimal equilibrium, the first best policy is to correct the underlying distortion at its source. Once this is done, there is no reason to intervene elsewhere in the economy. Thus, if the market happens to produce suboptimal labour standards, we should correct this distortion directly rather than through an indirect instrument such as trade sanctions. Under the direct approach, once labour standards have been set at the optimal level, free trade remains the optimal trade policy in the traditional sense. Purely from an efficiency standpoint, a case cannot be made for linking trade and labour standards.[54]

The theorem referred to here concerns distortions in the economic sense, i.e., instances in which the true social cost of an act of production or consumption diverges from the private cost experienced by those responsible for making a production or consumption decision, or in which the true social benefit of an act of production or consumption diverges from the private benefit of those responsible for making a production or consumption decision. How might this conception of a "domestic distortion" apply to the case of "suboptimal" labor standards? In order to apply the "economic" framework in this way, it would be necessary to think of acts of production in which labor standards are inadequately high as being ones in which the true "social cost" of the act of production is greater than its perceived private cost.[55] For this to be true, however, the increment between private cost and true social cost would have to be a cost experienced by *someone* other than those involved in the production process itself who are parties to the wage labor transaction, or a cost attributed to those persons but not perceived by them. If one of the parties to the wage labor transaction (worker or employer) perceived the cost, then it would be fully "internalized" within the contracting decision, and a "distortion" would not exist. Who might these others who experienced the social costs generated by production with poor labor standards be? They could only be other individuals in the country concerned, or indeed individuals in other countries.

In either case, a "correction of the domestic distortion at the source" in the form of a tax meant to bring the perceived private cost of production into line with the true social costs of production would indeed be a possible correction to the domestic distortion, and one which would potentially increase domestic welfare (if the "externality" is suffered by other individuals within the country) or world welfare (if the "externality" is suffered by individuals in other countries).[56] Although this is indeed an instance of the theory of the correction of a domestic distortion at the source, it is by no means obvious why the implementation of such a solution is inconsistent with linkage, contrary to assertions made in the literature. The theory recommends that domestic policies be used to correct domestic distortions and stresses that the existence of a domestic distortion fails to affect the optimal choice of trade policy. Indeed, linkage is a specific *means* of ensuring that countries adopt appropriate domestic policies and does not require that countries adopt any particular trade policy. It leaves countries free to choose the optimal trade policies that they would otherwise choose.

What of the claim that an appropriate system of international trading rules can be designed that does not incorporate linkage, leaving countries free to choose the level of labor standards appropriate to them (and achieving the objectives of linkage) while similarly fully reaping the gains from international trade?

Bagwell and Staiger (see the earlier presentation of their argument) present a scheme for eliminating the strategic incentive to depress labor standards in order to enhance domestic producers' market access. It incorporates a requirement to undertake Kemp-Wan adjustments, which require that when a country raises (or lowers) its labor standards it must correspondingly raise (or lower) its import tariffs so as to maintain the prices received by foreign producers. However, the game-theoretic insight they present and exploit is more widely applicable than they seem to recognize. In particular, whereas they assume that the maximand that *ought* to be pursued is also that which *is* pursued by governments, these two ideas should in general be distinguished. The value of enhancing labor standards may not be fully recognized in the "objective function" of the government. In the terms of Bagwell and Staiger, the social valuation placed on higher labor standards by the government may not correspond to the normatively appropriate valuation of these higher standards. This may be true for two distinct reasons. It may be thought that the appropriate normative valuation on labor standards is that which corresponds to an aggregate of the subjective preferences of the country's population.[57] In that case, it is necessary to ensure that the government's valuation of higher labor standards corresponds to that of the population's. However, there is no guarantee that the aggregation function used by the government appropriately reflects the subjective preferences of the population it represents. For example, the government may attribute overriding importance to satisfying the preferences of wealthier and more politically influential citizens while comparatively neglecting the preferences of workers and the poor. This is a pedestrian "political economy" insight of a kind that is familiar to trade economists, who often express concern that protectionist interest groups that engage in "rent seeking" or "directly unproductive activities" undermine the propensity of the state to pursue the public good.[58]

Second, it may be thought appropriate to assign a normative valuation to labor standards in which the valuation placed on higher labor standards is not based merely on the subjective preferences of the population. However, there is no assurance that the government of every country will value higher labor standards to an *appropriate* degree.

Hence, even a system incorporating adjustments of the kind recommended by Bagwell and Staiger may not lead to the socially optimal level of labor standards (i.e., that level which corresponds to the normative valuations or labor standards and other ends). Additional incentives may be required in order to encourage countries to raise their labor standards to the socially optimal level in each country (recognizing fully that this social optimum may depend on the country's present stage of development and other relevant conditions). A system of linkage incorporating burden sharing can provide these additional incentives. Ultimately, linkage is in its very essence a system for providing incentives for countries to choose freely to improve labor standards to a larger degree *than they might otherwise.*

No inherent conflict exists between the idea that the world trading system should incorporate linkage and the idea that it should require Kemp-Wan adjustments of the kind proposed by Bagwell and Staiger. Indeed, it may be desirable to incorporate both linkage *and* the requirement for such adjustments. Consider the following example. There are two countries, A and B, which possess some initial levels of labor standards. Now, suppose that country A's labor standards are below the level minimally demanded of it by the linkage scheme (determined in light of its present circumstances) and that country B's labor standards are above the level minimally demanded of it by the linkage scheme (determined in light of its present circumstances). The linkage scheme provides incentives for country A to raise its labor standards but does not provide incentives for country B to do so. Moreover, country B may have an incentive to *lower* its labor standards in order to confer greater market access to its domestic producers, for the reasons suggested by Bagwell and Staiger. The result that arises from the strategic interaction between countries will be suboptimal, because of the externality pointed to by Bagwell and Staiger: world gains from trade will be lower than otherwise. In order to eliminate the incentive of country B to lower its labor standards, thus ensuring an optimal outcome, the rule system could incorporate the requirement of Kemp-Wan adjustments in addition to linkage. In that case, country B could not lower its labor standards without correspondingly lowering its import tariffs. As a result, the incentive for country B to lower its labor standards purely to increase the market access of domestic producers of import competing goods would be eliminated. Similarly, the increase in labor standards in country A could be accompanied by a decrease in foreign tariffs on the items exported by country A (so as to maintain undiminished or indeed to enhance the level of access to foreign markets by the country's exporters) as we recommend.

We may imagine a range of labor standards–related considerations being incorporated into the world trading system. The linkage scheme could require that countries promote labor standards to a minimally adequate extent, as determined in light of the country's level of development and other relevant considerations. The scheme would require that the trading partners of countries that make improvements to labor standards in accordance with the requirements of the scheme lower their import tariffs for goods from the country, apply import subsidies, or offer other incentives that offset any cost these improvements may generate for the country. The rules of the trading system might also require that Kemp-Wan adjustments be undertaken by countries with labor standards above the level minimally required of them by the linkage scheme, in the event that they seek to lower these labor standards. This would be a means of discouraging countries from using reductions in labor standards as a means of seeking increased market access for their domestic producers as recommended by Bagwell and Staiger. Finally, the rules of the trading system might permit such countries to raise their labor standards further still without any such adjustments. The resulting world trading system, incorporating both linkage and an asymmetrical requirement for Kemp-Wan adjustments, would possess the attractive feature that it would be likely to encourage countries to improve their labor standards while ensuring high and stable levels of mutual market access. This is only a sketch of one possible form that a world trading system incorporating linkage could desirably take.

What of the claim that a linkage scheme is likely to reflect the preconceptions and priorities of external actors and will thus push developing countries to put in place labor standards that are inappropriate (or inappropriately high)? A linkage scheme need not reflect the preconceptions and priorities of external actors. Indeed, any unimposed scheme must appeal to some constituents within a country for it to be entered into by that country. As a consequence, such a scheme is likely to allow for the level of labor standards promotion expected of individual countries to vary with the level of development of the country and other relevant features of the national context. Indeed (as argued further below), such context-appropriate application is called for in order to meet other standard objections to linkage. The labor standards identified as worthy of promotion in any plausible linkage scheme ought to reflect the priorities of domestic activists and stakeholders. There is simply no guarantee that those domestic constituencies that best represent the interests of less advantaged persons will be able to influence policy sufficiently to achieve concrete measures to promote labor standards. By drawing on the experience of domestic actors that promote the interests of the less advantaged in identifying relevant standards, by strengthening their hand relative to other groups with different priorities, and by avoiding the cost in foregone trade and investment that would have been borne by countries that attempt to promote labor standards unilaterally, a linkage scheme will likely give rise to efforts to promote labor standards that are ultimately more beneficial to the less advantaged than those that could be achieved through domestic activism alone.

In all of this, we have assumed that labor standards are a good worthy in themselves of being promoted. If measures to improve labor standards are not worthy in themselves of being promoted but are only a means to an end (e.g., utility) then there may be other better ways of enhancing that ultimate end, namely, avoiding the labor supply "distortion" (and attendant deadweight loss) caused by labor standards improvements (which may be viewed as making working at certain jobs "artificially" attractive, thereby influencing both the labor-leisure decision and occupational choices) and undertaking instead ex-post redistributions of income. We reject this utilitarian framework, which assumes that all harms suffered can be compensated ex-post. We also note that this approach presumes the existence of adequately efficient tax and transfer instruments, adequate information with which to identify beneficiaries, and the actual use of the available instruments. The realism of each of these assumptions may be questioned. Further, the standard international trade models typically appealed to by linkage opponents feature fixed endowments of labor. Under this assumption, the concern that improved labor standards will distort the labor-leisure decision does not arise.

RESPONSE TO OBJECTION 3: LINKAGE CREATES
AN UNFAIR DISTRIBUTION OF BURDENS

It is argued by linkage critics that linkage is likely to most harm persons who are least advantaged. However, we have already shown, in addressing above the objection that linkage is self-defeating or inconsequential, that this argument is unconvincing. A linkage system can be designed in a way that minimizes or eliminates its possible adverse effects and ensures that it becomes an effective instrument on behalf of less advantaged persons.

Second, it is argued by linkage critics that linkage unfairly (because arbitrarily) affects only some persons, sectors, and firms. It is important to note that an agent has obligations to undertake certain actions (or avoid others) irrespective of what *other* agents are doing. For example, a husband's complaint that it is unfair to prevent him from beating his wife because others are not being prevented from beating their wives is illegitimate. It may be argued that an agent's obligations to promote at least some basic labor standards are independent of whether other agents fail similarly to promote them.[59] It is also argued by linkage critics that a linkage system will unfairly affect only those countries that are the physical sites of export production. However, there is no reason that a linkage system must take note of the failure adequately to promote labor standards *only* in those countries that are the physical sites of production. It seems likely that an effective and fair system of linkage will encourage appropriate actions by all countries involved in any stage of the production process, including those that are sites of registration, ownership, and management.[60]

Third, critics of linkage claim that linkage would unfairly penalize individuals for failing to promote specified labor standards, even where doing so is morally justified because of the consequences that are realized or the agent-relative moral ends that are thereby furthered. However, the mere fact that an individual's choice can be given a plausible rationale does not make costs that may be imposed on such an individual to discourage a particular choice unfair. Policies may rightly be designed so as to give greater weight to certain interests (e.g., those of workers) as compared to others (e.g., those of factory owners). Moreover, many of the hard choices faced in an environment in which incentives to promote basic labor standards are weak may disappear in an environment in which such incentives are present. If public policies discourage child labor, for example, a factory owner may no longer be forced to employ child labor in order to compete successfully with other firms. International burden sharing can also mitigate these costs and distribute them more fairly. The concern of critics of linkage that it will penalize individuals in poor countries for failing to promote labor standards can be sidestepped if international burden sharing adequately diminishes the necessity for poorer countries to be inattentive to poor labor standards if they are to pursue other valued ends.

The fourth claim of linkage critics is that it makes the citizens of one country bear the cost of satisfying the preferences of those of another country. In response, it should first be noted that the desirability of promoting basic labor standards arises not merely from the value of satisfying a preference (in this case, the "tastes" of the well-off) but rather arises from the moral value of promoting them.[61] Second, the premise of this objection to linkage is that poor countries will necessarily bear the cost of fulfilling the moral obligation to promote basic labor standards. However, this premise need not be true. As argued above, the costs to developing countries entailed by linkage may be small, especially if sufficient numbers of (otherwise competing) developing countries participate in the linkage system. Indeed, the remaining developing countries (those which do not undertake labor standards improvements) may experience *increases* in demand for their exports as a result of the efforts of other countries to improve labor standards (which will make goods produced in the former countries relatively cost competitive). Further, as argued above, all plausible approaches to linkage must include adequate burden sharing, in which developed countries transfer resources to developing countries. Finally, as described above, a plausible system of linkage will require actions to promote labor standards of all countries, not only those that are sites of production in which basic labor standards are not adequately promoted.

The fifth claim of critics is that linkage illegitimately abridges fundamental freedoms. It is claimed that individuals should be free to enter into contracts with one another and that rights to trade internationally without impediment are grounded in this principle. However, this proposition is exceedingly difficult to sustain—some contractual arrangements, although voluntary, may be unduly coercive or exploitative (and therefore illegitimate) because of the background conditions in which they are entered into. In such cases, it may be morally required either that the stronger party refrain from entering into the contract or that the contracts entered into guarantee terms superior to those that would merely suffice to entice the weaker party to enter the contract.[62]

Proponents of linkage need not deny that there are rights to trade or that these rights are important. Rather, they need only contest the nature and priority of rights to trade as understood by critics of linkage who emphasize these rights.[63] Few would argue that there is a comparable status to rights to trade within a domestic economy, where it is generally thought reasonable to forbid the trade of goods produced with stolen property, produced by employing slave labor or child labor, or that impose a serious risk of harm on intermediaries and consumers. The scope of rights to trade should be determined in light of their contribution to the fulfillment of valuable ends, which may plausibly include basic labor standards.

RESPONSE TO OBJECTION 4: LINKAGE IS CONTEXT BLIND AND POLITICALLY IMPERIALISTIC

Let us first address the claim that linkage is context blind because it is insensitive to a country's level of development. It can be responded that the requirement that countries promote basic labor standards need not be applied in a context-independent way. Rather, countries may be required to respect a few fundamental requirements (for example, to outlaw slave labor and child prostitution) regardless of their level of development, whereas they may be required to respect other requirements only if their level of development is sufficiently high.[64] Further, it must be recognized that it takes time and resources to achieve even basic standards. Limitations on rights to trade ought to be avoided and imposed only when absolutely necessary to deter the most egregious and persistent violations of basic norms (such as the prohibition of slave labor). Explicit allowance can and should be given to countries to demonstrate good faith efforts to promote standards to an extent and in a manner appropriate to their level of development. The obligation to promote labor standards can also be made contingent not only on the level of development of the country but on the pertinent facts, including the nature of the affected industry. Although increased costs may not greatly affect the competitiveness of "inframarginal" industries that enjoy significant cost advantages with respect to competing sources of the same goods and services, they may have large adverse effects on the competitiveness of "marginal" industries in which production within a country (or in the developing countries considered as a group) is barely viable. The empirical facts concerning an industry can and should be taken into account in determining the extent to which cost increases resulting from labor standards improvements can be reasonably absorbed.

Moreover, financial and technical assistance (made possible through international burden sharing) should be provided to countries to enable them to realize the improvements in labor standards that are feasible for them to achieve at their level of development. Although countries may reasonably plead that the costs of ensuring even basic labor standards are prohibitively high at their current level of development, they cannot make this plea if they are provided external assistance (material and technical) sufficient to reduce substantially or eliminate the costs they would face in promoting these standards. The burden-sharing element in plausible proposals for linkage ensures that developing countries will face diminished costs when enhancing labor standards.

For a linkage proposal to be context sensitive, it is important that the aims and procedures of the linkage system (including the basic standards to be promoted and the criteria for determining compliance) be defined through a process of fair negotiation, which (as noted above) is a requirement of all plausible systems of linkage.

Let us now consider the claim that inattention to basic labor standards is a necessary condition for development. This is an empirical claim and, as such, it may be questioned on empirical grounds. It is far from obvious that development requires (or even permits) that any (let alone all) basic labor standards be neglected. It is necessary to distinguish between the instrumental and the intrinsic relevance of basic labor standards to development. The attainment of at least some basic labor standards must be understood as constitutive of development; promoting these standards is a form of promoting development itself.[65] Further, labor standards may be instrumentally valuable because they facilitate other aspects of development. For example, the elimination of child labor may help to bring about universal basic education, which may in turn help to foster economic growth, or higher wages may foster increased productivity.[66] Indeed, countries often further certain basic labor standards without apparent impediment to their development.[67] Finally, even if the neglect of basic labor standards were causally relevant to the rapid development of specific countries in the past (for instance, during the British industrial revolution), it would not follow that this is so today, since economic and technological conditions have changed. For example, there now exist richer countries that can provide transfers to developing countries that can diminish the costs that would otherwise be entailed by the promotion of basic labor standards. The element of burden sharing that must be incorporated into all plausible linkage proposals can ensure that such diminution will take place.

If a system of linkage is legitimate, then the obligations that it ascribes to those who are party to it are ones that *morally* bind them. For a system to create moral obligations for those who are party to it, two conditions must hold. First, the country must have chosen to enter into the system voluntarily—it must not have been unduly coerced into joining it. This may be called the "criterion of external legitimacy." Second, its decision to join the system must have resulted from a process that took adequate account of the interests and perspectives of its citizens.[68] This may be called the "criterion of internal legitimacy." Processes can take adequate account of the interests of citizens in various ways. They may do so by allowing citizens and their representatives a direct say over such decisions through referenda or other democratic mechanisms, by providing them with opportunities to present their views in open public discussion in a manner that influences decisions, or by being otherwise systematically responsive to them.[69]

The tests of internal and external legitimacy must be satisfied in order for a system of linkage to be legitimate.[70] It must be underlined, however, that these criteria of moral legitimacy do not directly provide instructions for institutional design. A system of linkage may permit states to join it in the way that they have historically joined many international treaties—through governments becoming signatories—or it might require something more stringent, such as ratification by a popular assembly, as also demanded for certain existing international treaties. In either case, the moral assessment of the resulting system must take note not merely of whether the legal requirements of entry into the system were satisfied, but of whether the system satisfies criteria of internal and external legitimacy, thus resulting in legal obligations of membership which are also *morally* binding.

Let us now consider the specific claim that linkage represents a form of cultural imperialism. To rebut this charge it is not necessary to demonstrate that there exist specific universally applicable standards that bind all societies regardless of whether they endorse them. It need only be shown that a system of linkage can be designed to safeguard against the possibility of cultural imperialism. This can be done in three ways.

First, the standards that the system promotes must be *identified* in a manner that avoids the charge of cultural imperialism. The standards must be specified abstractly enough that they permit appropriate context-specific variation in their interpretation and application. Only standards specified in this way are likely to be a subject of the broad consensus that is required in order for a linkage system to enjoy wide acceptance. Standards that emerge from a process that takes due account of opinions within states as well as between states and that seeks to reasonably accommodate variation in the specification of the standards to the direction of opinion that is present will be more likely to be the subject of this type of broad consensus.[71] Thus, requiring that the standards promoted through the linkage system emerge from such a process is a means of avoiding the charge of cultural imperialism.

Second, the linkage system must be *applied* in a manner that avoids the charge of cultural imperialism. This may be partially assured by the requirements that the linkage system be impartial and rule based. There is, of course, a danger that the rules for applying the standards (as distinguished by the standards themselves) will be improperly culturally specific. One way of guarding against this prospect is to require that participation by states in the system of linkage not be unduly coerced. Such a safeguard against cultural imperialism may not suffice if states fail to adequately represent the range of interests of the diverse groups within them. For this reason, it is important also to require that the linkage system have two additional safeguards, relating respectively to the process by which the scheme is instituted and the process by which it functions on an ongoing basis.

First, to avoid the danger that states unfairly privilege the interests or perspectives of some, the linkage scheme must not only derive from a process of fair negotiation among states but also from a process that ensures that appropriate account is taken of viewpoints within states. Requiring that states engage in adequate internal consultation as a condition of entering into and participating in the linkage system is one way of ensuring this. Referenda or other means of direct democratic endorsement are forms that such consultation can take. However, it has been historically rare for such stringent mechanisms of gaining popular consent to precede the entry of states into international treaties. Many such treaties are widely held to be legitimate, including those that impinge on sensitive cultural issues (for example, international treaties concerning human rights), despite failing to receive explicit prior popular endorsement. The legitimacy of such treaties is often thought to rest on the fact that over time they have won wide retrospective endorsement by individuals throughout the world, despite their having failed to receive explicit prior popular endorsement. When states fail to engage in direct internal consultations prior to becoming signatories of an international treaty, their decisions may nevertheless reflect or come to reflect the opinions of a populace. This kind of responsiveness is often all that is demanded in order for an international treaty to be deemed (adequately) legitimate. Governments of countries with democratic institutions are typically presumed to reflect popular consent when they enter into international obligations. Insofar as they do not, governments in democracies open themselves to possible sanction and the possibility that withdrawal from the obligations may occur under successor governments. For these reasons, although prior popular endorsement of international agreements is desirable to avoid the charge of cultural imperialism, it is not always deemed strictly necessary.

Second, the system of linkage must incorporate measures that ensure that appropriate account is taken in an ongoing manner of viewpoints within states. Since nondemocratic regimes may neither engage in explicit internal consultation nor be adequately responsive to the views of their populations, it cannot be guaranteed that a nondemocratic regime will reflect the legitimate interests of its population. Further, regimes of all kinds may fail to give adequate weight to the legitimate interests of minorities. A safeguard against both of these possibilities is to create rule-based mechanisms within the linkage system by which complaints about either the content or the application of its standards can be heard. A system of linkage that incorporates these safeguards will fairly take account of viewpoints within states.

Although it is true that there are diverse and conflicting perspectives in the world concerning what is demanded by morality and justice, it does not follow from this fact (of moral and cultural diversity) that agreement on institutions that promote specified ends will be impossible.[72] Whether or not we can succeed in coming to agreement on the standards to be promoted and the means of promoting them is an empirical question.

It is important to note that cultural imperialism can flourish even in the absence of linkage. Indeed, in choosing which labor standards to uphold and to what extent, states often express the conceptions and interests of specific groups and deny those of other groups. In this context, a linkage system may even prove to be an important means of *combating* cultural imperialism. Further, though cultural imperialism is one evil to be avoided, it is not the only evil. The evils attending the neglect of basic labor standards must be weighed against the concern that linkage will be culturally imperialistic. To minimize the risk of cultural imperialism, a system of linkage may permit the conception of the basic labor standards that are to be promoted to reflect cultural specificities to an appropriate degree.

What of the allegation that linkage is a form of political imperialism? There are two responses to this allegation. First, the kind of system of linkage that we envision would not violate state sovereignty because it could only be brought about through the agreement of states that have not been unduly coerced. Once adopted, such a system would of course place constraints on domestic institutions and policies, but this is true of all other significant international agreements. Indeed, one of the features of state sovereignty is that sovereign states are at liberty to join or withdraw from agreements that selectively limit their freedoms.

It is fruitful here to distinguish between "proceduralist" and "substantivist" understandings of the criteria to be used to determine when contracts are freely entered into. A proceduralist understanding holds that contracts into which agents enter are freely entered as long as agents (in this case countries) are procedurally free to choose not to enter the contract. On this understanding, the outcomes arising from either choosing to enter the contract or not choosing to do so are irrelevant to determining whether or not the contract is freely entered into. A substantivist understanding asserts that whether a contract is freely entered into can depend not only on the existence of procedural freedom but also on the outcomes forseeably arising from choosing to enter the contract or not to do so, which together with the choices themselves comprise the structure of the choice system.[73] In particular, in the presence of specific kinds of "adverse background conditions" that make the decision not to enter into a contract extremely costly, we may have reason to conclude that a contract was not freely entered into. On a proceduralist understanding, the existence of the procedural freedom of action of countries to join an international agreement or not to do so is sufficient to determine that these contractual obligations, once entered into, morally bind them. In contrast, on a substantivist understanding, information about the procedural freedom of action countries enjoy in regard to whether to join an international agreement must be supplemented by information about the structure of the choice situation in order to determine whether these contractual obligations, once entered into, morally bind them.[74] An appropriately designed system of linkage can give to countries an adequate degree of freedom of choice (such that their entry into the system may be viewed as not unduly coerced) under both the substantivist and proceduralist understandings. We defer a fuller discussion of this idea to the section on feasibility considerations below.

This response, however, will not address the concerns of those who hold that international agreements (including the WTO) are objectionable not because they infringe upon state sovereignty but because they infringe upon popular sovereignty.[75] The concern of those who hold such views is that international treaties can limit the capability of a country's populace to exercise its prerogatives to govern itself in an ongoing way. For example, the WTO regime limits the freedom of governments to introduce certain domestic policies subsequent to joining the organization, even if they have widespread popular support. In response, it must be pointed out that, at least in this respect, international agreements are not altogether dissimilar from constitutions, which also limit the freedom of a populace to exercise its collective will. Whether the limits thus set can be viewed as legitimate is typically thought to depend on the content of the constitution as well as its origins (e.g., in a fair prior process of collective choice). Similarly, the acceptability of international treaty obligations in a democratic society depends on the extent to which these obligations help to express and promote ends viewed as valuable and the extent to which they derive from a fair prior process of collective choice.

International agreements need not always limit the ongoing exercise of popular sovereignty, even in the most immediate sense; some treaties may strengthen the likelihood that hitherto excluded persons and groups will have a role in decision making. Linkage may have such an impact, insofar as it enhances the associational freedoms of workers and strengthens their capacity to engage in collective bargaining and insofar as it lessens the material constraints they face in doing so.

RESPONSE TO OBJECTION 5: LINKAGE IS INFEASIBLE

It is sometimes objected that a linkage scheme would be infeasible because it would violate the existing rules of the international trading system. In particular, it is claimed that the rules of the WTO system preclude linkage. For example, it is suggested that a principle central to the WTO (and previous to it the GATT) is the "most favored nation principle" (which requires that all exporting countries' goods be treated identically by an importing country) and that this principle precludes linkage, since linkage potentially requires different treatment of exports from different countries.[76] To demonstrate that a proposal is infeasible, it must be shown that the changes to existing rules envisioned by it would be exceedingly difficult, or indeed impossible, to introduce or sustain. It is true that widely accepted rules may be difficult to overturn. For example, it may be necessary to convince many people of the merit of changing rules in order to change them, and they may have already made plans that are predicated on the existing rules. However, the objection that a proposal to change a system of rules is infeasible simply because the change would legitimate actions prohibited by the rules already in place is not *in itself* a sustainable objection.

It is far from obvious, in any case, that linkage need violate the existing rules of the international trading system. For example, exceptions to the MFN principle already exist. For instance, developed countries have long been permitted in the GATT and WTO to offer special and differential treatment to exports from developing countries. Further, under the Generalized System of Preferences, exports from some developing countries have received favorable treatment relative to exports from others. While the merits of these practices have been questioned, they have until recently been accepted.

The existing legal framework of the world trading system (and in particular the WTO) is open to interpretation and may be more flexible than commonly thought. For example, it can be plausibly argued that existing WTO rules demand that countries offer each other a specified level of market access without requiring that this market access be achieved through any specific combination of measures (such as tariff "bindings" or ceilings). Indeed, they can be interpreted as prohibiting countries from attempting to increase the access of their producers to foreign markets and to decrease the access of foreign producers to domestic markets by any means, including the lowering of labor standards.[77] Finally, it can be plausibly argued that GATT Article 20 permits a country to promote legitimate objectives (such as environmental or social goals) by using the level of market access it offers to other countries as an incentive to take actions that promote these ends (as long as this use does not constitute "a disguised restriction on international trade" or "a means of arbitrary or unjustifiable discrimination between countries").[78] We will not deal further with the objection that linkage is infeasible because it is not permitted by the existing rules of the world trading system, which we conclude is unconvincing. We now turn to the deeper objections that may be offered concerning the infeasibility of linkage.

It is alleged by linkage opponents that linkage is infeasible in two ways. First, an acceptable linkage system will be exceedingly difficult (or indeed impossible) to introduce. Second, a linkage system will be exceedingly difficult (or indeed impossible) to sustain.

For a system of linkage to be deemed feasible, it must be shown that there exists a feasible *transition path* to it, and that if it is brought into being, it would survive, i.e., that it is *stable*. In order to defend a proposal against the charge that it is infeasible, it is not necessary to demonstrate that efforts to implement it *will* succeed. It is sufficient to show that the likelihood that efforts to bring it about and maintain it will fail is *less* than some relevant threshold, which we may refer to as P. We will attempt to show that linkage is feasible in this sense. Any such demonstration will require empirical conjectures about which there may be reasonable disagreement. There may also be reasonable disagreement about the threshold of likelihood P that is relevant for determining feasibility in a given context. We cannot and do not therefore offer a definitive argument in favor of the feasibility of the kind of linkage scheme that we envision. Rather, we seek to show that the arguments critics of linkage have presented to show that such schemes are infeasible are unconvincing. To do so, we will identify conditions under which linkage of an appropriate form could be implemented that could plausibly arise or be brought about through the actions of agents. That successfully implementing the proposal may require prolonged political agitation is not in itself an embarrassment. History is replete with examples of institutional innovations that seemed at first infeasible either because their coming about appeared to require political conditions deemed highly improbable or because it was thought that they would, if brought about, be unsustainable. For example, the prospect for the emergence and sustenance of public support for the poor of a kind that is now widespread in advanced societies was once widely viewed as being very small.[79]

A central issue in determining the feasibility of the proposal concerns the motives that can realistically be attributed to agents (individuals, firms, or states). It is clear that some proposals will be feasible if moral agents are assumed to be significantly motivated by other-regarding moral principles but infeasible if the same agents are assumed to be significantly motivated by narrowly self-seeking concerns. There is considerable uncertainty about what motives agents actually have. It seems clear that agents are generally motivated neither purely by other-regarding concerns and commitments to moral principles nor purely by narrowly self-seeking concerns.[80] We take this minimal and unspecific claim as our starting point. We hope to show that on this reasonable understanding of agents' motivations, there is reason to believe that a normatively legitimate system of linkage can be brought about and maintained.

It is interesting to note that agents, including states, often affirm that moral ends inform their actions. Correspondingly, opponents of linkage sometimes argue that states should oppose linkage precisely for the reason that they do possess such concerns.[81] Although the motives that agents hold *at present* are certainly relevant to our judgments about feasibility, the possibility that agents' motives may change with the context (including institutional arrangements) that they inhabit must also be considered when seeking to determine what is feasible.[82]

To show that an international institutional arrangement is feasible, it is not necessary to prove that all countries would participate in the system or would always comply with its rules. No existing or past international institutional arrangement of note satisfies this demand. On the other hand, it is clear that a sufficient degree of participation and compliance is necessary for us to deem that a "system" exists.[83] We leave open the precise degree of participation and compliance required to deem that a system of linkage exists and aim merely to show that the normatively legitimate scheme can be designed in such a way as to secure an adequately high degree of participation and compliance.

For a system of linkage to be feasible it must secure the participation and compliance of countries to an adequate degree. In particular, the system must be incentive compatible in the sense that an adequate number of countries must find that their aims (however conceived) are more fully advanced by participating in the system and complying with its requirements than not. This requires that the system be designed so as to achieve its objectives by presenting an adequate number of countries with incentives of this kind. This problem of mechanism design may or may not be solvable.

We seek to identify whether a *morally legitimate* system of linkage is feasible. This requirement poses no significant challenge under a proceduralist conception of the conditions under which contracts are freely entered. According to such a conception, the system is legitimate as long as countries are procedurally free to choose whether or not to join it, which may be straightforwardly ensured through appropriate design of the rules of entry. However, under the contrasting substantivist conception it may be difficult to design a system of linkage that is both feasible *and* morally legitimate: establishing the set of incentives and disincentives necessary to make the system incentive compatible *may* make nonmembership so costly as to raise legitimate concerns as to whether membership in the system was freely entered into. If the substantivist conception is held to, the system of linkage should be designed so that countries (specifically those facing adverse background conditions) are not presented with incentives and disincentives of a kind and magnitude that gives rise to the concern that their decisions to participate and comply can plausibly be viewed as unduly coerced.

Consider, for example, two alternative designs for a system of linkage, each of which is aimed at creating a structure of incentives that will encourage participation (in the system and compliance with its rules). In the first design, member countries of the linkage system present a poor country ("Haitiopia") with the following choice: participate in the system of linkage or face an economic sanction. In the second design, member countries of the linkage system present Haitiopia with the following choice: participate in the system of linkage and receive a benefit that it would not otherwise receive. Given a sufficient magnitude of sanction or benefit, both systems would meet the incentive-compatibility requirement that they create strong incentives for countries to participate in the linkage system. However, they may not both meet the requirement of moral legitimacy. In both cases, Haitiopia is procedurally free to choose whether or not to become a member. Hence, the linkage system satisfies the proceduralist test of legitimacy irrespective of the magnitude of the benefit or sanction. On the other hand, from a substantivist point of view, sanctions (and even offers) can be unduly coercive. If the sanction would result in highly adverse conditions (such as widespread impoverishment and a breakdown of public security), for example, then it appears that Haitiopia may be unduly coerced by the threat of such a sanction. Similarly, where adverse background conditions severely limit the options available, it may not be possible for Haitiopians to consider seriously any action other than that which elicits the benefit, and to offer such a benefit may be unduly coercive. A substantivist perspective on choice and legitimacy requires that we consider the details of the background circumstances of Haitiopians and of the choices they are offered before a judgment can be formed as to whether they are unduly coerced to enter the system. In order for a system of linkage to be deemed legitimate from a substantivist perspective, it may have to be carefully designed. If it is not believed that all existing international agreements are illegitimate, then it seems plausible that it is possible to design a system of linkage that satisfies these requirements of legitimacy.

We will now sketch two possible approaches to creating and maintaining a system of linkage.[84]

The first approach we will consider involves the incorporation of linkage into the "single undertaking" that members of a trade agreement (e.g., the WTO) provide to one another. The second approach we will consider involves treating linkage as a "special undertaking" that may be entered into optionally by countries participating in the trade agreements. For simplicity, we refer to the WTO rather than to trade agreements in general in what follows.

It is important to note that some considerations regarding feasibility apply in both of these cases. For example, in discussing whether linkage is indeed "self-defeating or inconsequential" we have argued above that a policy "trade," in which developing countries offer to promote labor standards in return for additional trade liberalization, aid, or other concessions by developed countries, may be in the interest of both developed and developing countries. As a result, there is reason to reject the claim that linkage is clearly infeasible. However, let us explore the problem of feasibility more fully.

Let us first assess the approach of incorporating linkage into the single undertaking provided by WTO members to one another. The single undertaking refers to the idea that each WTO member has a single set of obligations that must be abided by *in toto* rather than "a la carte." Consider the stability properties of a system in which linkage is incorporated into the single undertaking of WTO members. A system, once it exists, can effectively collapse either due to the exit of participants from the system or due to the widespread failure to act in accordance with the rules of the system. A WTO system incorporating linkage as part of the single undertaking is likely to be stable in each of these respects. This is because the benefits to be gained by membership in the linkage system arise as part of a complete package of benefits provided by WTO membership, which is widely viewed as very attractive. Similarly, compliance with the rules of the system is made more likely by the fact that noncompliance may result in a wide range of consequences, including the possible loss of the range of benefits that would otherwise be gained from WTO membership and that can only be gained through acceptance of the linkage system. Consider now the feasibility of transition to such a system. Changes or extensions to WTO rules have in the past been instigated by coalitions consisting of a sufficiently large and influential number of countries, typically including some influential rich countries and some influential developing countries. Linkage could come about similarly. Why would countries find linkage to be in their interest and thus join such a coalition?

Some developing countries would wish to join an initial coalition for a number of reasons, of which we will mention four. First, as mentioned, linkage could (insofar as it is in the interest of developed countries) provide a useful bargaining chip with which to gain benefits of diverse kinds, including further liberalization of trade, investment, and resource transfers.[85] Second, it could help to protect workers in developing countries by diminishing the propensity of all countries to engage in a damaging regulatory chill or race to the bottom in labor standards.[86] Third, it could help to promote the interests of some influential groups in developing countries. Workers stand to benefit from the promotion of labor standards. Capitalists may also benefit, although this is less obvious.[87] Fourth, there may be a moral motive for joining. Such considerations may be of different importance in different developing countries, depending on individual circumstances (including transitory political factors). We have not tried to show that these factors would operate decisively in favor of linkage in any one developing country, but rather to argue that they would create reasons for a sufficient number of developing countries to view linkage favorably.

There are also reasons why developed countries might wish to join an initial coalition, of which we will mention four. The first reason is that workers in developed countries may have an interest in linkage insofar as it marginally diminishes the competition they face from developing countries, which have lower labor costs. Lower labor costs in developing countries may influence employment and wages in developed countries either directly, through the reallocation of production (as anticipated in the standard Heckscher-Ohlin-Vanek international trade theory), or through indirect "threat effects." More importantly, linkage may diminish the propensity of all countries (developed and developing) to engage in a damaging regulatory chill or race to the bottom in labor standards. It is important to note that from the standpoint of the feasibility concern, it is sufficient that workers perceive that there is such downward pressure on labor standards; it is not necessary that it actually exist. However, as noted above, Bagwell and Staiger have presented a powerful economic argument as to why such downward pressure is indeed likely to occur in the present WTO system and as to why minimal labor standards can be achieved in this system only by extending its scope to in some way incorporate labor standards. The second reason is that capitalists in developed countries may have an interest in linkage. This may be for a variety of reasons. For instance, as a group they may stand to benefit from improved labor standards in developing countries for much the same reason that capitalists in developing countries may do so. The promotion of basic labor standards may improve the quality and reliability of that portion of the developing country's labor force available to the developed country's capitalists to make use of directly through investment and indirectly through trade.[88] Further, some capitalists in developed countries (in particular, those who operate domestic labor–intensive, import-competing industries) may marginally benefit from measures that reduce the cost advantages of producers abroad. Yet another reason why some capitalists in developed countries may have an interest in linkage is that it would enable them to avoid the public scrutiny and prejudice that often accompanies the perception that they disregard basic labor standards. In particular, those firms that already take steps to protect themselves from this charge may have little to lose and much to gain from a system of linkage, as it may make it less necessary than at present for them to undertake costly private efforts to police the practices of their subsidiaries and suppliers; it may also diminish the competition they face from firms that do not promote labor standards. Of course, some individual firms that produce or source goods in developing countries and that rely on a reputation (contrasting with that possessed by other firms) for promoting labor standards as a central means of generating demand for their products may conceivably prefer to maintain the status quo.[89] The third reason is that countries that become initial members of a prolinkage coalition may gain a reputational advantage, which may increase the demand for products produced by firms owned or managed in the country or otherwise benefit them.[90] A fourth reason is that they may be motivated to support linkage for specifically moral reasons.

Would this "single undertaking" approach to implementing linkage be morally legitimate? In particular, would it avoid being unduly coercive? There are two kinds of concerns that may be raised about the legitimacy of introducing linkage in this way. A first concern may be raised by those who believe that the WTO is already unduly coercive and therefore morally illegitimate. It may be argued that a modified system involving linkage, incorporating it into the single undertaking, will also be unduly coercive, a fortiori. A second concern may be raised by those who believe that the WTO is at present a morally legitimate system but who may think that linkage will deprive it of its legitimacy because undue coercion will be required to implement and sustain it once linkage is incorporated into the single undertaking.

Among those who share the first concern (that the existing WTO is already unduly coercive), there are those who believe that a modified WTO system (perhaps significantly different from that which exists at present) incorporating the single undertaking is feasible and would be morally legitimate, and those who believe that *all* feasible WTO systems incorporating the single undertaking would be morally illegitimate. It can be argued in response to the first group that a revised WTO system that met the requirements of legitimacy would likely *remain* legitimate if it were to incorporate linkage. It is not clear why the incorporation of an appropriate form of linkage would disturb the legitimacy of such a system. Those who believe this to be likely must explain why. Indeed, the incorporation of linkage may be among the revisions to the WTO system that are required in order for it to become legitimate. The second group cannot, by definition, be convinced that even a radically revised WTO system incorporating a single undertaking could be morally legitimate. However, we will present reasons below why these critics may have reason to accept the legitimacy and feasibility of a linkage system based on a separate undertaking.

Those who possess the second concern (i.e., those who believe that the WTO is at present a morally legitimate system but who fear that linkage will deprive it of its legitimacy because it will require undue coercion to implement and sustain) should be reassured by the set of principles that we have identified above, which would protect a system of linkage against the charge of moral illegitimacy. Unless these critics can present reasons why these principles are insufficient to guarantee the legitimacy of a linkage system, their concerns appear unfounded. Based on these considerations, we reject the view that a morally legitimate system of linkage based on a single undertaking is evidently infeasible to bring about and sustain.

Let us now consider the second approach, in which linkage is adopted as a "separate undertaking" entered into optionally by some countries as a set of commitments additional to other trade-related commitments they may already have. We address the transition to the linkage system first. Why would a country participate in such a system of linkage? A developing country might wish to participate for at least six reasons, each of which has been discussed in detail above. First, the linkage system offers participants the possibility of gaining a quid pro quo in the form of market access, investment, or resources. Second, a participant may benefit from the reputation effects associated with participating in the system. Consumers may prefer to purchase goods produced in member countries, and socially responsible investors may wish to locate there. Firms concerned about consumer disapproval of labor standards violations will find it advantageous to locate in such countries. Third, it is in the interest of workers in a country for it to participate in the system. The reputation effects mentioned above only strengthen our earlier reasoning. Fourth, it may be in the interest of capitalists in the country for it to participate in the system. Again, reputation effects strengthen the reasoning presented above in relation to the single undertaking. Fifth, participating in the system is a way of solidifying ties with the other countries that are members, which may serve expressive ends or have instrumental benefits. Sixth, there may be specifically moral motivations for participating in the system.

A developed country might wish to participate for at least five reasons, each of which has again been discussed in detail above, in relation to the single undertaking. First, it may benefit from the reputation effects associated with joining the system. A developed country that participates in the system gains the benefit of appearing to be a praiseworthy supporter of workers' interests. Second, it is in the interest of workers in the country for it to participate in the system, for the reasons outlined above, including diminishing the propensity of all countries to engage in a damaging regulatory chill or race to the bottom in labor standards. Third, it may be in the interest of capitalists in the country for it to participate in the system, for the reasons outlined above. Fourth, participation in the system is a way of solidifying ties with the other countries that are members, which may serve expressive ends or have instrumental benefits. Fifth, there may be specifically moral motivations for participating in the system.

Let us now consider the stability properties of a system of linkage involving a separate undertaking. A system, once it exists, can effectively collapse either due to exit from the system or due to the widespread failure to act in accordance with its rules. There is reason to believe that at least some countries would have incentives to join the system. These reasons would also provide incentives to stay in the system. The reputation effects of joining, for example, may be more than undone by withdrawing from the system. There is no reason for us to think that the reasons why countries joined the system would disappear over time, even if the system sometimes results in individual rulings that are not in their interest.

Compliance with the rules of the system of linkage can be promoted by designing the system of linkage in a manner that gives countries compelling incentives. The role of the rule-based mechanism in governing the system and in defining the consequences of noncompliance will play an important role here. Since large sanctions for noncompliance may trigger withdrawal from a linkage system based on a separate undertaking, positive incentives, public pressure, and moral suasion will likely need to play a significant role. Ultimately, compliance results from the fact that the countries that participate are self-selecting. In joining the system they have affirmed their willingness to comply with its requirements.

Finally, let us consider the moral legitimacy of the separate undertaking approach. As before, we may consider the legitimacy of the system from proceduralist and substantivist perspectives. The procedural legitimacy of this approach is as strong as in the single undertaking model, since countries are free not to participate. From a substantivist perspective, the legitimacy of this approach is if anything stronger than in the case of the single undertaking approach, since the costs of nonparticipation are lower.

Based on these considerations, we reject the view that a morally legitimate system of linkage based on a separate undertaking is evidently infeasible to bring about and sustain.

We have argued that there exist two plausible approaches to creating and maintaining a system of linkage that are morally legitimate. Critics of linkage may contend that although our arguments are sufficient to show that efforts to achieve linkage may not necessarily fail, they are not sufficient to show that they will fail with likelihood less than the threshold required, P, and that this turns the argument in their favor. Those who argue in this way must show two things: they must justify their chosen threshold P and they must argue convincingly that we have not shown above that the likelihood of failing to achieve linkage is less than this level.

There are thus two types of disagreements that can arise with respect to feasibility: disagreements about whether the threshold is met and disagreements about what the threshold should be. Disagreements about whether the threshold is met are empirical in nature, for example, relating to divergent estimates of the power of different agents to change the world through specified actions. Disagreements about what the threshold should be are ultimately normative in nature (though they are influenced by empirical facts). This is because the charge that a proposal is infeasible (in the sense that efforts to achieve it are likely to fail with likelihood P) is intended to dissuade efforts to bring it about. The mere fact that efforts to achieve a desirable outcome are likely to fail is not reason enough to neglect those efforts, unless there is a cost (including an opportunity cost) to doing so for which we ought to account. Whether such costs are sufficient that they ought to dissuade us from striving to achieve the desirable outcome will depend on their nature, magnitude, and the normative significance we attach to them. The appropriate threshold P, which determines linkage's feasibility, cannot be specified without reference to broader judgments concerning, for instance, the value to be attached to attaining the ends of the scheme and the disvalue to be attached to failing to attain these ends, the availability of alternative means of achieving the same ends, and the likelihood that these alternative means will fail or succeed. It is necessary to take note of the actions that are available, the outcomes these actions could result in, the likelihoods associated with each of the outcomes, and the value to be attached to distinct potential outcomes in order to make well-founded decisions. Thus, the identification of the threshold of likelihood according to which infeasibility is to be judged demands addressing a problem of decision making under uncertainty, requiring attention to a range of relevant normative and empirical considerations.

OUTCOME OF THE CONSTRUCTIVE PROCEDURE

We have identified features of a linkage system that, appropriately understood, are sufficient for it to withstand the standard objections to linkage. We saw earlier that in order for proposition L to be satisfied, the system of linkage to which it refers must at the least be *unimposed, transparent, rule-based, and involve adequate burden sharing*. The constructive procedure has once again highlighted these requirements and has led to the identification of two additional conditions, which are that a linkage system must incorporate measures ensuring that adequate account is taken of viewpoints within states, and that the system be applied in a context-sensitive manner. Therefore, for proposition L to hold, it is sufficient that the linkage system to which it refers satisfy the following conditions, as defined above: *it should be unimposed, transparent, and rule-based; involve adequate burden sharing; incorporate measures that ensure that appropriate account is taken of viewpoints within states; and be applied in a context-sensitive manner.* We have noted that a fair and effective system of linkage will likely demand action to promote labor standards not only from countries that are the sites of production but also by countries in which firms involved in the process of producing or marketing goods are located, owned, or managed. We have argued that there is reason to believe that systems of this kind can be brought about and maintained. Therefore, proposition L is satisfied.

CHAPTER SEVEN

Sketch of One Possible Linkage System

We have identified above a class of linkage systems that withstands the standard objections made to such systems. In
order to provide a more concrete starting point for discussion, we offer
below a detailed description of a member of this class.

Any system of linkage will require administration. Who should be responsible for this? In order to answer this question, we should take note
of some relevant facts. First, there are existing institutions (in particular,
the WTO) that govern rights to trade. If a system of linkage is put in place,
these institutions will either have to cede some of their responsibilities or
incorporate the principles of linkage into their activities. Suppose that the
members of a linkage system also belong to a trade agreement that guarantees them a right to trade with one another. Since the linkage system
makes their right to trade with one another conditional upon the promotion of labor standards, but the trade agreement does not, the rights guaranteed by the two systems conflict. Second, there are existing institutions
(in particular, the ILO) that have the authority to define, monitor, and
promote labor standards.

One way to maintain the mandates and relevance of existing institutions (such as the ILO and the WTO) while introducing linkage is to
make them jointly responsible for its administration. We emphasize that
by doing this we do not thereby assume either the legitimacy or the de-

sirability of the current form of these institutions. It is possible that both institutions should be substantially reformed in order to play a legitimate role in the system of linkage sketched below.[1] One means of deferring to the expertise of the ILO in matters of labor standards and the WTO in matters of trade is to propose an Agency for Trade and Labor Standards (ATLAS) jointly governed by the WTO and ILO. We sketch the elements of such a proposal below. Many features of the proposed system are already part of the ILO's approach to labor standards promotion even in the absence of linkage.[2]

ACTIVITIES OF THE AGENCY

The agency will undertake two different types of activity. The first is *developmental* and the second *adjudicative*. In its developmental role, the agency will help countries to identify and execute measures that promote adherence to labor standards. In its adjudicative role, the agency will determine whether serious neglect of labor standards has occurred, and if so what steps ought to be taken by the country to remedy this neglect. Neither of these activities will alone suffice to address a complex global problem such as the inadequate promotion of labor standards. Neglect of adjudicative activities may both undermine the rule-based nature of the regime and lead to inadequate incentives for countries to conform to their obligations under the system, whereas neglect of developmental activities may lead to an inadequate focus on constructive measures that can help to promote labor standards.

INSTRUMENTS OF THE AGENCY

1. The Secretariat

The primary function of the secretariat is to provide administrative support.

Every country will be invited periodically (for example, every two years) to submit a "labor standards progress report" to the secretariat outlining the extent to which it is meeting its obligations under the system to promote labor standards at home and abroad. These obligations include those to share the burdens generated by efforts to promote labor standards abroad and promoting good practices by firms registered or managed in the country or owned by its citizens. The report will identify priorities for action. The requirement to submit such a report is one that will bind *all* member countries, whether rich or poor. A country's repeated failures minimally to meet its agreed obligations to share burdens and to foster sound practices on the part of its firms may expose it to censure or withdrawal of preferences, just as a country's repeated failure minimally to ensure that basic labor standards are adequately promoted on its territory may similarly expose it.

The secretariat will make publicly available the labor standards progress report submitted by each country and related documents resulting from the scrutiny of this progress report by a peer-and-partner review committee (introduced below). The secretariat will provide aid and technical assistance to countries to formulate and implement their action plans, whenever requested. It will maintain and develop required expertise internally and maintain strong links with organizations and individuals who possess relevant expertise.

The secretariat will manage a multilateral burden-sharing fund, collecting contributions from countries and disbursing them to countries to support their action plans. These funds will be disbursed according to various criteria and will be triggered by the recommendation of a peer-and-partner review committee (introduced below), the recommendation of the linkage system's adjudicative body (introduced below), or the request of countries themselves.

The secretariat will actively provide information to the worldwide public concerning member countries' current obligations under the system of linkage and the procedures for expressing concern or initiating an investigation.

The staff of the secretariat will be selected on the basis of open competition according to merit-based criteria. The performance of the secretariat will periodically be reviewed by a governing council consisting of representatives of the ILO, the WTO, and member countries, and by a visiting committee of experts. The reports of the governing council and the visiting committee will be publicly distributed. The governing council will have final authority over the organization and operation of the secretariat. Its individual members will be elected for single terms without possibility of reelection.

2. Peer-and-Partner Review Committees

The governing council of the agency will periodically constitute a peer-and-partner review committee (PPRC) to assess each country's progress, according to transparent criteria established by the linkage agreement. The PPRC's membership will be chosen to be broadly representative and will include members from geographically diverse developed and developing countries. Its members will include representatives of states and nonstate organizations, including workers' organizations. The PPRC will assess each country's labor standards progress report. It may supplement public sources and submissions with its own research concerning practices of a country's firms and conditions prevailing in the country. The PPRC may conduct site visits and public consultations in any member country or otherwise gather evidence. For example, a PPRC may examine conditions at production sites in countries other than the country being reviewed if firms owned or registered in the country being reviewed operate there.

The secretariat will provide advice and technical assistance to the PPRC as requested. The PPRC will recommend actions that the country can take to enhance its compliance with the requirements of the system. The country will then be invited to respond to these recommendations through the provision of an action plan for promoting agreed-upon labor standards, including explicit goals, time-bound schedules, and verifiable targets. The PPRC will respond formally to the country's action plan. It may make public recommendations as to how a country should modify its action plan. It may recommend the disbursement of funds from the multilateral burden-sharing fund to support the action plan as a whole or specific components of it. If a country is deemed to be in serious breach of its obligations under the system, then the PPRC may inform the advocate's office, for its possible action.

3. The Advocate's Office

The advocate's office will investigate potentially egregious instances of indifference to agreed labor standards and determine whether or not formally to initiate a complaint in the adjudicative body. It may do so on its own initiative or as the result of a notice brought to it by a PPRC, a country, or a member of the public. In addition to filing complaints itself, it will provide information and assistance to potential complainants who wish to submit grievances to the adjudicative tribunal.

4. The Adjudicative Tribunal

The adjudicative tribunal will decide on the merits of concerns brought to its attention and identify actions that are feasible and desirable for countries to undertake. Any person, organization, or country may submit a complaint to the adjudicative body. The tribunal will decide which concerns to consider (on the basis of established criteria). The tribunal may commission studies and research that it finds pertinent to the investigation of concerns registered with it. Upon completing their study of an issue, the tribunal has several options. It may determine that a concern has no merit and prescribe no actions. Alternatively, it may rule that the concern is substantiated and call for one of a number of actions. These may include recommending that technical and financial assistance be disbursed to a country from the burden-sharing fund to help it promote agreed labor standards, requiring that a country formulate an action plan to promote agreed standards and report back in due course on the actions that it has taken, or, as a last resort, recommending that other countries (perhaps all of them) withdraw trade preferences or other supports accorded to a country in a commensurate manner and to an appropriate degree. The members of the tribunal will be elected by an appropriate supermajority of the governing council on the basis of their qualifications, including technical expertise and contribution to geographical and social diversity.

5. Participation in the System of Linkage

WTO rules must be made consistent with the rules of the system of linkage. It does not follow from this, however, that all WTO members must be bound by the rules of the linkage system. Indeed, at an early stage in the introduction of a system of linkage it seems more likely that it would form part of a "separate undertaking" (i.e., a system that WTO members join by choice) rather than a part of the "single undertaking" of WTO membership (which binds all WTO members). At least some countries are likely to find benefits in joining a linkage system. Moreover, the voluntary character of such a system would defuse fears that it constitutes an attempt to impose the agenda of developed countries. Over time, as confidence in the system of linkage increases, it is possible that it will develop into a system all countries enter.

CHAPTER EIGHT

Conclusion

W e have demonstrated that there exists a class of proposals for linkage that would withstand the standard objections advanced against such proposals. Indeed, we have argued that there are systems of linkage that would help to promote a goal of both linkage opponents and advocates (increasing the level of advantage of the globally less advantaged) to a larger extent than would any proposals for the governance of international trade that do not include linkage, without notably detracting from other goals that they have.

Proposals for linkage have been criticized on the ground that they allegedly reflect the priorities of developed countries and are likely to harm the interests of those they are meant to help. However, it has been shown above that this conclusion rests on a narrow interpretation of the form linkage must take. An appropriately designed system of linkage may in fact promote the interests of poorer countries, by decreasing the costs they incur at present when pursuing policies to enhance labor standards. Further, such a system may powerfully further the interests of less advantaged persons in poorer countries by creating incentives for governments to implement policies that benefit them. A linkage system can extend the range of considerations to which transparent rules are applied in the governance of international trade, and it can be a compact between countries through which they advance shared moral aims and equitably distribute the burdens that arise in pursuing these aims.[1]

The debate on linkage has been overly narrow due to a lack of institutional imagination. The assumptions of its participants regarding the form that linkage must take have led to a widespread conclusion that it is evident that linkage is undesirable. We have challenged this assumption. We have not argued that bringing about linkage should be the most important priority for action. We have simply claimed that the possible benefits of a linkage system of the type we have described are sufficient to warrant further intellectual and practical exploration. Whether linkage should be a priority for action cannot be determined in advance of such exploration. This is true not only of proposals for linkage but for all policies and institutional changes that may be proposed and which have yet to be brought about. There are of course other competing priorities for action, the choice among which ought to depend upon the probable long-term effects of pursuing them. The proposal for linkage advanced above is only one of many possible means of increasing the extent to which global economic institutions and rules better serve the interests of globally less advantaged workers specifically and globally less advantaged persons generally.

Should linkage of the kind we have described turn out to be infeasible because certain influential agents remain implacably opposed to it (perhaps for no other reason than that it would somewhat erode the privileges they enjoy at present), this would show not that linkage is undesirable but that reforms that would make international institutions more just are being resisted by those who do not prioritize the goal of justice. At the least, this finding would help us better to ascribe moral responsibilities for the inadequacies of the world in which we live. Whether linkage is infeasible for this or any other reason can only be determined in the crucible of experience.

At the heart of the reasoning we have adopted is the idea that worthy institutional reforms must bring about desirable consequences, involve legitimate processes, and be possible to implement and sustain. Through reasoning we have tried to free the imagination. This is but a beginning. Practical knowledge and worldly experiment must make the imagined real.

Empirical Evidence on the Likely Effects of Improvements in Labor Standards

We have shown above that the arguments from economic theory most often adduced against linkage not only fail to demonstrate that linkage is undesirable but suggest instead that the opposite may be true. In this appendix, we consider the empirical evidence concerning the likely effects of improvements in labor standards in developing countries.

It is widely feared that enhanced labor standards will diminish the comparative advantage possessed by countries with relatively low labor costs and thus impede their ability to export relatively labor-intensive goods to developed countries. It is argued that the incentive to invest in such countries in order to export to developed countries will thereby also be diminished. This will in turn, it is suggested, damage the development of currently poorer countries.

Does current evidence offer support for these fears? At least two types of evidence are relevant to examining this question.

ESTIMATING THE IMPACT OF LABOR INCREASES: ACCOUNTING EXERCISES

The first type of evidence concerns the share of total (direct and indirect) labor costs embodied in the unit production costs of goods exported from developing countries to developed countries. If this share (which we will refer to henceforth as the "share of labor costs in unit costs") is low, then the argument that increases in labor costs will significantly erode the relative advantages poor countries possess in producing labor-intensive products may be implausible.[1] For example, if the share of labor costs in unit costs is 20 percent, then a doubling of labor costs would in turn result in a 20 percent increase in production costs. If the initial cost advantage associated with producing the good in poor countries is large enough, then this increase would not be sufficient to eliminate the cost advantage of poor countries in the production of the good. Existing evidence suggests that the cost advantages associated with producing goods that employ labor intensively in their production in developing countries rather than developed countries are indeed significant.[2]

What is the evidence on the share of labor costs in unit costs? Evidence from individual industries and countries suggests that the share of direct labor costs in unit costs is relatively low. Of course, these figures may significantly understate the share of labor costs in unit costs, as they do not account for the labor costs indirectly embodied in the cost of other inputs to the production process.

In order to advance beyond the existing (largely anecdotal) evidence, we have undertaken a calculation of our own, based on the UNIDO industrial statistics database.[3] We have calculated that for the year 2000 the share of direct labor costs (wages and salaries) in total input costs and in the total (ex-factory) value of output for enterprises producing manufactured goods of any kind in all countries for which sufficient data existed (about forty in total, with some variance in this number across industries). Direct labor costs as a share of total input cost were calculated by dividing the reported "wages and salaries of employees" by total input costs (conceived based on the definitions in the UNIDO database as the value of output minus value added plus wages and salaries). Direct labor costs as a share of the total ex-factory value of output were calculated by dividing the reported "wages and salaries of employees" by the value of output. The results of this calculation for distinct income-based country classes and the highly aggregative "total manufactures" category of goods are reported in table 2 below. Results for all specific industries at the three-digit level are available online.[4] The labor costs included refer to all wages and salaries, including those of managerial workers.

TABLE 1. Some Evidence on the Share of Direct Labor Costs in Unit Costs

"Most knowledgeable experts agree that in-country production costs in these [developing] countries rarely exceed 10 percent of the end-user prices of these products in MNC major markets, which are usually in industrially advanced countries. It is estimated that direct labor costs range from 2 to 5 percent of the ex-factory cost of the product."[1]

"A well-known brand of sneakers may retail for $75 in the United States and contain less than $2 in direct labor costs in Vietnam, China, or other overseas locations."[2]

"A typical branded men's polo shirt retails for between $30 and $50 in the United States, whereas the direct labor cost of manufacturing this shirt in a developing country is less than $1."[3]

"Tang Yang Indonesia . . . gets around $13 for every pair of shoes it makes for Reebok, paying only $1 for labor. . . . The shoes typically sell for $60 to $70 a pair."[4]

The average share of direct labor costs in the retail price of toys produced in southern mainland China is very low (mean across types of toys: 2.5 percent and the standard deviation across types of toys: 1.34 percent).[5]

The share of labor costs of nonsupervisory workers in unit costs of men's casual shirts produced in Mexico is 11.2 percent.[6]

The share of wages in total production costs for a television manufacturer in Tijuana, Mexico, is 10 percent.[7]

---

[1] S. Prakash Sethi, *Setting Global Standards: Guidelines for Creating Codes of Conduct in Multinational Corporations* (New York: Wiley, 2003), 58.
[2] Ibid.
[3] Ibid.
[4] Ibid., 59.
[5] See Hong Kong Christian Industrial Committee, *How Hasbro, McDonald's, Mattel, and Disney Manufacture Their Toys* (Hong Kong: HKCIC, 2001), table 2 (available online at http://www.cic.org.hk/download/CIC%20Toy%20Report%20Web%20eng.pdf).
[6] See Robert Pollin, Justine Burns, and James Heintz, "Global Apparel Production and Sweatshop Labour: Can Raising Retail Prices Finance Living Wages?" *Cambridge Journal of Economics* 28, no. 2 (2004): table 5.
[7] See Ian Carson, "The Tijuana Triangle: Mexico's Northern Border Is Modern Manufacturing on the Move," *Economist*, June 20, 1998.

As may be seen from table 2, the average share of direct labor costs in the total input costs for "total manufactures" is 9.9 percent for the low-income countries and 12 percent for the lower middle-income countries. As may also be seen from the table, the average share of direct labor costs in the total ex-factory value of output for "total manufactures" is 7 percent for the low-income countries and 8.5 percent for the lower middle-income countries in the sample. These results do not account for the difference

TABLE 2. Wages and Salaries as a Share of Input Costs and the Values of Output[1]

TOTAL MANUFACTURES

	Wages and Salaries in 2000 as:	
	Share of total input cost	Share of total ex-factory value of output
Average (High Income Countries)	0.165	0.135
Standard Deviation	0.046	0.045
Average (Upper Middle Income Countries)	0.12	0.093
Standard Deviation	0.04	0.031
Average (Lower Middle Income Countries)	0.12	0.085
Standard Deviation	0.029	0.02
Average (Low and Middle Income Countries)	0.116	0.086
Standard Deviation	0.014	0.025
Average (Low Income Countries)	0.099	0.07
Standard Deviation	0.03	0.012

[1] Sources: UN Industrial Development Organization, Industrial Statistics Database at the 3-digit Level of ISIC (INDSTAT3), CD-Rom, rev. 2 (Vienna: UNIDO, 2004); see World Bank, "Country Classification," World Bank Data and Statistics (2007), http://worldbank.org/data/countryclass.html.

(arising from marketing, transportation, and markups) between the ex-factory value of output and its retail value, and therefore substantially overstate (perhaps by a factor of ten, as suggested by table 1) the share of direct labor costs in final retail costs. On the other hand, the data is based on *all* manufacturing enterprises (not just those producing goods for export). If manufactured goods produced for export are more labor intensive than those produced at home for home consumption, then the figures reported below will understate the share of labor costs in total costs and in the value of output of exported manufactures. It is necessary to study exported items specifically before coming to firmer conclusions. Unfortunately, there is no data source that makes this straightforward to do.

It would be right to object that these figures may be relatively uninformative for the present purpose, as a general improvement in labor standards would raise the indirect as well as the direct labor costs of production and thereby have a much larger impact on final costs of production in developing countries than these figures suggest. Unfortunately, we have not been able to identify any studies that calculate these indirect costs for industries of interest in developing countries. Such a study would have to identify the labor costs incurred at each stage of a (possibly quite complex) domestic and international production chain culminating in the production of a final good for export.

We have attempted to address this concern through an analysis based on the empirical data reported above and some simplifying assumptions. Using a simple arithmetical model, we can calculate the total (direct and indirect) labor costs that would arise under various assumptions.[5] We allow the number of stages of the process leading to the production of a good in the South to vary between two and five. We also allow the share of direct labor costs in the total costs specific to each stage either to be a constant or to vary in an increasing or decreasing arithmetic progression.[6] We constrain the share of direct labor costs in total costs at the final stage to correspond to that observed in the UNIDO data. On the basis of these assumptions, it is straightforward to calculate the share of total (direct and indirect) labor costs in the unit costs of manufactured goods in the South (θ). Total labor costs are much higher than direct labor costs alone and increase with the number of stages of the production process that are assumed. Finally, by assuming a certain ratio of the unit cost of production of the good in the North as compared to the South (λ),[7] it is possible to calculate the multiple by which wages in the South would have to increase in order to eliminate the cost advantage of production in the South. We refer to this multiple (α) as the indifference ratio. It is defined by the requirement that $\alpha \theta + (1 - \theta) = \lambda$. That is, $\alpha = (\lambda + \theta - 1) / \theta$. Implicit in the calculation of an indifference ratio is constancy of the production technique (and thus, of the labor and nonlabor inputs employed to produce a unit of output). Of course, if adjustments to the production technique as a result of increases in labor costs are permitted, this will only increase the extent to which wage increases in the South may be absorbed without eliminating the cost advantage of Southern production, since any adjustments made by producers can only decrease their costs. Moreover, if improvements in labor productivity result from the increase in wages or labor standards (for any of a range of reasons, such as the existence of nutrition-productivity linkages), this too will increase the extent to which wage increases in the South may be absorbed without eliminating the cost advantage of Southern production. As well, since the Southern labor costs estimated in the data refer to all wages and salaries, including those of managerial workers, the multiple by which labor costs of line workers may be increased without eliminating the cost advantage of Southern production may be significantly underestimated by these figures. From these standpoints, the estimates of indifference ratios provided here are conservative.

Since the ratio of the unit cost of production of goods in the North as compared to the South is in general unknown, we calculate indifference ratios for various scenarios (ranging from a cost differential of 2:1 to a cost differential of 10:1).[8] We present results for a benchmark scenario in which the share of direct labor costs in unit costs is assumed to be constant across stages of production and equal at each stage to that reported in the empirical (UNIDO) data for 2000. In table 3, we present these results for "total manufactures" and selected industries. The full range of tables is available from the authors, but it may also be constructed by the reader employing her own preferred scenario (using the provided spreadsheet and UNIDO data). It may be observed that the multiple by which labor costs must be increased across the board to eliminate the cost advantage of Southern production is usually very large, and it is at least three even under a highly conservative assumption (that the unit cost of manufacturing a good in the North is only twice the unit cost of manufacturing the same good in the South). In short, there is room to *at least* triple real wages of workers in the South without there arising any possibility of the cost advantage of Southern production being lost. Of course, the possibility of substitution occurring among Southern producers is not considered in this counterfactual. However, the likelihood of such substitution may be less than is widely believed. There is evidence to suggest that labor costs are a less important determinant of decisions concerning which developing country to locate production and investment in than are infrastructure quality, reliability of suppliers, and other considerations.[9]

A related but distinct question concerns the impact of higher Southern labor costs on final retail prices and thereby on consumer demand. As already argued, the ratio of costs of production to final retail prices of most Southern exports sold in Northern markets is small, as a result of which these sales effects may be minor. This case is made very ably in the context of global apparel production by Pollin, Burns, and Heintz, who demonstrate that a doubling of wages of nonsupervisory production-level workers in the garment industry in Mexico would result in increases in final retail prices of garments exported to the U.S. of between 1 and 3 percent.[10]

ESTIMATING THE IMPACT OF LABOR STANDARDS
IMPROVEMENTS: CROSS-COUNTRY COMPARISONS

The second type of evidence concerns the apparent impact of labor standards on export performance and foreign direct investment, as revealed through cross-country comparisons. A number of such studies, most adopting regression analysis, have been conducted recently. Such studies are difficult to interpret for a variety of reasons. For example, commonly used measures of the enforcement of labor standards (such as ratification of ILO conventions) may not signify actual enforcement. More importantly, the association of labor standards enforcement with economic outcomes (export performance or intake of foreign investment) may be informative with regard to the impact of unilateral improvements in labor standards but may be entirely uninformative with regard to the potential impact of *coordinated* improvements in labor standards. Such coordinated improvements are likely to diminish the revenue and employment impact of increases in each country's labor costs, by reducing the possibilities for substituting for imports from a given country with imports from a lower-cost producer elsewhere. Such coordination reduces the magnitude of the elasticity of product demand faced by each country for its exports when increases in price are driven by improvements in labor standards.

Despite the methodological difficulties just highlighted, it is worthwhile to examine the results of recent studies based on intercountry comparisons of the apparent impact of labor standards on export performance and foreign direct investment. Dehejia and Samy offer a thoughtful survey of this literature. They find, based on their own work and that of others, that "there is no clear-cut link, either in theory or in practice, between the level of stringency of labor standards and a country's comparative advantage, whether it is measured by its terms of trade (in the theoretical model) or the extent to which it affects export performance (in the empirical work)."[11] Whereas Mah found that ratification of ILO conventions was associated with inferior export performance, "OECD found no evidence that countries with low labour standards achieved a better export performance than countries with high labour standards."[12] Mah did not control for "natural determinants of comparative advantage," thereby justifying some skepticism. Rodrik found that "labor standards are significant determinants of labor costs when one controls for productivity, but they are not important determinants of comparative advantage, the latter being determined mostly by factor endowments."[13] Dehejia and Samy find in their cross-country regressions that when "realistic" indicators of labor standards are used, there is no significant association between labor standards and export performance.[14] However, when less informative indicators (in particular possibly unenforced ILO ratifications) are used, then lower labor standards are associated with a higher level of export performance. The authors conclude that "we obtain rather weak evidence (especially given that we do not put too much faith in conventions ratified as realistic indicators) supporting the view that countries characterized by low labor standards have a comparative advantage in trade."[15] It is also interesting to note that in their time-series analysis of Canada-U.S. trade, Dehejia and Samy find that two of three measures of labor standards "indicate that higher labor standards have led to an *improvement* in export performance."[16]

Singh and Zammit also present an illuminating survey of the evidence. They report that the UK Department for International Development "has recently reviewed evidence on core labor standards and competitiveness. . . . However, these studies find no evidence of a negative relationship between higher labor standards and the FDI that a country receives."[17] They report that

> other studies indicate that higher labour standards tend to reduce labour-intensive manufactured exports. . . . Although there are very few economy-wide or comparative international studies of the effects of labour standards on economic development, there is considerable research which investigates the micro-level effects of standards on both firms and workers in developing countries. . . . In general, these indicate both negative and positive outcomes, and suggest that the effect of labour standards in developing countries is likely to be complex, depending on country- and industry-specific factors.[18]

The fear that increased labor standards will diminish the comparative advantage possessed by countries with relatively low labor costs and thus impede their ability to export relatively labor-intensive goods to developed countries has thus far received little empirical support.

TABLE 3. Indifference Ratios for Total Manufactures and Sample Industries

				TOTAL MANUFACTURES					

Share of total labor costs in unit costs (South)				Indifference ratios (Alpha)					
Beta	Delta	N	Theta			Number of production stages			
0.099	0	2	0.240			2	3	4	5
		3	0.337	Assumed	2	6.31	4.72	3.93	3.46
		4	0.422	ratio of	3	11.63	8.45	6.87	5.92
		5	0.496	unit costs	4	16.94	12.17	9.80	8.39
				(North/South)	5	22.25	15.89	12.73	10.85
					10	48.82	34.51	27.39	23.16

				FOOD PRODUCTS					

Share of total labor costs in unit costs (South)				Indifference ratios (Alpha)					
Beta	Delta	N	Theta			Number of production stages assumed			
0.066	0	2	0.240			2	3	4	5
		3	0.337	Assumed	2	8.83	6.40	5.18	4.46
		4	0.422	ratio of	3	16.67	11.80	9.37	7.92
		5	0.496	unit costs	4	24.50	17.20	13.55	11.37
				(North/South)	5	32.34	22.60	17.74	14.83
					10	71.51	49.59	38.66	32.12

				LEATHER PRODUCTS					

Share of total labor costs in unit costs (South)				Indifference ratios (Alpha)					
Beta	Delta	N	Theta			Number of production stages assumed			
0.128	0	2	0.240			2	3	4	5
		3	0.337	Assumed	2	5.17	3.97	3.37	3.02
		4	0.422	ratio of	3	9.35	6.94	5.74	5.03
		5	0.496	unit costs	4	13.52	9.90	8.11	7.05
				(North/South)	5	17.69	12.87	10.48	9.07
					10	38.56	27.71	22.34	19.15

(continued)

TABLE 3. Indifference Ratios for Total Manufactures and Sample Industries (*continued*)

PLASTIC PRODUCTS

Share of total labor costs in unit costs (South)				Indifference ratios (Alpha)					
Beta	Delta	N	Theta			Number of production stages assumed			
0.108	0	2	0.240			2	3	4	5
		3	0.337	Assumed	2	5.89	4.45	3.73	3.30
		4	0.422	ratio of	3	10.79	7.89	6.45	5.59
		5	0.496	unit costs	4	15.68	11.34	9.18	7.89
				(North/South)	5	20.58	14.78	11.90	10.19
					10	45.05	32.01	25.53	21.68

RUBBER PRODUCTS

Share of total labor costs in unit costs (South)				Indifference ratios (Alpha)					
Beta	Delta	N	Theta			Number of production stages assumed			
0.125	0	2	0.240			2	3	4	5
		3	0.337	Assumed	2	5.27	4.03	3.42	3.05
		4	0.422	ratio of	3	9.53	7.06	5.83	5.11
		5	0.496	unit costs	4	13.80	10.09	8.25	7.16
				(North/South)	5	18.07	13.12	10.67	9.21
					10	39.40	28.27	22.75	19.48

TEXTILES

Share of total labor costs in unit costs (South)				Indifference ratios (Alpha)					
Beta	Delta	N	Theta			Number of production stages assumed			
0.147	0	2	0.240			2	3	4	5
		3	0.337	Assumed	2	4.67	3.64	3.13	2.82
		4	0.422	ratio of	3	8.34	6.27	5.25	4.65
		5	0.496	unit costs	4	12.01	8.91	7.38	6.47
				(North/South)	5	15.68	11.54	9.50	8.29
					10	34.04	24.72	20.13	17.41

WEARING APPAREL

Share of total labor costs in unit costs (South)				Indifference ratios (Alpha)		Number of production stages assumed			
Beta	Delta	N	Theta			2	3	4	5
0.250	0	2	0.240						
		3	0.337	Assumed	2	3.29	2.73	2.46	2.31
		4	0.422	ratio of	3	5.57	4.46	3.93	3.62
		5	0.496	unit costs	4	7.86	6.19	5.39	4.93
				(North/South)	5	10.14	7.92	6.85	6.24
					10	21.57	16.57	14.17	12.80

Beta is the average share (for low-income countries) of direct labor costs in unit costs at the final stage of the production process. Delta is the increment by which the share of direct labor costs in unit costs is assumed sequentially to increase (i.e., in arithmetic progression) at each stage of production prior to the final stage. Theta is the share in unit costs of the total labor costs incurred directly and indirectly over the *entire* production process. N is the number of stages in the production process.

Economic Theory, WTO Rules, and Linkage

COMMENTARY BY KYLE BAGWELL

In this thoughtful essay, Christian Barry and Sanjay Reddy consider the important and timely issue of linkage.[1] In particular, they address the following question: should some rights to engage in international trade be made conditional on the promotion of labor standards? This is a complex question that may be approached from many angles. Concerned citizens of the world can all agree that less advantaged individuals in some developing countries work under very difficult conditions. There is thus some immediate appeal to the notion that trade sanctions might be used to motivate the governments of such countries to strengthen their labor standards. At the same time, with some reflection, it is also easy to appreciate the arguments made by critics of linkage. For example, higher labor standards may harm developing countries by raising costs in their export industries and undermining their ability to compete in world markets. Linkage could thus be a form of "disguised protection" that ultimately provides a financial benefit to firms and workers in import-competing industries in developed countries.

Linkage is a contentious issue that elicits passionate commentary from both advocates and critics. By comparison, Barry and Reddy offer a refreshingly balanced and comprehensive discussion. They first identify and summarize the standard objections to linkage and acknowledge that these objections provide a basis for rejecting the usual interpretation of linkage. They then consider the features a linkage system would require in order to withstand these objections. They conclude that an appropriate system of linkage *"should be unimposed, transparent, and rule-based; involve adequate burden sharing; incorporate measures that ensure that appropriate account is taken of viewpoints within states; and be applied in a context-sensitive manner"* (79, italics in original). This conclusion informs their discussion at the end of the essay, in which they contemplate the appropriate institutional expression of linkage.

An important and overarching theme throughout the essay concerns the value of sticks versus carrots. As Barry and Reddy explain, the usual interpretation of linkage, under which developed countries use sticks (the threat of punitive tariffs) to promote high standards in developing countries, is unduly narrow and has encouraged the impression that linkage is undesirable. Barry and Reddy favor an alternative linkage paradigm that also utilizes carrots. In essence, they suggest a "policy trade" whereby developed countries offer the reward of lower tariffs or other compensation to developing countries that achieve high labor standards.

If linkage is desirable and feasible, what is the appropriate institutional expression? Some have called for labor standards to be explicitly negotiated and/or enforced in the WTO, while others have argued that agreements over labor standards are best handled in the ILO. What do Barry and Reddy suggest? They address the institution question in broad terms on pages 56–57, when they describe one approach for incorporating labor standards into the world trading system. They propose a linkage system in which countries must achieve a minimal level of labor standards, though this minimal level may vary across countries in light of development considerations. The proposed linkage system utilizes carrots: if a country improves its labor standards to meet its labor-standards requirements, then its trading partners would be required to lower their import tariffs on goods from this country and perhaps offer other financial incentives as well, so as to share the burden and compensate the country for the additional costs that these improvements may generate. As a complement to this linkage system, the authors suggest that the trading system also include rules requiring within-country policy adjustments. Consider a country whose labor standards exceed the level minimally required under the linkage system. If this country were to lower its labor standards, then the authors suggest that it be

required to make further policy adjustments to ensure that foreign producers do not suffer diminished market access. For example, if labor
standards were lowered in an import-competing industry, then a corresponding reduction in the import tariff would be required. Barry and
Reddy suggest an asymmetric system, though, in the sense that they
would not allow such adjustments if this country were to raise its standards further still. Thus, their approach would not allow a country to
raise its standards in an import-competing industry and also raise its
import tariff.

Barry and Reddy further address the institution question in chapter
7. Here they provide additional institutional detail and sketch the possible design of a new international agency, called ATLAS, which would be
jointly governed by the WTO and ILO to administer linkage. The authors
note that WTO rules would require some modification in order to be
consistent with the rules of the system of linkage; in particular, punitive
tariffs may be authorized under the linkage system if agreed-upon labor
standards are not achieved. Additionally, while under WTO rules only
member governments are allowed to submit complaints, the authors propose (page 84) that ATLAS be designed so that any "person, organization,
or country may submit a complaint to the adjudicative body." However,
Barry and Reddy envision that participation in the linkage system would
be voluntary, so that a WTO member would be under no obligation to be
bound by the rules of the linkage system.

Barry and Reddy offer a thoughtful proposal for a class of linkage systems. The criteria they propose (in italics, above) rightly eliminate from
consideration the most objectionable linkage systems. In particular, I
agree that the linkage proposals they consider have important advantages over the usual and narrow interpretation of linkage. One important advantage is that the usual interpretation does not feature a role for
carrots. As I argue below, a system in which developed countries utilize
carrots might be especially useful when humanitarian concerns are pro-
nounced. A further advantage is that the usual interpretation focuses
on the level of labor standards rather than changes in labor standards
and thus does not describe a role for within-country policy adjustments.
I argue below that a (symmetric) system of rules for within-country
policy adjustments is of great value when market-access concerns are
significant. At the same time, I am not fully convinced that the authors'
proposal for a new overarching institution (ATLAS) represents the best

path forward. Below, I focus on the potential role of the WTO and argue that many of the benefits the authors seek might be achieved by harnessing the power of existing WTO rules and principles.

Barry and Reddy position their essay as a starting point for further discussion. In that spirit, I describe below a perspective on trade agreements and labor standards that is developed in my work with Robert W. Staiger and Petros C. Mavroidis.[2] Barry and Reddy's discussion of within-country policy adjustments draws in part from this work, as they graciously acknowledge, but some important distinctions remain. As I develop this perspective, I will point out other areas of agreement and disagreement. On the whole, my discussion provides some additional support for the view that ambitious new forms of linkage might not be needed and thus for the second standard objection that the authors identify.

Let me begin with a methodological point. In my view, when evaluating an existing or proposed international agreement among governments, the first step is to identify the problem the agreement is designed to solve. This can be accomplished once any assumptions regarding the objectives of governments are made explicit. It is then possible to describe the policies that governments would choose in the absence of any agreement. In turn, these unilateral policies can be contrasted with the policies that are efficient, where efficiency is measured in relation to the objectives of governments. A problem is then present when the unilateral policy choices are inefficient. In this event, governments have reason to form an international agreement: an appropriately designed international agreement could eliminate inefficient policy choices and thus generate a mutually advantageous outcome for participating governments. Moreover, if the precise source of this inefficiency is identified, then it becomes possible to evaluate whether, in fact, an existing or proposed international agreement is well designed for encouraging efficient policy choices.

Barry and Reddy adopt a distinct methodological approach. In proposition O, they state that a "very important factor in determining whether an institutional arrangement for the governance of the global economy should be viewed as superior to another is whether it improves the level of advantage of less advantaged persons in the world to a greater extent." I agree with this statement. On page 3 and in their subsequent discussion, they then generally refer to "improving the level of advantage of less advantaged persons in the world" as "the objective." Here, I would simply reinforce that it is important also to give due consideration to the implications of institutional arrangements for those individuals who are not less advantaged. In any event, as discussed above, the authors' methodological approach is then to argue that an institutional arrangement that features linkage in an appropriate fashion is superior to nonlinkage proposals in promoting this objective. The authors make their argument by constructing a class of linkage systems that better withstands the standard objections to the usual notion of linkage.

The approach taken by Barry and Reddy is informative and leads to valuable insights. It is important to stress, however, that the criterion that they use in assessing institutional arrangements is not the objectives of participating governments. Consequently, their approach does not focus on the reasons for a discrepancy between the labor standards that governments would choose unilaterally and those that governments would choose as part of a mutually beneficial agreement. Oversimplifying, the authors' position is that labor standards are currently too weak and that an appropriately designed institutional arrangement that raises standards should be pursued. But if improved labor standards are a good thing, one may wonder why governments haven't already raised standards to the appropriate degree. Why, exactly, do we need an international institution?

One good answer to this question is that many governments are corrupt and/or incompetent and thus do not appropriately represent their citizens.[3] Without question, this is sometimes the case. Even so, as a general matter, I am not sure this answer provides the best starting point from which to propose and evaluate international economic institutions. In its extreme version, this answer suggests that the underlying rationale for an international economic institution is that the designers of the institution understand better the interests of individuals than do the governments that represent those individuals. This rationale may conflict with standard notions of national sovereignty and seems especially problematic when the governments in question are democratically elected. For the purposes at hand, I prefer to start at the opposite extreme and assume that the preferences expressed by the government of a country are the best available indicator of the aggregate preferences of the individuals in that country. Under this assumption, which also has clear limitations and is admittedly more realistic for some countries than others, it is reasonable to evaluate an international agreement in terms of the extent to which it facilitates mutually advantageous policy choices among governments. This perspective in turn suggests a different answer to the question raised above: an international agreement might be needed in order to correct the inefficiencies that arise as a consequence of the international externalities that flow from one government's policy choices to another government's welfare. This answer directs attention to the identification of the pecuniary and nonpecuniary international externalities that might be associated with policy choices.

Let us next apply this methodology to the trade-policy setting and provide thereby a rationale for the WTO.[4] As the rationale I provide does not require a nonpecuniary international externality, I will focus the discussion and consider here only pecuniary international externalities. In the absence of a trade agreement, when setting its import tariff, each government would be mindful of the effects on its consumers, import-competing firms, and tariff revenue. A higher import tariff would hurt domestic consumers, help import-competing firms, and perhaps raise tariff revenue. After considering these various effects and weighing the extents to which they contribute or detract from its political-economic objective, each government would determine its optimal unilateral tariff. In making this determination, however, each government neglects one important group: foreign exporters. When a government of a large country imposes an import tariff, the export price received by foreign exporters is reduced, and some of the incidence of the tariff thus falls on foreign exporters. This pecuniary international externality is known among trade economists as the terms-of-trade externality.[5] The terms-of-trade externality thus induces each government to select import tariffs that are inefficiently high, since each government fails to internalize the negative effect of its tariff on foreign exporters and thus foreign government welfare.

In the trade-policy setting, governments thus face a terms-of-trade-driven prisoners' dilemma problem. Due to the terms-of-trade externality, governments adopt tariffs that are inefficiently high even though they could achieve mutual gains from an agreement to reciprocally lower their tariffs. Equivalently, each government offers its trading partners inefficiently little market access, even though governments could mutually gain from an agreement to reciprocally exchange greater market access. According to this view, the WTO can be understood as a trade agreement whose fundamental purpose is to facilitate an escape from a terms-of-trade-driven prisoners' dilemma. This perspective also suggests that an appropriately designed trade agreement would feature reciprocal (rather than unilateral) tariff liberalization and utilize the threat of retaliation as a means to deter cheating and thereby enforce negotiated reductions in tariffs. At a broad level, the design of the WTO is consistent with this description.

Let us now consider the application of this methodology to labor standards. What pecuniary and nonpecuniary international externalities might be associated with a government's choice of labor standards? To begin the discussion, I initially suppose that labor standards choices do not create an international nonpecuniary externality.[6] In the discussion of trade agreements above, governments are allowed to choose tariffs only, and the fundamental problem that a trade agreement might address is the insufficient market access that arises as a consequence of the terms-of-trade externality. In the extended framework now under consideration, where governments can choose both tariffs and labor standards, the basic analysis is unchanged: the problem is insufficient market access and the source of the inefficiency is the terms-of-trade externality.

To see the basic point, let us suppose that governments have negotiated lower tariffs through a trade agreement but have placed no restraints on the choice of labor standards. It is easy to understand that such an agreement cannot achieve an efficient outcome. Intuitively, when a government lowers its labor standards in an import-competing industry, the firms in this industry enjoy lower costs and are thus in an improved competitive position relative to foreign exporters. In other words, lower standards act like a higher import tariff: both policies generate a terms-of-trade externality and thus reduce the access of foreign exporters to the domestic market. Since a government does not internalize the costs that its labor standards choices impose upon foreign exporters, it sets labor standards in its import-competing industries at levels that are inefficiently low.

It is now possible to provide an interpretation of the race-to-the-bottom and regulatory-chill concerns that are associated with the choice of labor standards. A race to the bottom is present in the sense that each government perceives some advantage from improving the competitive position of its firms relative to that of foreign exporters and thus chooses inefficiently low labor standards in import-competing industries. In the same way, a regulatory chill can arise in the sense that a government may refrain from adopting an efficient improvement in its labor standards in an import-competing industry, since some of the benefits from such a regulatory change would flow to foreign exporters who would then enjoy expanded access to the domestic market.

When the choice of labor standards is completely unrestricted, negotiations over tariffs alone are thus insufficient for achieving an efficient outcome. This observation offers apparent support for a linkage system. In principle, an efficient outcome could be achieved through an agreement in which governments explicitly negotiate both tariffs and labor standards. Negotiations over labor standards, however, raise concerns about national sovereignty. It is thus important to ask: is it necessary that governments explicitly negotiate both tariffs and labor standards?

At a conceptual level, the answer to this question is clearly "no." In the absence of international nonpecuniary externalities, a government's policy choices affect a foreign government's welfare only by altering foreign exporters' access to the domestic market. Thus, an efficient outcome could be achieved through tariff negotiations alone, if the rules of the trade agreement ensured that the resulting negotiated market access commitments were secure against unilateral government infringement, where the infringement could result from subsequent changes in tariffs or labor standards. A two-step negotiation approach would do the trick.[7] First, given their existing labor standards, governments could negotiate tariff reductions that achieved efficient market access levels. Second, subsequent to the initial negotiations, either government would be free to adjust its policy mix (i.e., its tariffs or labor standards) as desired, provided that any such adjustment maintained the government's negotiated market access commitment. An appealing feature of this approach is that it focuses on the underlying problem (insufficient market access) and otherwise leaves governments free to enjoy national sovereignty with respect to their policy mixes.

The approach described here utilizes within-country policy linkages. If following a tariff negotiation a government were to lower its labor standards in an import-competing industry, then its market access commitment would be maintained only if it were also to reduce its import tariff. Such within-country linkages can thus reduce the potential for a race to the bottom in labor standards. I am delighted to see that Barry and Reddy agree with this point and have featured it in their discussion. Likewise, if a government were to raise its labor standards in an import-competing industry, then it would be allowed to raise its import tariff in a commensurate fashion. An adjustment of this kind reduces the potential for a regulatory chill.[8] Here I take issue with Barry and Reddy, who do not advocate a tariff adjustment of this kind. In my view, their proposal (page 57) of an "asymmetrical requirement for Kemp-Wan adjustments" does not adequately address the potential for a regulatory chill in labor standards.

Is this approach reflected in WTO rules? The WTO does not place explicit restrictions on the labor standards choices of member governments; however, if a government changes its labor standards and thereby erodes the market access of foreign exporters, then the policy change could invite a nonviolation complaint (NVC). An NVC is permissible if concessions (e.g., tariff cuts) have been negotiated and a subsequent measure is then adopted that could not have been reasonably expected at the time of negotiation and that has the effect of reducing the value of the negotiated concession. While changes in labor standards have not been the focus of any NVCs to date, Bagwell, Mavroidis, and Staiger discuss recent WTO case law and argue that NVCs plausibly might be used if labor standards were relaxed in import-competing industries following a negotiated concession.[9] When an NVC succeeds, one possible remedy would utilize within-country policy adjustments of the kind described above: the infringing government could restore market access by offering a further (nondiscriminatory) tariff reduction as compensation. On the basis of the approach described above and further discussion by Bagwell, Mavroidis, and Staiger, I thus propose an expanded role for NVCs.[10] A more active use of such WTO rules could help to secure market access commitments against unilateral government infringement through lower labor standards and thereby limit the potential for a race to the bottom in labor standards.[11]

With some augmentation, WTO rules can also limit the potential for regulatory chill. If a government considers strengthening its labor standards in an import-competing industry, the market access of foreign exporters would increase. If the increase in labor standards were coupled with a commensurate increase in the import tariff, then foreign market access would be unaffected. From this perspective, it is reasonable to regard an increase in labor standards as "compensation" for a renegotiation to a higher tariff. WTO rules already allow for renegotiation to a higher tariff under GATT Article XXVIII, provided that compensation is given. Traditional notions of compensation envision a corresponding reduction in the import tariff for some other good. Bagwell, Mavroidis, and Staiger propose that GATT Article XXVIII be amended so as to make explicit the following understanding: "If they so decide, WTO Members wishing to raise their labor standards and implement the standards reflected in the ILO Conventions will be allowed to raise the level of their bound duties without incurring the obligation to compensate injured WTO members."[12] A within-country policy linkage of this kind would ensure that the market access of foreign exporters is preserved (rather than increased) and thereby reduce the potential for regulatory chill.

The discussion to this point has addressed labor standards in import-competing industries. Consider now the pecuniary externality associated with the choice of labor standards for an export industry. From the point of view of the importing country, an increase in labor standards in the export industry is akin to an export tax. The higher labor standards result in a higher price for importing consumers and thereby generate a negative terms-of-trade externality for the government of the importing country.[13] This country would suffer additional terms-of-trade losses if it were to offer a carrot to the exporting country in the form of a reduced import tariff. If labor standards only impart pecuniary externalities, the interesting policy trade discussed by Barry and Reddy may fail to appeal to importing countries. In this case, I am more optimistic about an arrangement that would allow the exporting government to provide its export industry with a subsidy when labor standards are increased in this industry. A within-country policy adjustment of this kind would eliminate the terms-of-trade externality on other countries and thereby enable the exporting government to select the efficient policy mix.

At a practical level, however, a couple of objections may be made. First, the WTO imposes strong restrictions on subsidies. In my view, these restrictions are too strong, and the WTO rules should be modified to be more accommodating of within-country adjustments in tariffs and subsidies that maintain negotiated market access commitments.[14] In this context, I suggest that WTO rules be modified and made more receptive toward subsidies that accompany an increase in labor standards in export industries.[15] Second, some of the countries in which labor standards are weak may lack the resources to provide such subsidies. In this case, it would seem reasonable to encourage programs that facilitate low-interest loans and other financial compensation.[16]

Up to this point, I have focused on the pecuniary externalities associated with the choice of labor standards. The main policy implication of the discussion is that such externalities do not require explicit linkage agreements and can be handled with modifications of existing WTO rules. I consider now the possibility that nonpecuniary externalities may be associated with the choice of labor standards. A nonpecuniary externality arises, for example, if low labor standards in one country lead to humanitarian concerns among altruistic citizens in another country. In that event, the government of the latter country has a direct interest in the well-being of workers in the former country.

When such a nonpecuniary externality exists, a government's unilateral labor standards choices are inefficiently low, since the government does not value the benefit of an increase in its standards to other governments. The presence of nonpecuniary externalities thus provides a rationale for international negotiations over labor standards. Furthermore, if one government benefits when another government strengthens its labor standards, then a mutually advantageous strengthening in labor standards may be possible only if the former government shares the burden of the consequent costs. A carrot-based system, where a concerned government rewards another government when the latter increases labor standards, may then enhance efficiency among governments.[17] A cross-country resource transfer that takes the form of cash (or other financial assistance) would be one attractive way to provide such a carrot. As Barry and Reddy indicate, a tariff cut would also be a good means of providing a reward.

When nonpecuniary externalities lead to international negotiations, asymmetric information may be an important consideration. Barry and Reddy do not emphasize this concern in their essay, but it raises some interesting issues. In particular, when asymmetric information is a concern, it is interesting to compare a carrot-based system, such as Barry and Reddy consider, with the standard linkage system, which utilizes only sticks. As I argue below, asymmetric information favors a carrot-based system in many (but not all) circumstances.

Suppose first that the asymmetric information concerns the extent to which a given government would really benefit were another government to raise its labor standards. When the nonpecuniary externality is associated with humanitarian concerns, this case is quite plausible. A carrot-based system seems advantageous in this scenario. Intuitively, when the former government makes a request that the latter government raise labor standards in an export industry, only the former government knows whether the request reflects genuine humanitarian concerns or disguised protection. It may be efficient, however, to raise labor standards only when humanitarian concerns motivate the request. Under the usual interpretation of linkage, the request is accompanied by a threat to impose a retaliatory tariff (i.e., a stick) in the event of noncompliance. It is then difficult to tell what motivation underlies the request. By contrast, if the request is accompanied by an offer to make a resource transfer (such as a reduced tariff) in the event of compliance, then it is unlikely that disguised protection motivates the request. A carrot-based system thus has an "incentive-compatible" structure that facilitates the identification of humanitarian concerns and the implementation of efficient responses.

A second possibility is that the government of the country with low standards is asymmetrically informed as to the cost of raising standards. As Howard F. Chang argues in the context of environmental standards, a carrot-based system may perform poorly in this situation.[18] Under a carrot-based system, this government may wish to represent that the cost of an increase in labor standards would be high. If it can create this impression, then it can expect a larger resource transfer from other concerned governments. In turn, this government can signal that an increase in labor standards would be costly by setting very low labor standards in the prenegotiation phase. A carrot-based system can thus create perverse incentives by encouraging, at least initially, the behavior it is designed to eliminate. The potential for such distortions seems especially relevant if the system allocates carrots in a manner that is highly context sensitive (i.e., highly dependent upon industry and country circumstances).

My discussion above indicates that international negotiations on labor standards may be mutually advantageous for governments when nonpecuniary externalities are present. This discussion indicates an important role for the ILO. I turn now to consider the possible role for the WTO when labor standards generate nonpecuniary externalities. In general, when nonpecuniary externalities are present, it is no longer possible to achieve efficient policy outcomes with negotiations over tariffs alone. This is because nonpecuniary externalities do not travel through the terms of trade and thus need have no close connection with market access considerations. Accordingly, the rules of the WTO are not well designed for addressing nonpecuniary externalities such as humanitarian concerns. Even so, it is possible to entertain two ways in which the WTO might play a role when the choice of labor standards generates a nonpecuniary externality.

A first possibility is that agreements on labor standards might be directly negotiated in the WTO. In principle, it can be useful to combine issues into a single negotiating forum, if doing so better enables governments to divide the gains created by their negotiations. But does a government need to negotiate a new WTO tariff binding in order to induce another government to raise labor standards? Following Bagwell, Mavroidis, and Staiger, I would argue that the answer may be "no."[19] First, as mentioned previously, a government can use other instruments (cash, financial assistance, debt relief) to reward an improvement in labor standards. Second, even if a government prefers to offer a reward in the form of enhanced market access, it need not negotiate a new WTO binding. For example, it could apply a nondiscriminatory tariff that is below its bound rate in exchange for higher standards abroad. In the case of a developed country that wishes to induce higher labor standards in a developing country, WTO rules also provide some scope for rewards that take the form of discriminatory tariff reductions. Specifically, the Enabling Clause and the Generalized System of Preferences (GSP) introduce the potential for a government of a developed country to promise additional preferential market access to a developing country conditional upon the labor standards in the latter country. The European Community and the United States link labor standards and preferences in their respective GSP lists. In short, this discussion suggests that current WTO rules already provide scope for a range of carrots.

A second possibility is that the WTO dispute settlement procedures might be utilized to help enforce an agreement on labor standards negotiated outside of the WTO. The idea here is that labor standards agreements negotiated in the ILO, for example, could be more effectively enforced if a violation were to trigger retaliatory trade measures authorized by the WTO. Recent game-theoretic work suggests that explicit linkage of this kind, which facilitates cross-issue retaliation, can be beneficial to governments.

In some circumstances, linkage may result in greater cooperation in both policies; however, in other circumstances, linkage may imply a reallocation of cooperation across policies. In the latter case, enhanced cooperation in labor standards could come at the cost of diminished cooperation in trade policies. Overall, this line of research arguably provides the strongest theoretical foundation for Barry and Reddy's proposed international agency ATLAS.[20]

Following Bagwell, Mavroidis, and Staiger, I would argue, however, that the potential benefits of cross-issue retaliation might also be captured by utilizing existing implicit linkages between the WTO and ILO.[21] Both explicit and implicit linkages involve the possibility that the WTO could authorize retaliatory trade measures in the event that, say, a government chose labor standards that were in violation of an ILO commitment. When the linkage is explicit, the retaliatory trade measure would come about through the use of new retaliation rights that arise as consequence of augmented WTO rules; by contrast, an implicit linkage would correspond to harnessing the power of existing WTO rules. For example, suppose that a government has ratified an ILO convention and bound its tariffs in WTO negotiations and that the government subsequently violates its ILO obligations in a way that has market access implications. It then may be possible to argue that the ratification of ILO obligations creates reasonable expectations among trading partners that the government will respect the ILO convention; as a consequence, if the government fails to honor this convention, then the stage is set for its trading partners to use existing WTO rules and file an NVC. If the NVC is successful and the infringing government does not adjust its labor standards or otherwise appropriately compensate its trading partners, then its trading partners could be authorized under WTO rules to impose retaliatory tariffs. Notice that the linkage here is implicit—a violation of an ILO commitment is not regarded as a violation of WTO commitments—and yet existing WTO rules are used to help enforce negotiated ILO commitments on labor standards.

In summary, when unilateral labor standards choices generate nonpecuniary externalities, an international agreement on labor standards can produce mutual gains for participating governments. To achieve these gains, however, it might not be necessary that such an agreement be negotiated in the WTO or that an explicit link be established between the

WTO and ILO for enforcement purposes. In any case, I suggest that the use of existing implicit links between the WTO and ILO be encouraged.

I now wrap up with some general remarks on the WTO. In my view, the WTO (and GATT before it) has far-reaching and positive effects on the functioning of the world economy. The WTO facilitates the exchange of reciprocal market access commitments, and the resulting increase in trade and national income is on the whole beneficial for developed and developing countries alike. The nondiscrimination principle of the WTO deserves special attention: it "multilateralizes" negotiated concessions and thus ensures that exporters from developing countries can enjoy the tariff cuts that are negotiated between the governments of developed countries. While this approach has limitations (for example, negotiations among developed countries may give inadequate attention to products that are of greater importance to developing countries), a developing country would surely fare less well if bilateral negotiations were the only means through which it could achieve greater access to the markets of large countries. In turn, the resulting national income gains that WTO negotiations facilitate can be a very important catalyst for reduced poverty and improved working conditions within developing countries. With regard to the specific issue of labor standards, these general considerations give me further reason to favor modest changes to WTO rules that maintain a close coherence with WTO principles. Arguably, changes of this kind are least likely to threaten the long-term performance and stability of the WTO. I identify a few such changes above.

Barry and Reddy offer a very thoughtful proposal on a complicated and important issue. My comments above identify several areas of agreement with their proposal. I certainly agree with the authors that the usual linkage proposal is narrow and unattractive, and I welcome their call for greater "institutional imagination" and broader discussion. I also strongly agree that superior arrangements would place greater reliance on within-country policy adjustments and the use of cross-country policy trades (carrots). My main area of difference with the authors is in the institutional prescription. I argue that race-to-the-bottom and regulatory-chill concerns derive from a pecuniary (terms-of-trade) externality and are thus market access issues. With some augmentation, WTO rules are well designed to address these concerns. I also argue that inefficiencies resulting from nonpecuniary externalities such as humanitarian concerns might be addressed through the development of implicit links between the WTO and the ILO. In broad terms, I thus argue that many of the benefits Barry and Reddy seek may be best achieved by harnessing the power of existing WTO rules and principles. This is a more modest proposal than the ATLAS proposal advanced by Barry and Reddy.

Fine-Tuning the Linkage Proposal

COMMENTARY BY ROHINI HENSMAN

A cross-country comparison that finds "strong evidence that countries with open trade policies have superior labor rights and health conditions and less child labor"[1] suggests that openness to the world economy does not undermine workers' rights and may even enhance them. However, the finding that in any particular country openness to the world economy can go with high labor standards is not incompatible with the proposition that globalization as a process undermines labor rights globally.

One process by which this could and does take place is by the transfer of production from countries with higher labor standards to countries with lower standards, leaving workers in the former unemployed. Thus in developed countries, jobs in the labor-intensive textile and garment industries have been decimated as production has shifted to developing-country export sectors.[2] This has also caused job losses in developing countries, when production moved from higher-wage countries such as Korea to lower-wage ones such as Cambodia. Outsourcing in the service sector led to a further transfer of employment from developed to developing countries, leading to calls for a curb on outsourcing in the United States.[3]

A less obvious and more insidious way in which labor standards are undermined is by the spread of low labor standards to countries that did not formerly suffer from them (or at least not to the same extent), as employers and governments compete for investment and markets. The global expansion of informal labor—workers who do not have any formal employment contract with an employer and therefore are extremely vulnerable to abuse—is a case of this. Informal labor was always preponderant in India, but the expansion of homeworking, sweatshops, and the hiring of workers through intermediaries ("labor contractors," "agencies," "gangmasters," and so on) in countries that were formerly free of these problems[4] has caused serious concern within the ILO in the twenty-first century.[5]

In this context, the publication of *International Trade and Labor Standards: A Proposal for Linkage*, with its carefully crafted proposal for linking trade and labor standards in a manner that is both feasible and capable of stopping the downward pressure on labor rights, is of great importance. The authors have taken up objections to linkage in a step-by-step manner in order to formulate a proposal that meets almost all the arguments commonly put forward against it. This paper is an attempt to strengthen that proposal and make it more concrete.

UNFAIR TRADE PRACTICE OR VIOLATION OF HUMAN RIGHTS?

There are two connected but distinct arguments for linking labor standards with trade, which are not sufficiently distinguished in the proposal. One is that low labor standards are an unfair trade practice by means of which a country attempts to enrich itself at the expense of others, and the other is that basic labor standards embody fundamental human rights that ought to be upheld in all international treaties. The proposal starts off by suggesting that the ILO Core Conventions—dealing with freedom of association and the right to organize and bargain collectively, freedom from forced and compulsory labor, the elimination of discrimination in employment and occupation, and the abolition of child labor, all of which are characterized as fundamental rights of human beings at work—should be the basis for the definition of minimum labor standards, implying that it accepts a human rights definition. However, the suggestion that "the linkage system would require that countries attain to a minimally adequate level of labor standards, as determined in light of its degree of development and other relevant considerations" would make sense only if low labor standards were seen as trade practices for which allowances might be made if the country were very poor. Yet there is an implicit return to a human rights definition in the suggestion that "countries may be required to respect a few fundamental requirements (for example to outlaw slave labor and child prostitution) regardless of their level of development."

There is a danger that defining low standards as a labor practice that might be justifiable in poor countries could detract from the feasibility of the proposal; it is likely that there would be endless wrangling over a country's degree of development and thus its appropriate level of labor standards. More importantly, the moral force of the argument for linkage would be undermined, and this is, no doubt, why the paper proposes a few fundamental requirements that all countries should respect, regardless of their level of development. If there are, indeed, "fundamental requirements" all countries should be required to respect, there is a strong argument for defining these in terms of the ILO Core Conventions. While there has been some criticism of these—on one side, allegations that the rights embodied in these conventions are too restricted,[6] and on the other, that they go too far—they also have undeniable merits.

One great advantage is that the *ILO Declaration on Fundamental Principles and Rights at Work and Its Follow-up*, adopted in 1998, can be interpreted as agreement that these rights are applicable to all member countries, regardless of their level of development and regardless of whether they have ratified the conventions in question.[7] Given that most countries in the world are ILO members, that governments, employers, and unions are represented in it, and that the majority of members belong to developing countries, this is probably as close as we can get to standards on which there is universal agreement. Charges of cultural and/or political imperialism would be less plausible if it can be pointed out that the majority of the world's people have, through the ILO, endorsed these as fundamental rights.

If it is accepted that there should be at least *a few* requirements that are universally applicable, then there should be some rationale for them, and their status as human rights is the obvious one. It is true that slavery and child prostitution involve egregious violations of human rights, and, indeed, two of the core conventions are aimed at eliminating forced labor and the worst forms of child labor. But in what way are other forms of child labor different from slavery, given that it is the freedom to enter into—and exit from—a contract with the employer that distinguishes wage labor from slavery, and children do not have the legal right to enter into contracts nor do they have the freedom to exit from employment except in the same way as slaves, by running away? And is child prostitution so very much worse than other forms of child labor? The Indian government belatedly woke up to the problem of children in domestic service in 2006, after the torture, sexual assault, and murder of ten-year-old Sonu by her employers received widespread publicity, yet a report by Save the Children charged that subsequent amendments to the Child Labor Act were inadequate, pointing out that these children, most of them girls, were being forced to work for fifteen hours a day with no breaks and little or no pay, were routinely subjected to physical abuse, and were often sexually abused as well. The argument that *all* labor is a violation of children's human rights if it exposes them to occupational hazards or abuse, deprives them of adequate time for rest and play, interferes with their education, or does not give them the freedom to exit at any time has the merit of consistency. Including the abolition of child labor as a fundamental requirement would bring the linkage proposal into line not only with the core conventions but also with other UN instruments including the Child Rights Convention.

Again, discrimination against some section of the population, covered by two of the core conventions, is regarded as a violation of human rights by everyone who believes in the concept of human rights, and is prohibited by several UN instruments, starting with the Universal Declaration of Human Rights. The sanctions that helped to bring down the Apartheid regime in South Africa were justified as a means of ending the systematic discrimination practiced by that regime. The right to freedom of association and to form and join trade unions, covered in the remaining two core conventions, are also upheld in the Universal Declaration of Human Rights and other UN instruments. It should therefore be uncontroversial that all the rights articulated by the core conventions are universal human rights. It would then follow that making their protection dependent on the level of development of a country would be to condone the violation of fundamental rights under certain circumstances.

What about the contention that the rights embodied in the core conventions are unaffordable by poor countries, and that their enforcement may even block development? As the paper correctly observes, there are strong arguments for maintaining that these rights are in fact central to the very definition of development and that real development cannot occur in their absence, although it may certainly be possible for a few individuals or business houses to amass a great deal of wealth. Second, the point is also made that cashing in on the expansion of the tertiary sector, where most of the new jobs are being created, requires an educated workforce, which in turn depends on universal elementary education at the very least.

In fact, a model of development built on a disempowered and destitute population producing for export to rich countries is no longer viable. With the market for many consumer products saturated in developed countries, companies are seeking out "emerging markets" for investment. Qualifying for these investments depends on having a reasonably good infrastructure and creating mass markets for consumer products, which in turn depend on wages above the level required for mere survival. A. T. Kearney's survey of over one thousand top international companies in 2001 showed that the two major attractions of India as an investment destination were (1) the potentially huge size of its market, and (2) the availability of an educated, skilled English-speaking labor force at competitive wages.[8] However, China was considered more attractive because its market was seen as being disproportionately larger—ten times larger, in the view of some companies—probably because prices of consumer goods were much lower in China, creating a mass market for them.[9] Thus development, even in a narrow economic sense, involves the expansion of the domestic market and a tax base large enough to support state investments in infrastructure and education, both of which are promoted by implementation of the core conventions.

PRACTICAL MECHANISMS

The ILO is the only organization with the competence to monitor labor rights, investigate complaints, and assist governments in complying with the core conventions. It would have to perform these functions for a joint ILO/WTO body set up to oversee the operation of the linkage system and would need adequate funding for this purpose. In this context, "burden sharing" between developed and developing countries, as suggested in the proposal, would be an important element in implementing a linkage scheme, but it must be emphasized that countries with higher labor standards must not be understood as being synonymous with developed countries, nor those with lower standards with developing countries. Thus the transfer of resources should not necessarily be from countries with higher labor standards to those with lower standards; it would hardly be fair to transfer resources from Sweden to the United States, or from Sri Lanka to Bangladesh.

One suggestion for an equitable and feasible mechanism for resource transfer is that WTO member states should fund the linkage scheme by contributions that are a flat percentage of their GDP, while the amount of financial help countries are entitled to in order to fund improvements in labor rights should be inversely proportional to their per capita GDP: from each according to their ability, to each according to their need.

It should be possible for anyone to make a complaint, including workers' organizations. It would then be the task of the ILO to investigate the complaint and determine who is responsible for the violation, if it exists: the culprit might be a domestic company, a multinational or foreign retail company, the government, the IMF or World Bank (whose policies may undermine labor rights), or some combination of these. The next step would be to suggest a strategy to eliminate the violation and assist the government in implementing it. Only if the government refuses to cooperate should penalties be considered as a last resort.

What should the penalties be? An important condition for making linkage acceptable to Third World governments and even trade unions is that it should not be possible to use the system in a discriminatory manner against developing countries. In order to ensure an equal standard, ratification of the relevant conventions, their incorporation in national legislation, and genuine efforts to implement the laws should be required of a member state before it has a right to make a complaint against another state. This would take care of valid objections to the possibility of the United States taking action against other countries for violating rights that are being violated in the United States itself.

If a country is in fact in compliance with the ILO core conventions, it should then have the right to refuse to import products made in violation of them. For example, WTO rules should allow a developing country that has eliminated child labor to refuse to import products made by children, which might threaten it with a reappearance of child labor in its own economy if domestic producers tried to compete with these imports by employing children. And a developed country implementing these conventions should be allowed to discriminate in favor of imports made in compliance with them, in order to encourage respect for human rights in the global economy. It has been suggested that one way to achieve this is to expand Article XX(e) of the WTO agreement—which permits countries to ban the import of goods produced using prison labor—to include goods and services produced in violation of any of the core human rights conventions.[10]

However, there is a danger that such action by itself could have adverse effects: for example, children who are simply expelled from export production might end up in even worse occupations. The only way to preclude such an outcome is to ensure that the minimum labor rights embodied in the linkage system are enforced not just in production for export but in *all* production, and, indeed, this is what Barry and Reddy propose. But this raises a new problem: to use international trade sanctions as a penalty for the violation of labor rights in production for the domestic market would not be appropriate. Let us suppose, for example, that all the manufacturers producing garments for export are complying with the requirements of the linkage system while those producing for the domestic market are not, and the government refuses to take action against them. The first victims of international trade sanctions would be the manufacturers—and their workers—who are in compliance with the requirements. The government too would suffer, no doubt, but less immediately. The companies violating labor rights might not be affected at all, unless the government is finally pressured into taking action against them.

This "punishment" of the innocent, like all collective punishment, would be perceived as being unjust and would therefore discredit the linkage regime. Instead, putting pressure on recalcitrant governments to take action against offending companies producing for the domestic market could, for example, take the form of fines; if the violations are by a Third World subsidiary or subcontractor of a multinational based in a developed country, both countries could be fined in proportion to their GDP. The fines could then be used by the ILO to help eliminate the violation: to take children out of employment and assure them of a livelihood and education, to set up machinery to deal with cases of bonded labor, union busting or discrimination, and so on. The system could be linked to international trade in a less direct fashion, by making it mandatory for every member of the WTO to participate in it.

Such a system would help to rule out the possibility that linkage might harm those it is meant to help, while at the same time putting pressure on recalcitrant governments to change their policies. It would also help to raise money to fund the reforms from governments that could afford to spend more on labor standards but instead had other priorities, such as military spending or subsidies for companies. A cross-country study of child labor, for example, concluded that "poverty is not even a significant reason for child labor when the influence of other explanatory factors for child labor are taken into account,"[11] and suggested that it is lack of will on the part of governments to provide a good education for every child that is responsible for child labor. This is confirmed by examples within India, where state governments with a commitment to providing an education for all children have succeeded in eliminating child labor despite being poor, while richer states continue to have a much higher level of child labor.[12] In such circumstances, the threat of fines would be an appropriate way to put pressure on WTO member states to undertake the policy changes required to protect these basic human rights.

INFORMAL LABOR

Perhaps the biggest challenge faced by a linkage system—as, indeed, by any attempt to defend basic labor rights—is dealing with informal labor. Workers who are employed but have no legal status as workers nor any formal relationship with an employer can easily be denied basic rights and dismissed with impunity if they try to demand them; indeed, this happens all the time in India. They constitute a large and growing section of the global labor force, and it can be argued that any system of labor rights protection fails unless there is a strategy for including them in it.

This is a problem that goes beyond linkage. Informal women garment workers in Bombay suggested that registration of all employers and employees and some form of legal employment contract—in other words, measures to formalize their employment—would be necessary if they were to have the right to organize and other basic rights; labor legislation that currently excludes them should also be extended to cover all employees.[13] The ILO could, and should, do something to remedy this situation. At a seminar on informal workers organized by IRENE (International Restructuring Education Network Europe), the Clean Clothes Campaign, and the Evangelische Akademie in Meissen in September 2004, one of the proposals was that the right to proof of identity as workers and proof of employment should be incorporated in one of the ILO Core Conventions. The most appropriate would be No. 98, on the Right to Organize and Collective Bargaining (1949), which deals (among other things) with protecting workers from victimization for belonging to a union or taking part in its activities.[14]

If one of the ILO Core Conventions is amended as suggested, inclusion of informal workers would automatically become part of the linkage scheme. This would undoubtedly add to the cost of implementation, since it would then become necessary to set up the machinery to register informal employers and employees, and the employment contracts entered into by them, as well as to monitor the application of labor laws to these workers. But the costs of not dealing with this problem would be infinitely greater, although not so easily measured in financial terms: the lives, limbs, health, and democratic rights of a large and growing section of the world's labor force.

CAMPAIGNING FOR LINKAGE

The campaign for a workers' rights clause to be part of WTO's international trade agreements, which was so vociferous at the time of the 1999 ministerial meeting in Seattle, has died down considerably. There could be several reasons for this. Resistance from Third World employers and governments that saw such a measure as threatening the cheap labor regimes in their countries is one. Governments of developed countries that were pushing for it may simply have been playing to their working-class constituencies in an opportunistic manner, abandoning the proposal when it no longer served their political purposes.

However, the main reason was probably the fact that the constituency that could have derived the most benefit from it—workers in both developed and developing countries—were confused and divided on the issue. Unions in developed countries proposed a linkage mechanism that could, conceivably, be used for protectionist purposes. This antagonized unionists in developing countries, who concluded that the purpose was to attack their employment and therefore opposed it. Conversely, unionists from developed countries were shocked at what they thought was endorsement of child labor by their counterparts in developing countries who opposed the proposal. Antiglobalization activists saw the WTO as being by its nature neoliberal and neoliberalism as being inimical to labor rights; they therefore concluded that the proposal was eyewash and should be dismissed along with the WTO itself; this attitude made its way into some sections of the labor movement. The debate, if it could be called that, was not conducted in an orderly manner.

One unfortunate consequence was that the international and developed-country unions that had been the strongest supporters of the "social clause" turned to other strategies, especially International Framework Agreements and Codes of Conduct. Yet the implementation of both of these faced enormous difficulties,[15] and even when they were able to protect labor rights, the number of workers affected were minuscule by comparison with those who might have been reached by a clause in WTO agreements. This does not mean that these strategies should be abandoned, only that it is still necessary to supplement them with a more inclusive measure.

Nonetheless, there were some gains. One was the attempt by some of those who supported linkage in principle to craft a proposal that would meet valid objections that had been made to the earlier one. If a campaign for such an improved scheme can be launched at this point, it could result in a more satisfactory debate. And if the measure is actually incorporated in WTO agreements, it would do much to legitimize the international trade body in the eyes of unions and labor activists throughout the world. Hopefully, this volume will help to launch such a campaign.

The Ethics of Political Linkage

COMMENTARY BY ROBERT E. GOODIN

In the negotiations leading up to the Helsinki agreement of 1975, Western negotiators proposed linking nuclear arms reductions to respect for international human rights. There were widespread complaints at the time. Arms control and human rights were two wholly separate issues having absolutely nothing to do with one another, it was said, and it was simply inappropriate to make one conditional in any way on the other. Such complaints came naturally enough from the Soviet bloc. But they were also heard from Westerners who were genuinely serious about nuclear arms reductions and who suspected that the linkage was intended by the U.S. administration as a "killer amendment" to guarantee that the negotiations collapsed altogether.

Subsequent history proved different. The Soviets grudgingly accepted the conditions and imperfectly implemented them, and those human rights reforms, limited though they were, constituted a first foot on the slippery slope that eventually led to the unraveling of the Soviet empire.[1] That happy historical ending notwithstanding, the more general problem persists. What sorts of issues may properly be linked together in international agreements?

An analogy from domestic law might provide some traction. In U.S. constitutional law, there is something called the "impermissible conditions" doctrine. There are all sorts of things the state is legally free to do or not to do, just as it pleases, but even though the state would be perfectly within its rights to refuse to do the thing altogether, it is not necessarily permissible for it to set any condition it pleases upon its doing them. In one leading case, for example, the state of California was deemed to be entirely free to grant or withhold a building permit for alterations to an owner's beachfront house, but it was deemed impermissible for the state to make granting that permit conditional upon the owner's agreeing to granting a right of way through the property for the public to access the beach.[2]

The principles for deciding what sorts of conditions are permissible in such domestic law situations might give us some insight into what sorts of conditions ought be deemed appropriate in international law situations. Those standards can, in turn, cast important light on the moral appropriateness of Berry and Reddy's proposed linking of trade and labor standards.

Before proceeding with this exercise, one threshold question must be addressed. It is the hoary old question of "realism" in international relations. Realists insistently enquire, "what has morality got to do with it?" International relations, in their view, are entirely a matter of power and interests. States simply do (and should do, in the purely prudential sense of "should," which is the only sense known to realists) whatever they have the power to do in furtherance of their interests.[3]

In international negotiations, such realists would insist, states simply impose (and should impose) whatever conditions they want and have the power to make stick, as the price of their acceding to the desires of others. International negotiations are bargaining games, pure and simple, with no external standards of what is and is not "appropriate" to put on the table. States demand (and should demand) whatever quid pro quo they want, and have the power to secure, in reaching agreements with one another.

The principles that I will suggest ought to govern such international negotiations are indeed moral principles, but ones with a prudential bite. They are akin to the principles that Lon Fuller identifies with the inner logic of law: "lower law," rather than "higher law," because those principles need to be respected for law to function as law at all.[4] The sorts of principles I shall discuss below are ones that similarly are required for states' behavior to be "rule governed" at all. And while it is obviously in every state's interests for everyone else to abide by rules while it itself flouts them, most states (even very powerful ones) usually come to realize that it better serves their own interests to be rule governed in their behavior toward other states, since that is generally the price of their being rule governed in their behavior in return.

The main principled reason for thinking that states may impose any conditions they like on agreements negotiated with other states is akin to the main realist reason for thinking so. From a moral point of view, the key point is simply that states are under no obligation to conclude any (particular) agreement with any (particular) other state. Since they are morally at liberty to refuse to conclude any agreement at all, it seems that states should be morally at liberty to refuse to conclude an agreement unless whatever conditions they care to impose are met. Lawyers express this thought by saying that the "greater power" (i.e., the power to refuse altogether) subsumes the "lesser power" (i.e., to refuse unless certain conditions are met).[5]

Early liberal writers infamously deployed this principle in defense of slavery. In the classical world, slaves were conquered warriors. Early social contract theorists justified their enslavement in the following terms. Under standard just war theory, warriors had every right to kill those who were attempting to kill them. Since "the greater power subsumes the lesser," it follows that if you have a right to kill someone unconditionally, then you have a right to kill or not kill that person, depending on whether some condition is met: conditional, for example, on that person's becoming your slave.[6]

Similar logic has long governed thinking about the permissibility of imposing conditions on trade. Vattel, for example, thought that it would be perfectly legitimate for a state to impose especially onerous burdens on aliens and foreign traders doing business within their borders "since the lord of the territory may, whenever he thinks proper, forbid its being entered he has, no doubt, a power to annex what conditions he pleases to the permission to enter." Although subjecting aliens and foreign corporations to differential treatment (higher tax rates or whatever) is no longer legally permissible in most jurisdictions, such practices were justified on precisely those grounds right to the end of the nineteenth century.[7]

What is wrong with the "greater power subsumes the lesser" doctrine is immediately evident from the slavery case. Powers are conferred on people, by positive law and moral law alike, for some specific purpose.[8] It is an abuse of those powers to use them for some purposes other than those for which they are granted. In the slavery case, the purpose of conferring the "power to kill one's opponent in armed combat" is "self-defense." Once one's opponent has been vanquished and no longer constitutes a threat to one's own life, one's right to kill the opponent lapses. Victors thus have no right to kill the vanquished or hence to do anything short of killing them (like holding them in ongoing slavery) either.

If people are given a certain power for a certain purpose, that constitutes an earmarked sort of resource. It is right to use it for the purpose for which it is granted, and it is wrong to use it for any other purpose. Specifically, it is wrong to use that power as a bargaining chip in pursuit of some other purpose altogether. If you are given a right to kill people in self-defense, it is wrong to use that power to enslave them, offering not to exercise your right to kill them in exchange for their agreement to become your slaves. Morally and legally you are within your rights either to kill them or not to kill them, unconditionally. You are even within your rights not to kill them, on certain sorts of conditions: on condition, for example, that they lay down their arms, for example. But you are not within your rights not to kill them on condition that they become your slaves. Imposing that condition would be impermissible, morally, because that condition is wholly unrelated to the purpose for which the power is granted.[9]

That principle generates a straightforward test for which conditions may or may not legitimately be imposed on the exercise of a discretionary power. The condition is permissible if and only if it is "germane"—relevant to the purposes—of the discretionary power.

To see how this "germaneness" test might work in connection with international trade policy, consider the U.S. ban on trade with Cuba. It is an open question whether that is a good or bad policy, whether it actually furthers its designated aims, and whether it causes suffering disproportionate to those aims.[10] I shall set all those important questions to one side. All I shall be concerned with is whether the conditionalities embodied in that policy are permissible under the "germaneness" test.

The trade ban was initially imposed in 1960 in response to Cuba's refusal to pay just compensation for U.S. property it had nationalized. The condition on the United States' lifting that initial ban was simply that Cuba pay "prompt, adequate, and effective compensation" for the nationalized U.S. assets. Over time, a regime-change rationale was superimposed on that original policy. This is particularly evident in the Helms-Burton Act—tellingly entitled the "Cuban Liberty and Democratic Solidarity (LIBERTAD) Act of 1996"—which declares:

The purposes of this Act are—

(1) to assist the Cuban people in regaining their freedom and prosperity, as well as in joining the community of democratic countries that are flourishing in the Western Hemisphere;

(2) to strengthen international sanctions against the Castro government;

(3) to provide for the continued national security of the United States in the face of continuing threats from the Castro government of terrorism, theft of property from United States nationals by the Castro government, and the political manipulation by the Castro government of the desire of Cubans to escape that results in mass migration to the United States;

(4) to encourage the holding of free and fair democratic elections in Cuba, conducted under the supervision of internationally recognized observers;

(5) to provide a policy framework for United States support to the Cuban people in response to the formation of a transition government or a democratically elected government in Cuba; and

(6) to protect United States nationals against confiscatory takings and the wrongful trafficking in property confiscated by the Castro regime.[11]

Only 6 and the second part of 3 speak to issues of nationalization without compensation. All the rest are clearly regime-change purposes. The condition for lifting a trade ban, based on that rationale, would be that the Castro government cease to rule Cuba.

Now, the original rationale for the trade ban with Cuba, whether good or bad policy, was at least germane to the purposes of trade policy. Trade is trade in titles to property. Taking is the antithesis of trading. So trading with people only on condition that they pay for what they take is to impose a condition that is wholly germane to the purposes of trade policy.

Trading with people only on condition that they install a government more to your liking is not. Set to one side the larger issue of national self-determination and the question of whether it is ever permissible for one country to interfere with the internal affairs of another. Whichever way we go on that larger issue, there is a narrower issue on which I think we can all agree, which is simply that whatever public purposes are served by allowing governments to permit or prohibit trade, altering the form of government of their trading partners is not one of them. That is simply not "germane" to any of the plausible purposes for allowing governments to set policies on international trade in the first place.

With this background in place, let us now turn to the Barry-Reddy proposal. Their suggestion is to make trade with other countries conditional upon their enforcing minimal labor standards. Is that condition "germane," and hence permissible, or not? Is it more like the original "compensation" rationale for the ban on trade with Cuba, or is it more like the later and less legitimate "regime change" rationale for that ban?

The case for seeing the Barry-Reddy proposal in the latter light, I suppose, is that it amounts to an interference with the domestic policy decisions of one's trading partner. The interference is less dramatic than the Helms-Burton Act's. No change in the basic "form of government," or even governor, is envisaged. But a change of policy clearly is, at least in one crucial dimension. Whatever reason we might have for letting governments set international trade policy, the argument might then go, it is not to alter the domestic policies of one's trading partners.

The contrary argument, of which I am more persuaded, holds that there is indeed a tight connection between the rationales underlying trade policy and labor standards. Both are justified as means of promoting welfare. Trade is justified because it increases the welfare of both trading partners. Labor standards are justified because they protect the welfare of the people who produced what is being traded. Linking trade to respect for labor standards is justified because that prevents the welfare of some (the trading partners) being promoted at the (maybe—probably) greater expense of the welfare of the workers producing the traded goods.

Of course, that argument merely suggests that it would be morally permissible—not morally obligatory—for governments to adopt the Barry-Reddy proposal and make trade conditional upon honoring minimal labor standards. That might seem like a minor contribution to this debate. It would be obviously more impressive to be able to show that that proposal is right, not merely all right—obligatory, not merely permissible.

My own hunch, however, is that the main argument against the proposal is not going to be that it is "wrong" in the sense of being incorrect or ill-advised. Rather, I suspect, the main counterargument is likely to be that the proposed linkage is "wrong" in the sense of being an inappropriate insinuation of social concerns into purely economic realms where they have no proper place. The objection that most needs to be countered is that it would be somehow inappropriate to impose that sort of labor-standard condition upon trade policy. That is the objection that my contribution anticipates and is intended to refute. By the germaneness test, which I argue is the most appropriate standard in these realms, it would be wholly appropriate for governments to embrace the Barry-Reddy proposal and link trade to respect for labor standards.

Will they? Here political realism reasserts itself. Principle is always most powerful when allied with interest. And it is of course in one country's economic interest that its trading partners not obtain an unfair economic advantage by enforcing more lax labor standards. Therein lies the source of the "social program" (such as it is) of the European Union. Therein, too, lies the practical political hope that countries may well actually be tempted by the Barry-Reddy proposal.

The Transformative Imagination and the World Trading System

COMMENTARY BY ROBERTO MANGABEIRA UNGER

Christian Barry and Sanjay Reddy have made a contribution to the alliance of reason with hope. In this note, I suggest four ways of developing their view.

1

In an argument about the linkage of trade to labor standards, it is important to address squarely the content of these standards. Their definition presents a problem of great importance and of vast scope. Wage labor is supposed to be free labor, in contrast to slavery and serfdom. If, however, workers must sell their labor under circumstances of economic duress or dependence, the break with slavery and serfdom may remain unfinished. The contractual form of the employment relations may be a sham.

The large question buried in the invocation of labor standards and of their linkage to trade is whether free labor in the emerging world economy will be really free. Will this economy be built on the basis of a form of wage labor that remains tainted by the residues of the oppression that salaried work is thought to replace? Or will the development of an open world economy be accompanied by arrangements that help ensure the freedom of free labor?

Given the importance of this issue, it would be a mistake to leave undeveloped the content of the labor standards that are to be linked to trade, focusing almost all the argument on the linkage and almost none on the standards themselves. I propose that, in defining these standards, we distinguish four elements and a horizon. The four elements combined amount to only a modest broadening of the conventional, established approach to the definition of labor standards. What changes the meaning of this familiar combination and reveals its transformative potential is the idea that it might represent a step in a certain direction: what I call the horizon.

The first element is the prohibition of outright coercion or oppression, including child labor. The second element is the rejection of all discriminations that would reward different groups of people unequally for the same work. The third element is the assurance of a living wage: a wage by which workers can ensure the necessities of life and secure their personal dignity according to the standards of their society. If certain countries are too poor and unproductive, the whole world—as partners in the world trading system—must make up the difference. Otherwise, the degradation of some will threaten the trade regime by undermining the integrity of its foundation in free labor. The fourth element is the empowerment of workers, through labor laws and democracy, to struggle effectively over their share in national income and in the earnings of the firms for which they work. There is no self-evident standard of the appropriate take of labor from national income; the idea that the real return to labor must of necessity accompany the rate of rise of productivity is a superstition of contemporary economics unsupported by fact.

Consider the horizon toward which these four elements should be directed. The organization of world trade and of the world economy should facilitate the completion of the break with slavery and serfdom so that free labor, as the foundation of an open world economy, be or become indeed free. Free labor can take one of three forms: wage labor, self-employment, and partnership.

Of these, the first is always suspect as a realization of the ideal of free labor. The second cannot, by itself, satisfy imperatives of scale in production and of discretion in management. Self-employment can address those imperatives only when associated with partnership. Partnership is therefore the most fully realized expression of free labor. Its translation into practical forms of economic organization requires experiments with the institutional arrangements of the market economy, including the rules of contract and property. Alternative regimes of private and social property might come to coexist experimentally within the same national economy, in different sectors or at different scales of economic activity.

It is therefore not enough for the world trading system, and the emerging global economy of which it is the heart, to protect wage labor against extremes of economic duress and subjugation. They should also develop in a direction that would ultimately reduce wage labor to the status of an exception. The horizon is free labor through partnership, achieved through the institutional reorganization of the market economy.

At a minimum, nothing in the rules of world trade should inhibit such an advance. The reconciliation of alternative trajectories of national development, not the maximization of free trade, should be the commanding principle of the world trading system. Accession to the global trade regime should not serve as an excuse to impose on the whole world a single version of the market economy, one that helps entrench wage labor given under economic duress as the general and ineradicably deficient form of free work.

2

The linkage of trade to labor standards may produce two opposite results.

The benign outcome is to spur a continuing rise in productivity. The most important form of such a rise in productivity is the substitution of work that we already know how to repeat by formulas expressing this knowledge and by the machines embodying such formulas. The goal is to devote more of our time and attention to activities that we do not yet know how to repeat and that we are consequently not yet able to express in formulas and to embody in machines. The rise in labor productivity may in turn be part of a chain of events resulting in higher total-factor productivity.

The harmful outcome is to help push an economy into a low-productivity trap. Higher labor standards may mean higher costs without higher productivity. Unit labor costs may rise and trap a national economy in a position of relatively high labor costs (compared to the countries of cheapest labor) but of relatively low productivity (compared to the countries that have advanced in the substitution of repeatable activities by formulas and machines).

I conjecture that a particular set of national and international factors may be decisive in promoting the benign outcome and in avoiding the harmful one.

The national factors fall into three categories. The first national condition is that a country be able to shield the "heresy" in its development strategy. In today's circumstances, such a shield will ordinarily be made of forced mobilization of national saving, of innovations in the institutions of finance that are designed to tighten the links between saving and production and to prevent the squandering of the productive potential of saving in a financial casino, of fiscal discipline achieved by a high tax take and an enhanced capacity for public investment, and of selective and temporary restraints on the comings and goings of foreign capital. Foreign capital is more useful the less one needs it. The notion of the shield represents a special case of a general idea. Defiance to the interests and ideas dominant in the world will not guarantee a country success. Without defiance, however, nothing of consequence is feasible in world history.

The second national condition is that development be based on a broadening of economic and educational opportunity: to afford more people access to more markets in more ways. To broaden access to the market economy will usually require changing the institutions and the practices that define what the market economy is. Ultimately, the experimental logic of the market economy should be freed from attachment to any single institutional formula. As in the previous argument about the content of the labor standards linked to trade, different versions of the market economy, including different types of private and social property, should coexist experimentally within the same economy.

The third national condition is that the advanced forms of productive experimentalism, with their attenuation of stark contrasts between conception and implementation as well as among implementing roles, their mixture of cooperation and competition in the same domains and activities, and their ceaseless use of the repeatable to turn our attention to the not yet repeatable, spread through large parts of economy and society. They must not remain quarantined within advanced sectors of production, weakly linked to other, more backward sectors. Their diffusion is unlikely to occur unless it is made to take place through social action and governmental initiative.

The two models of government-business relations on offer in the world today—the American model of arms'-length regulation of business by government and the Northeast Asian model of formulation of unitary trade and industrial policy by a bureaucracy—are inadequate to carry out this task.

The international condition is that, in return for their adherence to labor standards, developing countries secure access not only to the markets of rich countries but also to the ideas and the technologies of the whole world. The implication is radical reform of a regime of intellectual property that turns inventions into assets. It is to develop alternatives to that regime, including alternatives that take as their points of departure the experiments of the nineteenth century in providing public rewards and subsidies for invention.

3

In making their proposals for an agency to administer the labor standards that they want to see linked to trade, Christian Barry and Sanjay Reddy exemplify a principle that should be rendered radical and universal: the reinvention of the institutional forms of the market and of an open world economy. We are not limited to either regulating the market or to compensating for its inequalities and insecurities through retrospective redistribution. We can reimagine and remake the market economy. We are not restricted to either accepting globalization in its current form as an inescapable fate or to resisting it and trying to slow it down. We can have globalization on different terms. To do justice to the proposals in the book, we must see them from this perspective.

4

The argument of *International Trade and Labor Standards* seeks to demonstrate that there is no sound basis in economics, properly understood, on which to reject the linkage of labor standards with trade. One by one, objections to linkage turn out to depend on an abuse of economic analysis, through the confusion of this analysis with stipulations of fact, claims of causality, or proposals of direction that have no basis within economic theory itself but that are made to wear a specious semblance of economic authority. The method in this book is to turn the tables on these abusers of economics, impaling them on their own weapons and letting the world go free of mumbo jumbo in the service of injustice.

There is a limit to this operation. Restored to its analytic purity, economics is indeed innocent. However, it is innocent because, in the form of the dominant, marginalist tradition, it is empty of both causal explanation and normative prescription. It acquires explanatory and prescriptive power only by teaming up with ideas from somewhere else: from other disciplines and intellectual traditions.

Let us not delude ourselves into supposing that the chastisement of the abusers of economic analysis will relieve its powerlessness to explain or propose. Christian Barry and Sanjay Reddy reach their affirmative conclusions in this book by combining the criticism of illusion with the appeal to descriptions, explanations, and ideals that the established economics is unable, by itself, to justify or inspire.

The temptation is great to say that nothing is wrong with the core of economic analysis once it is rescued from its mishandling. It is the path of modesty. It avoids a thankless struggle with the self-satisfied votaries of a discipline suffering from arrested development. However, something is indeed wrong. It is necessary to turn away, once and for all, from the intellectual strategy, first devised in the late nineteenth century by the generation of Walras, Jevons, and Menger, of treating facts, causation, and normative judgment on the basis of ad hoc stipulations, to be deployed at will when no one is looking and to be disavowed whenever someone insists on the purity of economic analysis.

The point is neither to win arguments nor to seek, in a citadel of analytic innocence, immunity to causal and normative controversy. The point is to understand the world by imagining its transformative variations under varying conditions and then to change the world by the light of the imagination.

Reply to Commentators

CHRISTIAN BARRY AND SANJAY G. REDDY

KYLE BAGWELL

The international trade economist Kyle Bagwell sees merit in our proposal for linkage and presents thoughtful criticisms of it. He characterizes the "alternative linkage paradigm" that we present as differing from the "unduly narrow" standard interpretation of linkage. While the standard interpretation of linkage emphasizes the threat of application by developed countries of "sticks" in the form of trade sanctions or punitive tariffs, we emphasize the role of a diverse range of "carrots," in which developed countries "offer the reward of lower tariffs or other compensation" to developing countries that "achieve high labor standards."

This distinction certainly captures a very important dimension of the difference between our proposal and previous linkage proposals—our proposal envisions a cooperative and promotional approach to improving labor standards, as contrasted with a punitive one. It is important to note, however, that drawing the distinction between sticks and carrots requires background judgments that are more complex than is often recognized. Let us imagine, for example, some country (A) that provides incentives to another country (B) to improve its labor standards. Further, let us imagine that one such incentive (MA) is that its provision of some level (x) of market access to B's exports is conditioned upon B's making specified efforts to improve labor standards within its territory. If B fails to make these efforts, its exports will enjoy only level $(x - 1)$ of market access to A. Given this background, how should we characterize incentive MA? Is it a carrot or a stick? By "offering a carrot," we usually mean that some agent offers to make another agent *better off* if the latter undertakes some course of conduct. The notion of "using a stick," on the other hand, suggests the idea of some agent making another agent *worse off* if it fails to undertake some course of conduct. In this light, how should A's use of MA be interpreted? B will have lower access to A's markets (and presumptively be made worse off as a result) if it fails to take steps to improve labor standards. This suggests that market access is indeed being used as a stick to get B to take steps to improve its labor standards—the *threat* of market access level $(x - 1)$ is being used to provide incentives to B. It is also the case, however, that B will have greater access to A's markets (and presumptively be made better off as a result) if it takes steps to improve its labor standards. This suggests that market access is being used as a carrot by A to get B to improve its labor standards—the *promise* of market access level (x) is being used to provide incentives to B.

Why can this case be so easily interpreted either as involving carrots or sticks? It is because different *baselines* can be invoked, relative to which the introduction of MA can be seen either as introducing a carrot or a stick. A baseline may be defined temporally or counterfactually, and the choice of the baseline may lead to different judgments about the nature of the incentives offered. If the baseline invoked is the level of market access prevailing at some particular time T1, and if the level of that access is less than (x), then MA may appear to be a carrot. If the baseline invoked is the level of market access prevailing at some other time T2, and if the level of that access is (x), then MA may appear to be a stick. Now, does it make sense to claim that, this relativity not withstanding, MA *really is* either a carrot or a stick? Perhaps, but only if there is some compelling reason that can be given for treating some particular baseline as privileged and thus as the baseline against which MA should be interpreted and assessed. The present empirical status quo is only one such baseline and it should not simply be assumed that it ought to be privileged when characterizing the types of incentives offered by a linkage scheme. Our suggestion that countries seeking to promote labor standards should be provided incentives such as preferential access to export markets cannot therefore straightforwardly be viewed as differing from existing proposals in substituting carrots for sticks. It certainly does differ from standard approaches in having a nonpunitive orientation—it does not involve one group of countries unilaterally casting judgment and imposing penalties on others. It also differs from standard approaches in insisting that the costs of improving labor standards must not fall solely on the countries in which the labor standards improvements are being sought, but that these costs should instead be appropriately shared by all countries that are party to the linkage system.

Bagwell discusses at length our proposals regarding the possible application within a linkage scheme of Kemp-Wan adjustments of the kind that he and his coauthors have advocated elsewhere. These adjustments require that a country bring about a specified level of access to the domestic market for foreign producers by applying some *combination* of labor standards (which influence the costs of domestic producers of import-competing goods) and tariff rates (which influence the domestic market price of imported commodities), which function *together* to provide the specified level of market access to foreign producers. Under such a scheme, a decrease in the level of labor standards must be compensated for by a decrease in tariff rates so as to maintain the specified level of domestic "market access" for foreign producers. The motivation for this proposal is to remove the incentive that is present (in an environment of imperfect competition) for countries to reduce labor standards as a means of gaining competitive advantage, thus bringing about through the back door the competition (to promote the interests of one's own producers by building barriers to trade and thus to "beggar thy neighbor") that trade agreements are designed to prevent.

By the same logic, an increase in the level of labor standards in a country handicaps domestic producers (whether they are in an import-competing or an export-producing industry) and increases the level of market access of foreign producers (respectively at home or abroad). There is thus not only *no* incentive for governments to *increase* labor standards as a means of furthering the commercial interests of domestic producers, but such a measure brings them harm. Governments may thus not seek to improve labor standards unless domestic producers can in some way be insulated from the adverse effects of such improvements. Such insulation of domestic producers from the effects of labor standards improvements can in principle be achieved either through within-country adjustments or through international adjustments.[1] In particular, in the case of an import-competing industry the country may employ countervailing wage subsidies or production subsidies or raise tariffs on imports, or foreign countries may be required to undertake measures (such as increasing production or export taxes or improving labor or production standards) that raise their export prices. In the case of an export-producing industry, the country may undertake wage, production, or export subsidies, or foreign countries may be required to undertake measures (such as tariff reductions, import subsidies, or labor or environmental standards reductions) that lower the relative competitiveness in their home markets of goods produced by their domestic producers. These measures will of course differ in their efficiency properties and overall welfare impact.

The goal of eliminating the harm experienced as a result of improvements in labor standards by producers in a country can in principle be achieved by permitting or demanding either appropriate within-country or international adjustments. Should one of these methods be preferred? In the case of exporting industries (of special interest from the standpoint of developing countries), international adjustments in which foreign countries undertake measures such as tariff reductions (which neutralize the competitiveness-reducing impact of labor standards improvements at home) are especially desirable, since the alternative is for the country to apply subsidies to domestic production or export, which it may find difficult to finance and implement (for example, because of the possibility that such schemes may be undermined by rent seeking and administrative weaknesses). We do recognize that such domestic policies are nevertheless in principle desirable and can provide an important means through which countries can neutralize the cost-raising impact of labor standards improvements, with or without additional international assistance either in the form of financial assistance or of tariff reductions abroad. We believe, however, that there is a conceptual and practical case for international adjustments (formalized in a system of linkage) in diminishing the disadvantages countries will otherwise suffer as a result of improving labor standards that does not as straightforwardly apply to within-country adjustments. Although it can be preferable to "correct domestic distortions at the source," the argument for doing so depends on various empirical judgments, such as that the international trade policy being contemplated to correct the distortion is to increase protection at home (not decrease it abroad, as in our case) and that there exist efficient tax-and-transfer instruments for redistributing resources and adequately compensating harms.

In order to understand better the distinction between the approach suggested by Bagwell and his coauthors and that which we suggest, it is essential to note a central difference in our respective motivations. Bagwell proposes that countries be required to make within-country adjustments in order to maintain a minimum level of market access for foreign producers in the domestic market. He envisions that the international trade commitments made by countries will take the form of commitments to maintain specific levels of market access for foreign producers, rather than merely to bind their tariffs at a particular level. Thus countries would be permitted to raise or lower labor or environmental standards to the level they desire as long as they apply a *combination* of policies in regard to trade and standards sufficient to ensure that they meet their treaty commitments in regard to minimum market access for foreigners. Although an effect of the approach is to permit countries to set labor standards at the level that they desire, its *goal* is to prevent countries from undermining their treaty commitments concerning market access for foreigners through a back door.

In contrast, we require *foreign* countries to make adjustments in order to maintain a minimum level of market access for *domestic* producers in the foreign market. The goal of our approach is not to prevent countries from undermining their treaty commitments concerning market access for foreigners (although that is an end that may be independently worthy of attainment) but rather to remove the incentive countries have to reduce their labor standards (in order to achieve greater market access for their producers at home and abroad) and indeed to go beyond this to create incentives for countries to improve labor standards. The role of international adjustments (as required in a linkage system) is therefore central in our approach. We conceive of within-country adjustments as playing a potentially supplementary role in such a system, because they may not by themselves be sufficient to further the ends that we envision (because of empirical costs or obstacles to their application and the resulting need to provide countries with incentives to apply them) and because there may be multiple objectives (one of which is to promote higher levels of labor standards where that is desirable and another of which is to maximize the gains from trade by providing secure commitments of mutual market access) that one may reasonably seek to promote through the world trading system.

Finally, we envision a role for both within-country and international adjustments in promoting labor standards up to the level presently deemed minimally desirable for each country to achieve, but not necessarily beyond that. In contrast, the role envisioned for within-country adjustments by Bagwell is not to promote a particular level of labor standards but to ensure a specified level of market access for foreigners, and, as a result, *any* level of labor standards that the country chooses is deemed acceptable as long as the specified level of market access is attained. In our proposal, in contrast, countries that possess labor standards falling beneath a level deemed minimally adequate within the system may not be permitted to lower their labor standards further (even if they undertake Kemp-Wan adjustments to maintain the level of market access of foreigners), but countries that possess labor standards above the level minimally demanded of them may be permitted to lower their labor standards (as long as they undertake Kemp-Wan adjustments to maintain the required level of market access of foreigners). This is the sense in which our approach to the incorporation of Kemp-Wan adjustments into the trading system allows for their potentially asymmetric application. The discretion of countries to choose their own level of labor standards is thus qualified within our proposed system (unlike in the system proposed by Bagwell).

We fully recognize the concern that an important objective for the world trading system has been to guarantee secure levels of market access in each country for foreign producers. This is a potentially important goal that need not conflict with the other goals we identify. The extent to which the different objectives we have highlighted (viz., enhancing labor standards and guaranteeing such access) should each be pursued within the architecture of the system should be a matter for subsequent discussion.

As Bagwell rightly notes, we believe that higher levels of labor standards are worthy of promotion under current empirical conditions (in particular, those prevailing in developing countries). We do not depend on the premise that governments value these labor standards improvements in order to make our case. Indeed (as Bagwell notes), we have argued that there are a number of reasons that the objectives pursued by governments may not fully reflect the interests of the populations they ostensibly represent. Bagwell suggests that claiming to understand the interests of individuals better than do the governments that represent these individuals "conflicts with notions of national sovereignty" and is especially suspect "when the governments in question are democratically elected."[2] It is not immediately obvious why this is the case, since the formation of judgments about the interests of others is not in itself equivalent to impeding the *actions* of the states that claim to represent them (which would seem to be required in order actually to interfere with sovereignty). However, it is certainly true that the *application* of such judgments in a manner that affects the opportunities and constraints faced by nations may conflict with particular understandings of national sovereignty. The same can be said, however, for core human rights, antidiscrimination norms, or any other standards now widely accepted to constrain what governments may legitimately do. Many labor standards concerns may not fall in this domain. Nevertheless, the example serves to demonstrate that the prerogatives of national sovereignty may need to be appropriately qualified and the boundaries attached to these prerogatives adequately justified.

While there is certainly reason to suppose that democratic governments may be more likely to represent the interests of their populations than nondemocratic governments, it is also widely recognized that even democratic governments can implement policies that can (illegitimately) harm sections of their populations. We may form external judgments to this effect without applying these judgments. Moreover, we may apply such judgments to the negotiation of international agreements without necessarily diminishing state sovereignty—which may, for example, be thought to be adequately protected as long as countries are free to enter and exit international agreements.

Even if governments do fully represent their populations, however, there is still a reason that international agreements over trade and labor standards may fail to achieve the goals of governments to the extent desired. As we have noted, governments are at present punished for efforts that they may take to improve labor standards through diminished market access for their producers abroad. This international externality generated by a domestic effort to improve labor standards (the existence of which is implied within Bagwell's own framework) can be corrected through an externality internalizing mechanism. An appropriate international (linkage) scheme is one such mechanism. From this standpoint, it is indeed the case that "unilateral policy choices are inefficient" under current international trade arrangements. We, with Bagwell, possess the view that "an appropriately designed international agreement could eliminate inefficient policy choices and thus generate a mutually advantageous outcome for partici-pating governments."[3] That is a motive for our proposal (although not the sole one). The lens of whether "in fact, an existing or proposed interna-tional agreement is well designed for encouraging efficient policy choices" is fully appropriate to the analysis of the linkage system of the kind that we propose.[4] For this reason, we do not "adopt a distinct methodological ap-proach" from that proposed by Bagwell, as he suggests (although we may have been insufficiently explicit about this point).[5]

Our method allows for the possibility that the objectives of govern-ments do not always have decisive normative significance (and indeed we take the view that this perspective of possible divergence is rather impor-tant in practice), but we also allow for the possibility that the objectives of governments already fully incorporate all of the normative concerns that ought to be taken into account. Faced with the latter perspective, we emphasize that the existing world trading system is inefficient for the reason that there is at present an important international externality of domestic policy choices. The externality arises because of the adverse terms-of-trade and revenue impact of improvements in labor standards. It arises irrespective of whether labor standards are viewed merely as an instrument for achieving competitive advantage or whether they are viewed as being directly valuable (as we have proposed). The role of a linkage scheme is, in this perspective, to ensure that an efficient outcome is reached. There is thus no necessary gap between the methodology we adopt and that espoused by Bagwell and other economic analysts. The methodology of assessing proposed international agreements from the perspective of whether they respond to an inefficient realization of states' own objectives can offer support for a linkage system requiring between-country adjustments just as it can offer support for a system requiring within-country adjustments (as favored by Bagwell). We note that noth-ing in an efficiency-based argument for linkage would hinge on a focus on the interests of the less advantaged alone. Although we do give special importance to the interests of the less advantaged (following the apparent consensus of participants in the debate on linkage), we share Bagwell's view that the interests of all persons should be a matter of concern in evaluating institutional arrangements.

Bagwell insightfully notes that the use of carrots rather than sticks to create incentives for labor standards improvement has the convenient feature that it helps to separate efforts on the part of developed countries that are motivated by disguised protectionism from ones that are driven by concern for labor standards abroad as such. Of course, the use of carrots may not *fully* suffice to separate these motives for a variety of reasons (such as that protectionist motives may be strong enough to create a self-interested rationale for the provision of carrots as well as the wielding of sticks, and that these distinct motives can coexist). Bagwell also notes Chang's important point that a carrot-based system can potentially become hostage to the opportunistic behavior of recipient countries, which may overstate the cost that they face in improving labor standards in order to increase the level of resources transferred to them, the level of tariff reductions abroad, or other benefits made available through the system. These are certainly valid concerns about the implementation of such a system. Indeed, they further underline the importance of ensuring that a linkage system be rule based and that it adequately and explicitly specify the measures to be taken by countries, the benchmarks against which their efforts are judged, and the principles to be used to determine the level of resources transfers to be made available to countries. It is crucial that such a system provides for the independent adjudication of disputes, including disputes about the costs of improving standards.

We are encouraged that Bagwell shares our view that "with some augmentation, WTO rules are well designed to address these concerns" and that limited reinterpretation, addition, or change to these rules may suffice to implement an appropriate labor standards–promoting scheme.[6] However, as existing rules focus on the provision of secure and mutual market access alone, even a progressive interpreter must recognize their limits. For example, is not difficult to imagine cases in which there may be grounds for a market access–based complaint but not for a labor standards–based complaint and vice versa. Although the system proposed by Bagwell allows a country to choose a level of labor standards that immunizes it from such complaints, it does not ensure that a country will do so. Our proposal would allow for a country's failure to take action to promote or to maintain labor standards above a level deemed minimally adequate for it to become a ground for action under the system even if this failure did nothing to alter the mutual market access commitments of the country involved. The difference in the underlying motivation of the scheme proposed by Bagwell and his coauthors and that which we propose can in this way be brought to the surface.

ROHINI HENSMAN

Despite general agreement with our analysis and proposal, the labor activist and scholar Rohini Hensman insists in her illuminating comment that there is a need to develop further our arguments in favor of linkage (in particular concerning the definition of basic labor standards in our proposal).

As a prelude to characterizing our argument, Hensman asserts that there are two distinct types of arguments that can be advanced in favor of linkage. In her view, the first type of argument (which might be called the "intercountry fairness argument"), suggests that linkage is needed to prevent countries with lower labor standards from unfairly enriching themselves at the expense of those with higher standards. By maintaining lower standards, countries can tilt the playing field in favor of their producers, by enabling them to incur lower labor costs than do competing producers of tradable goods in countries maintaining higher standards. In her view, the second type of argument (which might be called the "human rights argument") emphasizes that the demand to respect basic labor standards derives from fundamental human rights that ought to be treated as essential requirements in all international treaties, including trade agreements. Hensman believes that our use of the concept of basic labor standards—levels of wages and working conditions that are deemed minimally adequate—suggests that we are making a human rights–based argument for linkage, but that we do not do so consistently. The inconsistency is alleged to arise because we suggest that the standards that ought to be considered minimally adequate within a linkage system should be understood in the context of a country's level of development, prevailing norms, and other relevant considerations. Hensman claims that human rights–based demands are by their very nature "universally applicable and categorical" and interprets this as entailing that such demands apply to countries regardless of their level of development or other characteristics. She claims that we slide back into human rights–based arguments when we suggest that the linkage scheme may nevertheless require countries to respect a few requirements irrespective of their level of development.

Our argument for linkage does not fall neatly into either of the categories of arguments for linkage proposed by Hensman. We argue that a class of linkage proposals should be explored on the ground that arrangements for the governance of the global economy incorporating such proposals could improve the living standards of less advantaged people throughout the world to a greater extent than would arrangements for the governance of the global economy that do not incorporate them, and could do so without imposing undue costs on others. While we do not doubt that arguments concerning intercountry fairness can be made against some countries' practices with respect to labor standards, our argument is not of this kind. The case we make in favor of exploring linkage is not based on the wish to diminish the extent to which some countries take "unfair" advantage of others but rather on the aim of improving the outcomes generated while recognizing fundamental procedural constraints (such as the need to avoid political and cultural imperialism). Our focus is not on the unfairness of the benefits that countries with lower labor standards derive from their correspondingly lower costs of production, but on the desirability of diminishing the disadvantage experienced by less advantaged persons as a group, who may be collectively less well off than they would be under alternative arrangements for the governance of the global economy. We argue that existing arrangements effectively punish countries that undertake measures to enhance labor standards, as (insofar as these measures increase labor costs) in order for labor standards to rise, they may bring about a diversion of trade and investment toward countries that do not take such actions. Under the existing international trading system, the real freedom of countries to undertake reforms to improve labor standards is therefore constrained. By offering countries that promote labor standards to a greater extent privileged access to export markets in rich countries, by requiring rich countries to provide financial and other resources to poor countries that promote labor standards, and by isolating countries that systematically and egregiously fail to take even the most minimal of such steps, a system of linkage could substantially increase the real freedom of poorer countries to improve the level of advantage of their people.

While we do not explicitly refer to human rights in defense of our proposal, we do think that our view is consistent with, and could indeed be supported by, some human rights–based arguments. We also think that our approach is consistent with the claim that human rights are universally applicable and that they should be recognized and promoted in international treaties.

What does it mean to affirm that some practices, such as slave labor, constitute violations of human rights? Such affirmations are usually taken minimally to involve the assertion that human beings have ethical claims, simply by virtue of being human, and that they may not be subject to certain kinds of treatment or be unnecessarily deprived of the material and social resources required to be capable of attaining certain ends there is reason to value.[7] The claims involved are of two main kinds. The first is an ethical claim *against* other agents, such as employers, that obligates these agents to undertake or to refrain from certain types of conduct (e.g., to not enslave or to facilitate the enslavement of other persons). The second is an ethical claim *on* social institutions, which requires that they be designed and that they function in such a way that all persons' rights are fulfilled to the extent that is feasible without imposing unacceptable costs (including the nonfulfillment of rights) on others.[8] Our proposal is fully consistent with both of these kinds of ethical claims. Indeed, the point we are making about prevailing arrangements for governing international trade is that they may not protect the vital interests of people as well as would feasible alternative arrangements, plausibly including some that incorporate linkage between trade and labor standards.

Does the fact that our proposal does not require the same inflexible minimum of labor standards in all countries show that it is inconsistent with human rights concerns? Hensman claims that it does, stating that making the protection of basic labor standards dependent on the level of development of a country "would be to condone the violation of fundamental rights under certain circumstances." To insist that a particular institutional arrangement should not include rules that discriminate against countries on the ground that they have not met some context-invariant set of requirements, however, is not tantamount to indifference to the fact that they have not met these requirements. We may hold that all countries are obliged to fulfill the human rights of their citizens as appropriately conceived, while rejecting the application of specific penalties or sanctions against countries failing to fulfill these rights. Why might this be? One possible reason is that the application of a sanction may be a morally inappropriate response to nonfulfillment of rights, especially where the reasons for that nonfulfillment are complex and include the presence of constraints that make it difficult (even if not impossible) to fulfill completely the rights that are unfulfilled. Another possible reason is that the penalties or sanctions contemplated (for example, involving membership in international organizations or trade agreements) could have a counterproductive impact on important aims, including the fulfillment of the rights themselves. Denying the prerogative of specific countries to become members of international organizations or parties to trade agreements, for example, may lead regimes that do not adequately respect or promote human rights to become even more negligent of these rights. If arrangements that discriminate among countries on human rights grounds would be counterproductive, then establishing them appears to be inconsistent with furthering the fulfillment of human rights.

We are concerned that a linkage system that demands that a common minimum be inflexibly attained in all countries may be unrealistic, unreasonable, and possibly counterproductive, especially if that minimum is very demanding. Accordingly, we emphasize the importance of conditioning the level of labor standards promotion required *under the system* on the level of development of a country and other pertinent contextual factors. We have already argued that such an approach would be consistent with maintaining that countries should do (and indeed are ethically required to do) much more to promote labor standards than is required under the rules of the scheme. We do suggest, nevertheless, that countries may be required to take certain measures regardless of their level of development. One reason is that allowing countries the liberty to permit highly egregious practices (such as slavery) without there being any consequence within the system will very likely be counterproductive from the point of view of the aims of the system (i.e., increasing the level of advantage of less advantaged persons throughout the world). If it were be shown that *even these* requirements would have a counterproductive impact on the aims of the system, we would not incorporate them as minimal expectations within the system.[9]

In sum, it is necessary to distinguish two important and complementary tasks in defining the idea of basic labor standards. The first is determining which types of norms should be applied to assess whether people's rights are fulfilled. The second is determining the types of arrangements that should be implemented in international institutional arrangements to ensure that people's rights are fulfilled. Hensman's comment focuses on the first task, whereas our proposal for linkage attempts to undertake the second.

Hensman also worries that any linkage scheme that would make the labor standards–promoting activity that is demanded conditional on a country's level of development would lead to "endless wrangling over a country's degree of development and hence its appropriate level of labor standards." We do not see why this should be so. There are many international institutions (among them the WTO) that already incorporate special allowances or obligations for countries that vary according to their level of development and other pertinent characteristics. This idea is a commonplace in the arena of international human rights. Article 2.1 of the International Covenant on Economic Social and Cultural Rights, for example, demands that signatory states take steps to "realize progressively" the rights recognized by the covenant, rather than to realize them immediately. This may seem like a loose demand. Country reports of the Committee on Economic, Social, and Cultural Rights suggest, however, that assessments of a country's conduct can indeed make reasonably clear distinctions between shortfalls from human rights that arise due to resource and other constraints on the capabilities of the government and those that arise due to its failure adequately to prioritize these rights in its policy choices. The principle that developing countries (and, in particular, the least developed countries) must be accorded special and differential treatment is at the very heart of the WTO system and has been concretely implemented through a wide range of specific and legally enforceable provisions. These examples from actually existing international institutions suggest that this particular concern cannot be viewed as compelling.

A further objection to linkage identified by Hensman is that linkage will affect only those involved in production for export (in which labor standards may well be higher than in production for domestic consumption). An imaginable perverse effect of linkage would be to push workers from export production into other sectors in which labor standards are worse. This is one reason why the scheme we envision would make rights to trade internationally conditional on taking adequate steps to promote labor standards in *all* production sectors. While sympathetic with the motivation of this aspect of our scheme, Hensman objects that "to use international trade sanctions as a penalty for the violations of labor rights in production for the domestic market would not be appropriate," because it would amount to a form of "collective punishment" that would risk making those producing for export the "first victims" in the case that some of a country's rights to trade or other benefits offered by the linkage scheme were to be limited as a result of its failure adequately to promote labor standards in areas producing for the domestic market. Instead, Hensman advocates a system of fines independent of the trading system in order to provide incentives to improve labor standards in production for domestic consumption.

A main reason for employing trade-related incentives and disincentives for labor standards promotion (in any sector of production) is that they are likely to be potent. This reason for employing trade incentives remains present as long as an economy possesses a tradable goods sector, even though the international externality associated with labor standards promotion (i.e., that it influences the cost competitiveness of a country's producers of tradable goods and thereby their level of "market access") is not present in the production of nontradable goods. This having been said, there is no reason that nontrade incentives and disincentives (such as the system of fines advocated by Hensman) could not in principle be used to bring about improved labor standards. Even if there is agreement on the objective of encouraging countries to take steps to promote labor standards, the balance among various kinds of incentives, both within the linkage system and more broadly, must be a matter for empirical judgment.

It is true that firms producing for export in a country that does not enjoy the full benefits potentially offered by our proposed linkage scheme (such as additional rights of market access or funds made available through the international burden sharing element) because its government systematically neglects to take steps to promote labor standards in areas of production for domestic consumption may do worse than they would had their government taken such steps. If our argument about the potential efficacy of trade-related incentives is correct, however, it is also true that a great many more workers could be worse off under a system of linkage in which trade-related incentives are restricted to production for export than they would be under a system in which such incentives were present also in relation to the production of import-competing and nontradable goods. The issues involved in assessing whether this would be the case are complex and depend on the nature of the supply-and-demand interlinkages between distinct production sectors and the impact on domestic (as well as foreign) consumption of cost increases associated with labor standards improvements. It is not at all obvious that exempting import-competing and nontradable goods production from the obligations of a linkage system would further the interests of either firms or workers in those sectors.

Finally, if some persons and firms producing for export can be viewed as "innocent victims" of our proposed scheme, then so too can others be viewed as "innocent victims" of the type of linkage scheme proposed by Hensman, since they will be worse off than they would be under a scheme offering more robust trade-related incentives to improve labor standards. We think it inadvisable to use language of this kind, which presupposes specific moral conditions that may not be satisfied, in describing either our proposed scheme or that envisioned by Hensman.

There is much with which we agree in Hensman's comment. For example, Hensman rightly emphasizes the importance of dealing with the informal sector in any system of labor standards promotion applied by developing countries. Her proposal to make the right to proof of identity and employment one of the standards to be promoted by a linkage scheme strikes us as an especially promising one. In addition, we share her view that countries with higher labor standards should not be presumed to be countries that are more developed, and that the emphasis in burden sharing should be on the provision by richer countries of resources to those that are both poorer and are making attempts to improve labor standards. Finally, we are most encouraged by Hensman's optimism about the prospects for a renewed and improved debate on the topic.

ROBERT E. GOODIN

Determining whether some form of linkage of trade with labor standards may be justified depends on two types of considerations. The first type of consideration centers on the *effectiveness* of such linkage in achieving valuable outcomes. Much of the previous debate on linkage has centered on considerations related to its effectiveness in promoting desirable consequences. We too have emphasized such considerations extensively (although not exclusively) in our argument, attempting to establish that a linkage system of an appropriate kind would indeed promote outcomes that linkage critics and proponents alike hold to be desirable (more effectively than would proposals for the governance of international trade not incorporating linkage). The second type of consideration centers on nonconsequentialist factors that might be deemed relevant in determining whether such linkage is *appropriate*.[10] The political philosopher Robert E. Goodin's interesting comment draws attention to some such nonconsequentialist factors and offers us the opportunity to discuss them at greater length.

There are reasons other than effectiveness in achieving desirable outcomes that might be thought to militate *in favor of* linkage. Linkage might be thought to be desirable, for example, because it *expresses* an appropriate moral attitude toward certain types of practices. For example, a system of linkage that would suspend some of a country's rights to trade with other countries if it is known to permit and encourage the use of slave labor within its territory might be thought to be more desirable, all things considered, than another system of international trade that does not incorporate such measures, because such a system would express *condemnation* of egregiously wrong practices in an appropriate manner.[11] The public isolation of such countries within the world trading system would serve (to borrow Joel Feinberg's memorable phrase) as "a symbol of infamy," whatever its other effects might be.[12]

Goodin points out, however, that considerations other than effectiveness might also militate *against* linkage. In particular, he identifies the following objection to linkage: even if some form of linkage would be effective in achieving valuable outcomes, it is nevertheless undesirable since it would "involve the inappropriate insinuation of social concerns to purely economic realms in which they have no proper place."[13] It is argued that powers are conferred for specific purposes that have ethical justification[14]—and it is impermissible that agents to whom such powers are conferred use them for other purposes. If this test of permissible application of powers is satisfied when these powers are applied to a specific purpose, then the application of these powers to the purpose in question is called *germane*. In general, it is suggested that an agent's power should be deemed germane to some policy issue area only if one of the reasons why the agent should be granted the power would be to promote desired effects within that very policy issue area.[15]

Goodin illustrates this idea with the example of the U.S. ban on Cuban exports. Whatever one thinks of the potential efficacy of the U.S. ban on trade with Cuba in promoting valuable outcomes, one might question whether it is legitimate to use the extension or withdrawal of rights to trade as a means of bringing about regime change (a stated aim of the trade embargo at least since the passage of the Helms-Burton Act in 1996). Altering the form of government of one's trading partners simply does not, Goodin maintains, further the purposes that are served by granting governments the power to permit or prohibit trade. Since regime change is an objective that is not germane to the purpose of granting governments powers over trade policies according to Goodin, rights to trade may not in his view be restricted in order to achieve this objective.

Linkage too is a way of allowing countries to use trade policy to influence the domestic policy decisions of their trading partners. It might similarly be argued (though Goodin himself does not) that the reasons for which powers are conferred on governments to set international trade policy do not include the altering of the domestic policy decisions of their trading partners. It might be concluded that trade policy is not a germane instrument to apply in attempting to influence domestic policies concerning labor standards and that this provides a compelling reason to reject linkage. Let us call this the "nongermaneness" objection to linkage.

Goodin entertains three distinct types of arguments that might serve to counter such an objection. The first argument asserts that countries have the moral privilege[16] to link rights to trade to the promotion of labor standards because they may do just about anything they wish to promote their perceived interests, including insisting on whatever quid pro quo they can secure as a condition of allowing their potential trading partners access to their markets. We may call this argument, following Goodin, the "realist" argument. A realist would maintain that if some government wishes to bring about regime change in another country, they are not morally constrained from using trade policy to do so, whether or not trade policy is an instrument that is otherwise "germane" to the purpose of achieving regime change. Trade policy is just one more way that governments can promote (and are therefore entitled to promote) their perceived interests. Such a realist argument is not open to us. It is clearly inconsistent with many claims we make in our essay about the requirements that linkage systems would need to meet for them to be plausible. A realist would not, for example, object to a rich country's efforts to impose a system of linkage that was prone to opportunistic use by it and other rich countries when this would serve their interests, even if such use would engender serious hardships in poorer countries. Our foundational concern to promote the interests of the less advantaged in the world is in itself at odds with the realist perspective.

The second type of counterargument to the nongermaneness objection might be called the "privilege entailment" argument. This doctrine maintains that *if an agent has a moral privilege not to conclude any agreement at all, then it has also the privilege to insist on any conditions it wishes as part of any particular agreement.* The first premise of this argument is that states have the moral privilege to refuse to conclude trade or other types of agreements with one another. The second premise of this argument is what Goodin refers to as "the greater power subsumes the lesser" doctrine. If both of the premises of this argument are true (or at least seem plausible), then it seems reasonable to maintain that countries have moral privileges to demand that their trading partners undertake changes in their domestic policies relating to wages and working conditions as a condition of their making trade agreements with them.

Goodin vigorously attacks the second premise of this argument, drawing on various examples to show that the principle that the greater power subsumes the lesser leads to results that are morally counterintuitive in a broad range of cases.[17] Even if the doctrine that the greater power subsumes the lesser were deemed justified, however, we would not want our defense of linkage against the nongermaneness objection to depend upon the privilege entailment argument. This is because one might be uncertain about whether to affirm its first premise. It may be that states are not (usually, at least) under a duty to conclude any *particular* agreement with others. The scope of their moral privileges with respect to setting trade policy might nevertheless not be unlimited. It might be argued, for example, that it would often be impermissible for some country A to deny altogether access to its markets to producers in another country B. Some libertarians would view such conduct by A as an unacceptable infringement of the fundamental freedoms of individuals living within A and B to engage voluntarily in trade with one another, barring some special justification. A's denying market access to B might also be viewed as unacceptable if it would cause severe harm to the population of B, especially if B's producers had come to depend (or were even encouraged by A to depend) on access to A's markets to secure their livelihoods, unless some compelling reason could be given for such denial. Finally, we might think of A's conduct as unacceptable if it was undertaken with discriminatory intent, for example on the grounds that B's population was largely of a specific racial origin. The proper scope of countries' privileges to set trade policy is clearly a complex and controversial issue. For this reason (in addition to the reasons presented by Goodin to doubt its second premise), we do not wish to rely on the privilege entailment argument to counter the nongermaneness objection.

There are at least three remaining strategies for countering the nonger-maneness objection. The first is to deny the validity of the nongermane-ness objection, either in general or in its specific application to linkage. Act consequentialists, for example, would not consider germaneness to be a relevant consideration in evaluating how an agent should exercise their powers. The second is simply to allow that this objection has force but that it does not necessarily constitute a *conclusive* argument against link-age. If a system of international trade involving linkage could be shown to be much more effective than alternative systems that do not incorporate linkage in achieving valuable outcomes, it might be argued that it should be implemented because the effectiveness reasons in favor of linkage out-weigh reasons of other kinds against it. The third strategy is to try to meet the objection head on by showing that one of the reasons for conferring the power to set international trade policies on governments is indeed re-lated to the labor market policies of its potential trading partners. We pur-sue this third strategy here, although all three strategies may be fruitful.

To show that labor standards are indeed germane to international trade requires reflection on the reasons why powers should be conferred on governments to make trade policy. One reason, as Goodin points out, is that conferring such power can be welfare promoting, both for the coun-tries themselves and for their trading partners. Trade is an instrument for enhancing prosperity and welfare, of one's own citizens and of citizens of other countries. Insofar as linkage can help to promote such prosperity and welfare, it is therefore germane to trade policy. Another reason, particu-larly pertinent in this context, is that conferring such a power on govern-ments enables them to help to ensure that their citizens act in accordance with moral obligations that apply to them when they engage in trading activity. Such reasons relate both to the *types* of goods that are appropriate for trade and the *processes* by which goods may be brought to market. It is commonly held, for example, that there are restrictions on the types of goods and services that people may permissibly trade for their consump-tion or use. The services provided by assassins or child prostitutes, to take some extreme examples, are not thought to be legitimately tradable at all. Other goods and services are thought to be legitimately tradable, but only for certain things or in narrowly circumscribed contexts. As Michael Wal-zer puts it, "citizens can't trade their votes for hats."[18]

Even when goods and services can be legitimately traded, it is com-monly accepted that people have moral reasons not to trade them unless they have come to market via certain processes. At least three types of process considerations are important in this context, whether the trade in question be in widgets, labor, or financial services, although how the considerations apply may vary depending on the good traded. First, trades involving various kinds of bullying, coercion, or deception, for example, may be deemed impermissible. Second, however free of bullying, coercion, or deception a particular present trade may be, it may be impermissible if the good being traded was previously stolen from its rightful owner, or if past transfers of this good involved bullying, coercion, or deception of the relevant kinds. Third, the nature of the process by which some good or service is produced is relevant. Goods that are produced through the use of slavery or the worst forms of child labor, for example, may plausibly be deemed ineligible to enter into legitimate trade. People who know (or should have known) that they are buying stolen goods or goods produced via particularly egregious labor practices are viewed as having violated their ethical duties by *contributing to* or by becoming *complicit in* such practices.[19] Since governments can, to some extent at least, help to ensure that their citizens do not engage in such conduct by adopting appropriate trade policies, this provides a good reason to confer to them the power to set such policies.

Finally, one reason why the powers to set trade policy might reasonably be conferred upon governments is that doing so enables its citizens to act on their moral reasons, among which are reasons to help protect the vital interests of other people. One reason for employing trade-related incentives and disincentives for promoting labor standards that we have stressed throughout our text is that they are likely to be effective. If such effective incentives and disincentives are oriented toward promoting valuable outcomes, and if they can be (as we have argued they can be) embedded within an institutional framework that guards against the opportunistic and harmful misuse of such incentives and disincentives, then there is good reason to confer upon governments and institutional arrangements the power to employ them.

ROBERTO MANGABEIRA UNGER

The philosopher and social theorist Roberto Unger expresses appreciation for our argument, which he describes as "a contribution to the alliance of reason with hope." He suggests that we have demonstrated that "there is no sound basis in economics, properly understood, on which to reject the linkage of labor standards with trade," and that our argument demonstrates both the methodological inadequacy of the prevailing approach to economic analysis and its unduly status-quoist institutional prescriptions. However, he insists that it is essential to embed both the negative and the constructive aspects of our argument for linkage in a larger account of a transformative program for the general empowerment of persons and suggests that the salience of our argument is diminished by its inadequate attention to the content of the labor standards to be promoted through linkage.

Unger argues that it is essential to address squarely the content of the labor standards being linked to the trading system. If one fails to do so, these standards may be specified in such a way that the resulting linkage system may serve merely as an ameliorative device that does away with the worst excesses of the labor market without fundamentally reforming the system of wage labor itself and the structure "of economic duress or dependence" it engenders. The consequence would be that "the break with slavery and serfdom may remain unfinished." Unger insists, however, that if the labor standards to be promoted by the linkage system are specified in the right way, the system can have a transformative potential, bringing us incrementally closer to a desirable "horizon" in which labor becomes effectively freer (for instance through the realization of organizational forms that place partnerships among workers at the heart of the productive system). Unger imagines that the introduction of the system of linkage can constitute a step on a ladder of possible institutional reforms, giving rise to an ever wider range of emancipatory possibilities that progressively increase the effective freedom of workers and citizens.

We are wholly sympathetic to this suggestion. We have deliberately constructed an argument, however, showing only that the rejection of the claims of linkage opponents and the demonstration of the attractiveness of a linkage system in furthering the goal of improving the circumstances of less advantaged persons throughout the world do not crucially depend on the upholding of any particular conception of the labor standards to be promoted. This does not mean that we view the choice among alternative conceptions of labor standards as unimportant. Indeed, we believe it is extremely important. It is important intrinsically, since some standards may be directly valuable to promote because of their constitutive role in the flourishing of persons. It is also important instrumentally, since the promotion of certain labor standards may play a role in furthering other valuable ends. For example, as Unger rightly emphasizes, the promotion of certain labor standards (such as rights of workplace association and collective bargaining) may create favorable conditions for the subsequent freedom-enhancing transformation of societies.[20] For these reasons, our description of the features that a linkage system must have in order to escape the standard objections to such a system must be complemented by a more detailed account of the standards that ought to be promoted. We share Unger's view that the development of a larger economic and social program of freedom-enhancing institutional revision ought to be an aim of progressive thought. We hope that the proposal we have presented here can serve as an aid and not as an obstacle in this important task.

Unger also notes the danger that for many countries (especially those which begin neither with decisively cheaper labor nor with decisively superior technology than their potential competitors) an improvement in labor standards may raise costs without correspondingly raising productivity, thereby damaging the relative attractiveness of the country as a site for production, investment, and employment. He presents a series of proposals for enabling such countries to become sites of experimentation and innovation so as to gain competitive advantage and avoid this trap. One of the features of our proposal is that it aims to bring about coordinated improvements in labor standards in poorer countries that are potential competitors for production and investment, thus muting the adverse impact of improvements in labor standards on the competitiveness of individual countries. We also propose domestic policies that may be used to neutralize the cost-raising impact of labor standards. Nevertheless, we recognize the importance of Unger's concern. We strongly endorse the view that it is important to locate our proposal within a conception of the possible developmental strategies of nations that recognizes the need for countries to unlock the constraints they face in the implementation of transformative strategies, so as to avoid the trap of becoming relegated to a fixed (and perhaps unremunerative) position in the world division of labor. It is ultimately indispensable to conjoin our proposal not only with a compelling account of the labor standards to be promoted but also with broader proposals for development (concerning the choice of national policies that can best promote developmental dynamism and concerning the architecture of an international system that can permit and support these national choices).

Finally, Unger's call for the reimagining and the remaking of the market economy is one from which we take strength. We share his view that a reconceived economic analysis, freed of casuistry and better anchored to empirical knowledge, is an instrument of such a project. Through the renovation of our modes of reasoning and imagining we can liberate ourselves from straitjacketed perspectives, among which is the persistent prejudice that the market economy in the nation and in the world must take a single form.

NOTES

PREFACE

1. Martin Wolf, *Why Globalization Works* (New Haven, Conn.: Yale University Press, 2004), 4.

2. John Rawls, *The Law of Peoples* (Cambridge, Mass.: Harvard University Press, 1999), 13.

INTRODUCTION

1. Other such proposals have been made, all of which share some of the features of the proposal sketched below. E.g., see Daniel S. Ehrenberg, "From Intention to Action: An ILO-GATT/WTO Enforcement Regime for International Labor Rights," in *Human Rights, Labor Rights, and International Trade*, eds. Lance A. Compa and Stephen F. Diamond (Philadelphia: University of Pennsylvania Press, 1996), 163, 168; International Confederation of Trade Unions (ICFTU), *Building Workers' Human Rights Into the Global Trading System* (Brussels: ICFTU, 1999), 66 (available online at http://www.icftu.org/www/english/els/escl99BWRGTS.pdf); and Pharis J. Harvey, Terry Collingsworth, and Bama Athreya, "Developing Effective Mechanisms for Implementing Labor Rights in the Global Economy," Workers in the Global Economy Project Papers (International Labor Rights Fund, Washington D.C., 1998), sec. II.A (available online at http://www.laborrights.org/projects/globalecon/ilrf/intro.html).

2. It is possible that other valued objectives, such as promoting environmental quality or respect for human rights norms more broadly may also be promoted through linkage. We take no stand on these issues here.

3. We are assuming that global institutional reforms that promote better working conditions and living standards for less advantaged persons in the world without placing significant burdens on more advantaged persons advance the ends of justice. Widely varying conceptions of justice would affirm this view.

4. A number of preferential trading agreements, e.g., NAFTA, CAFTA, the U.S.-Cambodia trade agreement, the U.S.-Jordan trade agreement, and the U.S.-Chile trade agreement, contain provisions regarding labor standards. See also Tobias Buck, "Brussels to Offer Rewards to 'Good' Poor Countries," *Financial Times*, Oct. 21, 2004.

5. Specifically, we do not assume that free trade is always the policy that maximizes the gains from trade.

1. WHAT IS LINKAGE? TWO PROPOSITIONS

1. We deliberately formulate this proposition abstractly to accommodate the broad range of views present in the literature.

2. Although the way in which individual advantage is conceived will undoubtedly influence the specific policies and institutional arrangements deemed desirable, the arguments for and against linkage discussed in this essay are largely independent of the choice of a particular conception, within reasonable bounds of variation. See, e.g., Amartya Sen and Bernard Williams, eds., *Utilitarianism and Beyond* (Cambridge: Cambridge University Press, 1982); Martha C. Nussbaum and Amartya Sen, eds., *The Quality of Life* (Oxford: Oxford University Press, 1993); and John Rawls, *A Theory of Justice* (Cambridge, Mass.: Belknap Press, 1971), for a discussion of different conceptions of individual advantage.

3. General Conference of the International Labour Organization, 86th Sess., *ILO Declaration on Fundamental Principles and Rights at Work* (Geneva: International Labour Organization, June 1998), secs. 2.a–d (available online at http://www.ilo.org/public/english/standards/relm/ilc/ilc86/com-dtxt.htm).

4. It may be helpful to contrast proposals to further the achievement of basic labor standards with proposals to further the achievement of labor standards as such. Whereas the former are concerned with minimally adequate labor standards (however defined), the latter may seek the attainment of still higher labor standards regardless of the levels already attained. Proposals of the latter kind are not our focus here.

5. Many recent critics of linkage have characterized the idea of linkage much more narrowly than we have. Arvind Panagariya, for example, has claimed that the "trade-labor link effectively requires countries to raise standards to the level desired by importing countries or face trade sanctions by the latter. It is argued that a country that adheres to higher labor standards within its national boundaries has the moral right to suspend trade with another country that does not adhere to equally high labor standards." Arvind Panagariya, "Labor Standards and Trade

Sanctions: Right End, Wrong Means," (paper presented at the conference "Towards an Agenda for Research on International Economic Integration," East-West Center, Honolulu, Jan. 15–16, 2001), 5 (available online at http://www.columbia.edu/~ap2231/Policy%20Papers/Hawaii3-AP.pdf). Clearly it is possible to oppose linkage as Panagariya has characterized it without opposing linkage as we understand it. Indeed, few (if any) linkage proponents would endorse linkage as Panagariya understands it, and in what follows we express full agreement with the criticisms that have been advanced by Panagariya and others of this type of linkage. Similarly, Srinivasan frames disagreement about linkage in terms of differing views regarding whether diversity in labor standards among nations is legitimate. T. N. Srinivasan, *Developing Countries and the Multilateral Trading System: From GATT to the Uruguay Round and the Future*, 2nd ed. (Boulder, Colo.: Westview Press, 2000). This is misleading, since many linkage proposals (such as the one sketched below) not only allow that diversity of labor standards among nations is legitimate but insist that attempting to "harmonize" them under present conditions would be illegitimate. See ICFTU, *Workers' Human Rights*, 31; and Pharis J. Harvey, Terry Collingsworth, and Bama Athreya, "Developing Effective Mechanisms for Implementing Labor Rights in the Global Economy," Workers in the Global Economy Project Papers (International Labor Rights Fund, Washington D.C., 1998), sec. II.D (available online at http://www.laborrights.org/projects/globalecon/ilrf/intro.html).

6. The distinction between sanctioning and offering additional opportunities depends on having specified a baseline. Such a baseline can be identified on the basis of various (empirical and normative) criteria. A common misunderstanding is that it can only be defined on the basis of empirical considerations, such as whether a measure restricts or expands the opportunities possessed *ex ante* by the parties.

7. A system that provides a country with additional *permissions* (e.g., to impose tariffs on foreign products) if it adequately promotes labor standards is also a form of linkage as defined by proposition L, since the rights to trade that it accords to *other* countries are made conditional on the promotion of labor standards. We do not focus on linkage of this kind below but simply pause to note that proposition L accommodates it.

2. THREE TYPES OF LINKAGE, AND WHAT LINKAGE PROPONENTS MUST SHOW

1. We have borrowed the term "master-goal" from Thomas W. Pogge, "On the Site of Distributive Justice: Reflections on Cohen and Murphy," *Philosophy & Public Affairs* 29, no. 2 (2000): 137, 155. Formally, individual attainments $a^1, a^2, \ldots a^n$ contribute to the attainment of a master-goal defined by an objective function $U(a^1, a^2, \ldots a^n)$. It does not necessarily follow that this objective function is additively separable. As a result, it is often impossible to evaluate the marginal contribution of

each attainment to the master-goal, and thus of the optimal combination of attainments to be pursued, without determining the extent of other attainments.

2. This agent could be individual or "collective," i.e., a group or an organization.

3. Rights linkage as we understand it is linkage between the possession of rights and the undertaking of certain conduct (the exercise of their rights in a specific way) and is distinct from another type of linkage that might also deserve the term rights linkage: that in which an agent's possession of one right is made conditional on his or her possession of some other right.

4. Possibly more than one: agency linkage requires that at least some agents be charged with promoting distinct ends, but it does not require that each end be promoted by only one agent.

5. We are referring here to what is needed to demonstrate proposition L to those who accept proposition O. Different arguments may be necessary to persuade those who reject proposition O to accept proposition L.

3. WHAT LINKAGE OPPONENTS MUST SHOW

1. See, e.g., Consumer Unity and Trust Society, "Third World Intellectuals and NGOs' Statement Against Linkage," *CUTS International* (Sept. 6, 1999), pars. 1, 3 (available online at http://cuts-international.org/twin-sal.htm).

2. Some individuals have been hostile to such conditionality in both the domestic and international contexts (e.g., libertarians such as Robert Nozick and consequentialists who have favored the "unfettered" free market, such as Milton Friedman), but this is distinctly the view of a minority. Dani Rodrik notes a useful point that is related to, but distinct from, that which we raise above: trade may be viewed (in the abstract) as a technology that allows inputs to be transformed into outputs. Dani Rodrik, "Labor Standards in International Trade," in *Emerging Agenda for Global Trade: High Stakes for Developing Countries*, by Robert Z. Lawrence, Dani Rodrik, and John Whalley (Overseas Development Council, Washington D.C., 1996), 35, 41–42. It is widely agreed that production methods may not be employed in the domestic economy without regard to whether or not they entail the violation of minimal labor standards. Those who advocate some restrictions on the production "technologies" that may be used in the domestic economy but reject such restrictions in the global economy must, Rodrik argues, make clear why these two spheres should not be treated in a like manner. However, it may be argued that this comparison obscures the potentially morally relevant distinction between production at home and production abroad. Some moral conceptions may disvalue nonfulfillment of minimal labor standards within a country to a greater extent than they disvalue such nonfulfillment abroad.

3. Although it is certainly true, as Richard Freeman has argued, that the debate about trade and labor standards is often simply "one of a set of running battles between those

who believe the unfettered market can do no wrong and those who believe governmental regulations can make things better" (Richard Freeman, "A Hard-Headed Look at Labor Standards," in *International Labor Standards and Economic Independence*, eds. Werner Sengenberger and Duncan Campbell [Geneva: International Institute for Labor Studies, 1994], 80), it nevertheless does seem that many linkage critics affirm the role of various domestic regulations of labor and product markets.

4. ARGUMENTS AGAINST LINKAGE

1. In particular, it is argued that influential interests (such as labor unions and employers in some industries) in developed countries would benefit from reduced competition from countries with low-cost labor and therefore press for such opportunistic misuse. See, e.g., Gote Hansson, *Social Clauses and International Trade* (New York: Palgrave MacMillan, 1982), 34–38; Jagdish Bhagwati, "Policy Perspectives and Future Directions," in *International Labor Standards and Global Economic Integration: Proceedings of a Symposium*, eds. Gregory K. Schoepfle and Kenneth A. Swinnerton (Washington D.C.: U.S. Department of Labor, Bureau of International Labor Affairs, 1994), 57, 60; Jagdish Bhagwati, *In Defense of Globalization* (New York: Oxford University Press, 2004), 122–134; Jagdish Bhagwati, *The Wind of the Hundred Days: How Washington Mismanaged Globalization* (Cambridge, Mass.: MIT Press, 2000), 274; Drussila K. Brown, "Labor Standards: Where Do They Belong on the International Trade Agenda?" *Journal of Economic Perspectives* 15, no. 3 (2001): 89, 102–103; T. N. Srinivasan, "International Trade and Labor Standards from an Economic Perspective," in *Challenges to the New World Trade Organization*, eds. Pitou van Dijck and Gerrit Faber (The Hague: Kluwer, 1996), 219, 239; Arvind Panagariya, "Labor Standards and Trade Sanctions: Right End, Wrong Means" (paper presented at the conference "Towards an Agenda for Research on International Economic Integration," East-West Center, Honolulu, Jan. 15–16, 2001), 9 (available online at http://www.columbia.edu/~ap2231/Policy%20Papers/Hawaii3-AP.pdf); Kaushik Basu, "Child Labor: Cause, Consequence, and Cure, with Remarks on International Labor Standards," *Journal of Economic Literature* 37, no. 3 (1999): 1083, 1092; George Tsogas, *Labor Regulation in a Global Economy* (Armonk, N.Y.: M. E. Sharpe, 2001), 27–28; Jose M. Salazar-Xirinachs, "The Trade-Labor Nexus," *Journal of International Economic Law* 3, no. 2 (2000): 377, 380–381; Martin Khor, "Rethinking Liberalisation and Reforming the WTO," Third World Network, sec. 5 (available online at http://www.twnside.org.sg/title/davos2-cn.htm [accessed Dec. 13, 2006]); Muchkund Dubey, "Social Clause: The Motive Behind the Method," Alternative Information and Development Center (available online at http://www.aidc.org.za/?q = book/view/71[accessed Dec. 13, 2006]); and Gregory Shaffer, "WTO Blue-Green Blues: The Impact of U.S. Domestic Policies on Trade-Labor, Trade-Environment Linkages for the WTO's Future," *Fordham International Law Journal* 24, no. 3 (2000): 608, 621n44.

2. See, e.g., Consumer Unity and Trust Society, "Third World Intellectuals and NGOs' Statement Against Linkage," *CUTS International* (Sept. 6, 1999), par. 5 (available online at http://cuts-international.org/twin-sal.htm); Bhagwati, *Wind of the Hundred Days*, 320; and Jagdish Bhagwati, "Free Trade and Labor" (unpublished essay, Columbia University, 2001, available online at http://www.columbia.edu/~jb38/ft_lab.pdf).

3. See Nicholas D. Kristof and Sheryl WuDunn, "Two Cheers for Sweatshops," *New York Times Magazine*, Sept. 24, 2000; Vivek H. Dehejia and Yiagadessen Samy, "Trade and Labour Standards—Theory, New Empirical Evidence, and Policy Implications," CESifo Working Paper no. 830 (CESifo, Munich, 2002), 20–25.

4. See, e.g., Inter-American Dialogue and Carnegie Endowment for International Peace, "Breaking the Labor-Trade Deadlock," Carnegie Paper no. 17 (Carnegie Endowment, Washington D.C., 2001), 3.

5. See, e.g., Keith E. Maskus, "Should Core Labor Standards Be Imposed Through International Trade Policy?" World Bank Working Paper no. 1817 (World Bank, Washington D.C.: 1997), 33–35 (available online at http://ssrn.com/abstract = 44605); and Brown, "Labor Standards," 100.

6. See Lyn Squire and Sethaput Suthiwart-Narueput, "The Impact of Labour Market Regulations," Policy Research Working Paper no. 1418 (Policy Research Department, World Bank, Washington D.C., 1995), 7–11; Panagariya, "Labor Standards," sec. 2.5; Inter-American Dialogue and Carnegie Endowment for International Peace, "Breaking the Labor-Trade Deadlock," 3; Pranab Bardhan, "Some Up, Some Down," *Boston Review* 26 (Feb./Mar. 2001, available online at http://bostonreview.net/BR26.1/bardhan.html); and Pranab Bardhan, *Social Justice in the Global Economy* (ILO Social Policy Lecture, University of the Western Cape, South Africa, Sept. 1–6, 2000), 13 (available online at http://www.ilo.org/public/english/bureau/inst/papers/sopolecs/bardhan).

7. See, e.g., Inter-American Dialogue and Carnegie Endowment for International Peace, "Breaking the Labor-Trade Deadlock," 3; and Bhagwati, *Wind of the Hundred Days*, 143–144.

8. In particular, it will be undesirable according to those views that hold that the level of advantage is directly or indirectly influenced by the extent of inequalities (for example, in working conditions or command over resources).

9. T. N. Srinivasan, "International Labor Standards Once Again!" in *International Labor Standards*, 34, 37; see also Basu, "Child Labor," 1093; and Maskus, "Core Labor Standards," 22.

10. We deal in this section with the *outcomes* expected to arise as a result of alternative institutional arrangements. We are concerned here with "comparative static" comparisons of distinct outcomes. Comparisons of the cost of *transition* from the status quo to distinct institutional arrangements are dealt with below, under the heading of feasibility.

11. Note that the set of "superior means" (SM) arguments and the set of "inconsequential/self-defeating" (I/S) arguments overlap, and it is not necessarily the case that one is contained in the other. Any argument recognizing linkage as being at least partially effective in attaining its goals, though less effective than the alternatives, is an SM argument and not an I/S argument. Any argument that views linkage as unable to achieve its aims but also views all other feasible policy interventions as being unable to achieve those aims is an I/S argument and not an SM argument. The "tragic sense of life" underlying this perspective is one that does not appear to be prevalent in the debate on linkage. Most I/S arguments are also SM arguments.

12. E.g., Jagdish Bhagwati, "Trade Liberalisation and 'Fair Trade' Demands: Addressing the Environmental and Labour Standards Issues," *World Economy* 18, no. 6 (1995): 745, 757; Bhagwati, *Wind of the Hundred Days*, 160–162; Bhagwati, "Free Trade and Labor," 5 ("A good tongue-lashing... can unleash shame."); Jagdish Bhagwati, "Free Trade: Why AFL-CIO, the Sierra Club, and Congressman Gephardt Should Like It," *American Economist* 43, no. 2 (1999): 3, 11; see also Maskus, "Core Labor Standards," 67; and Ajit Singh and Ann Zammit, "Labor Standards and the 'Race to the Bottom': Rethinking Globalization and Workers' Rights from Developmental and Solidaristic Perspectives," *Oxford Review of Economic Policy* 20, no. 1 (2004): 85, 102.

13. Archon Fung, Dara O'Rourke, and Charles Sabel, "Realizing Labor Standards," in *Can We Put an End to Sweatshops?* (Boston: Beacon Press, 2001), 3–5.

14. See, e.g., Dani Rodrik, "Labor Standards in International Trade," in *Emerging Agenda for Global Trade: High Stakes for Developing Countries*, by Robert Z. Lawrence, Dani Rodrik, and John Whalley (Overseas Development Council, Washington D.C., 1996), 60; Kimberly Ann Elliott and Richard B. Freeman, *Can Labor Standards Improve Under Globalization?* (Washington D.C.: Institute for International Economics, 2003), 27–48; Panagariya, "Labor Standards," sec. 3.2; and Maskus, "Core Labor Standards," 21.

15. Srinivasan, "International Labor Standards Once Again!" 35.

16. Bhagwati, "Free Trade," 10; Bhagwati, *Wind of the Hundred Days*, 277–278.

17. Bhagwati writes: "[Linkage] wind[s] up harming both trade liberalization (which is the true objective of the WTO) and advancement of the social and moral agendas. . . . The underlying reason for such an unsatisfactory outcome is that you are trying to kill two birds with one stone. Generally, you cannot. . . . [By] trying to implement two objectives, the freeing of trade and the advancing of social and moral agendas, through one policy instrument such as WTO, you will undermine both. You will miss both birds." Bhagwati, *Wind of the Hundred Days*, 277–278. See also T. N. Srinivasan, *Developing Countries and the Multilateral Trading System*, 2nd ed. (Boulder, Colo.: Westview Press, 2000).

18. Bhagwati, "Free Trade and Labor," 4; Bhagwati, "Free Trade," 10–11; Bhagwati, *Wind of the Hundred Days*, 278. See also Srinivasan, *Developing Countries*, 72–73.

19. See Kyle Bagwell and Robert W. Staiger, "The Simple Economics of Labor Standards and the GATT," in *Social Dimensions of U.S. Trade Policy*, eds. Alan V. Deardorff and Robert M. Stern (Ann Arbor: University of Michigan Press, 2000), 195, 197. See also Srinivasan, *Developing Countries*.

20. See Bagwell and Staiger, "Economics of Labor Standards"; see also Kyle Bagwell and Robert W. Staiger, "The WTO as a Mechanism for Securing Market Access Property Rights: Implications for Global Labor and Environmental Issues," *Journal of Economic Perspectives* 15, no. 3 (2001): 69.

21. In principle, there is a corresponding rule involving export items and export subsidies, which the authors do not discuss.

22. See, e.g., Kristof and WuDunn, "Two Cheers for Sweatshops." Kristof and WuDunn's article is cited approvingly and at length in Bhagwati, *In Defense of Globalization*, 175. See also Basu, "Child Labor," 1114.

23. For examples of critics who have made that argument, see Maskus, "Core Labor Standards," 49; Brown, "Labor Standards," 105–106; Arvind Panagariya, "Trade-Labour Link: A Post-Seattle Analysis," in *Globalization Under Threat: The Stability of Trade Policy and Multilateral Agreements* (Cheltenham: Edward Elgar, 2001), 101, 110.

24. See, e.g., Singh and Zammit, "Race to the Bottom," 95–96.

25. Kristof and WuDunn, "Two Cheers for Sweatshops"; Bhagwati, *In Defense of Globalization*, 175; see also Inter-American Dialogue and Carnegie Endowment for International Peace, "Breaking the Labor-Trade Deadlock," 3.

26. See Bhagwati, *In Defense of Globalization*, 172–173 (citing the hypothesis that U.S.-run factories provide higher wages because they have higher productivity).

27. Panagariya, "Labor Standards," sec. 2.1.

28. A recent Cato Institute publication puts this point, rather gushingly, as follows: "The threat of using trade restrictions to advance human rights is fraught with danger. Free trade is itself a human right and rests on an individual's rights to life, liberty, and property—rights the U.S. Founding Fathers regarded as inalienable and self-evident. When the federal government closes U.S. markets to countries with governments that deny their citizens certain civil liberties, it robs those citizens of one more freedom and undermines the market dynamic that in the end is the best instrument for creating wealth and preserving freedom. . . . Free Trade Is a Human Right: The proper function of government is to cultivate a framework for freedom by protecting liberty and property, including freedom of contract (which includes free international trade)—not to use the power of government to undermine one freedom in an attempt to secure others. The right to trade is an inherent part of our property rights and a civil right that should be protected as a fundamental human right. The supposed dichotomy between the right to trade and human rights is a false one. Market exchange rests on private property, which is a natural right. As moral agents, individuals necessarily claim the right to liberty and property in

order to live fully and to pursue their interests in a responsible manner. The free-dom to act without interference, provided one respects the equal rights of others, is the core principle of a market economy and the essence of human rights. Without private property and freedom of contract, other rights—such as free speech and religious freedom—would have little meaning, because individuals would be at the mercy of the state. The human-rights fabric is not made stronger by unraveling economic liberties in the hope of enhancing other liberties. Protectionism violates human rights. It is an act of plunder that deprives individuals of their autonomy—an autonomy that precedes any government and is the primary function of just governments to protect. . . . The danger of buying into the argument that restricting trade with China will increase human rights is that such an argument diminishes the significance of the moral case for free trade, politicizes economic life, and weak-ens the market-liberal vision—a vision that needs to be strengthened in order to protect civil society and human liberty." James A. Dorn, "Trade and Human Rights: The Case of China," *Cato Journal* 16, no. 1 (1996, available online at http://www.cato. org/pubs/journal/cj16n1–5.html).

29. Robert Nozick, *Anarchy, State, and Utopia* (New York: Basic Books, 1974), 163.

30. Personal conversation with Kamal Malhotra.

31. The narrower objective of promoting basic labor standards of those who are employed will in this case allegedly conflict with the broader objective of improv-ing the level of advantage of less advantaged persons more generally. An implicit premise of the argument is that the gain in attaining the latter objective justifies the loss in attaining the former.

32. Srinivasan, *Developing Countries*.

33. This assumption is common in the literature. See, e.g., Basu, "Child Labor," 1100, 1103–1104.

34. See, e.g., Bhagwati, "Free Trade and Labor," 163; Paul Krugman, "One in the Eye with an American Pie," *Bangkok Post*, Feb. 17, 2000; Shaffer, "WTO Blue-Green Blues," 624–625; and Srinivasan, *Developing Countries*.

35. Srinivasan, *Developing Countries*, 73–77. The literature on "Asian values" is replete with such claims.

36. See, e.g., Brown, "Labor Standards," 91.

37. See, e.g., Basu, "Child Labor," 1089.

38. See, e.g., Inter-American Dialogue and Carnegie Endowment for Inter-national Peace, "Breaking the Labor-Trade Deadlock," 4; Jagdish Bhagwati, "The Question of Linkage," *American Journal of International Law* 96, no. 1 (2002): 126, 128, 131.

39. See, e.g., Theodore H. Moran, "Trade Agreements and Labor Standards," Policy Brief no. 133 (Brookings Institution, Washington D.C., 2004), 6 (available online at http://www.brookings.edu/comm/policybriefs/pb133.htm).

40. Bhagwati has cited a Human Rights Watch report on the United States' violation of the right to organize in connection with this claim. See, e.g., Bhagwati, *In Defense of Globalization*, 177, 192, 247, 251.

41. See, e.g., Mark Levinson, "Wishful Thinking," in Fung, O'Rourke, and Sabel, *Can We Put an End to Sweatshops?* 54.

5. RULING OUT LINKAGE PROPOSALS

1. We are not committing ourselves to the view that no imposed institution could under any conditions be legitimate. However, it is our judgment that under present conditions it is highly implausible that an imposed system of linkage could be legitimate.

2. This idea is associated with the work of Hans Kelsen. Cf. John Rawls, *A Theory of Justice* (Cambridge, Mass.: Belknap Press, 1971), 567.

3. See Philip Alston, "Labor Rights Provisions in U.S. Trade Law," in *Human Rights, Labor Rights, and International Trade*, eds. Lance A. Compa and Stephen F. Diamond (Philadelphia: University of Pennsylvania Press, 1996), 71, 73–83, for an interesting discussion of the reasons to reject the system of linkage imposed by the United States through its General System of Preferences (GSP).

4. See ibid. "The United States is . . . imposing its own, conveniently flexible and even elastic, standards upon other states." See also Terry Collingsworth, "International Worker Rights Enforcement," in *Human Rights*, 227, 229–233, for a discussion of some of the abuses of the GSP by the United States.

5. The baseline against which these costs can be measured can, of course, be specified in different ways, such as the status quo ex ante or an appropriate counterfactual, for example, what would have occurred pursuant to the previous rules or some other morally appropriate benchmark.

6. The Kyoto Protocol has a burden-sharing component (Article 11), as did the framework convention on climate change agreed to at the Rio conference in 1992. Rio "set explicit goals under which several rich nations agree to emission-level-reduction targets (i.e., to return, more or less, to 1990 levels), whereas the commitments of the poor countries were contingent on the rich nations' footing the bill." T. N. Srinivasan, *Developing Countries and the Multilateral Trading System: From GATT to the Uruguay Round and the Future*, 2nd ed. (Boulder, Colo.: Westview Press, 2000). Technical cooperation and financial aid are provided to countries so that they can comply with WTO rules. Bilateral trade agreements, such as the U.S. and Cambodia textile and apparel agreement (Article 10 (E)) also offer examples of this kind. The burden sharing that took place with respect to reforming the labor practices of the Bangladeshi garment sector is discussed in Kimberly Ann Elliott and Richard B. Freeman, *Can Labor Standards Improve Under Globalization?* (Washington D.C.: Institute for International Economics, 2003), 113. The link-

age proposals developed by the ICFTU (*Building Workers' Human Rights Into the Global Trading System* [Brussels: ICFTU, 1999], available online at http://www.icftu. org/www/english/els/escl99BWRGTS.pdf) and the ILRF (Pharis J. Harvey, Terry Collingsworth, and Bama Athreya, "Developing Effective Mechanisms for Implementing Labor Rights in the Global Economy," Workers in the Global Economy Project Papers [International Labor Rights Fund, Washington D.C., 1998], available online at http://www.laborrights.org/projects/globalecon/ilrf/intro.html) both demand burden sharing.

7. Unlike Srinivasan, who seems to view international burden sharing through income transfers and linkage as *alternative and mutually exclusive* means of promoting labor standards, we view such transfers as essential to any plausible linkage proposal. Srinivasan, *Developing Countries*, 74. We argue below that there are reasons why a scheme that employs income transfers alone as a means of promoting labor standards will likely be inferior to one that combines these with trade incentives, and that a plausible linkage scheme will combine trade and nontrade incentives. For a discussion of the kinds of complementary policies that may be necessary to combat objectionable forms of child labor, see Drusilla K. Brown, Alan V. Deardorff, and Robert M. Stern, "Child Labor: Theory, Evidence, and Policy," in *International Labor Standards*, eds. Kaushik Basu et al. (Malden, Mass.: Blackwell, 2003), 195, 225–237.

8. Cf. Robert E. Goodin, *Protecting the Vulnerable: A Re-Analysis of Our Social Responsibilities* (Chicago: University of Chicago Press, 1985), 186; Peter Singer, "Famine, Affluence, and Morality," in *World Hunger and Morality*, eds. William Aiken and Hugh LaFollette, 2nd ed. (Englewood Cliffs, N.J.: Prentice Hall, 1996), 26–27; Peter Unger, *Living High and Letting Die: Our Illusion of Innocence* (New York: Oxford University Press, 1996), 62–72. Even those who reject this claim may have reason to be sensitive to the distributional consequences of proposed institutional reforms if they believe that the present unequal distribution of advantages has emerged from a historical process in which rights they wish to see respected have been violated. See, e.g., Hillel Steiner, *An Essay on Rights* (Oxford: Blackwell, 1994), 266 ("Redress transfers are redistributions which, very broadly, *undo* the unjust redistributions imposed by encroachments on rights: they restore just distributions"); Thomas W. Pogge, *World Poverty and Human Rights: Cosmopolitan Responsibilities and Reforms* (Cambridge: Polity Press, 2002), 14.

9. See, e.g., Christian Barry, "Applying the Contribution Principle," *Metaphilosophy* 36, nos. 1–2 (2005): 210–213. For examples of other principles, see Goodin, *Protecting the Vulnerable*; and David Miller, "Distributing Responsibilities," *Journal of Political Philosophy* 9, no. 4 (2001): 453.

10. See, e.g., Barry, "Applying the Contribution Principle," 213–214.

11. This concern is not unique to a system for promoting labor standards, as mentioned earlier. Similar issues arise in other areas of international cooperation,

such as the promotion of environmental standards, as is ably discussed in Ragh-bendra Jha and John Whalley, "Migration and Pollution," Workings Papers in Trade and Development 2003/07 (Research School of Pacific and Asian Studies, Economics Division, Australian National University, Canberra, 2003, available on-line at http://rspas.anu.edu.au/economics/publish/papers/wp2003/wp-econ-2003–07.pdf). In discussing the conditions under which India might be willing to agree to a system of linkage, Rob Jenkins emphasizes the importance of developed countries sharing substantially in the burdens of linkage (as well as making greater progress in fulfilling their commitments under the Uruguay Round Agreements). Rob Jen-kins, "India and the Trade-and-Labour-Standards Controversy" (paper presented at the seminar "India at the Beginning of the 21st Century," Instituto do Oriente, Lisbon, Mar. 20–23, 2001), 4–7 (available online at http://www.gapresearch.org/governance/The%20Politics%20of%20Trade%20in%20India.pdf). A similar point is made in reference to other developing countries by Kevin Kolben in "The New Politics of Linkage: India's Opposition to the Workers' Rights Clause," *Indiana Journal of Global Legal Studies* 13, no. 1 (2006): 225–259.

12. The level and nature of burden sharing required to make a linkage scheme feasible may be different from that required to make it morally legitimate. The level of burden sharing that is adequate will have to be determined in light of both considerations.

13. This is borne out by studies of attitudes toward linkage among trade unions in the South, which show that they possess much greater receptivity to linkage proposals than is widely believed. See the results of the remarkable survey of developing-country trade unions reported in Gerard Griffin, Chris Nyland, and Anne O'Rourke, "Trade Unions and the Social Clause: A North-South Union Divide?" Working Paper no. 81 (National Key Center in Industrial Relations, Monash University, Melbourne, 2002), 8–11 (finding that 95 percent of union members in the global South favored international trade agreements that protect core labor standards); and see also the sources cited therein, reporting similar conclusions.

14. See Jenkins, "India," 3; see also Srinivasan, *Developing Countries*, 70.

15. See note 2 above and accompanying text.

6. A CONSTRUCTIVE PROCEDURE—IDENTIFYING LINKAGE PROPOSALS THAT MEET THE STANDARD OBJECTIONS

1. For our argument to succeed, it is sufficient to identify one class of proposals for linkage that satisfies the standard objections. It is therefore no embarrassment to fail to identify *all* the classes of proposals that satisfy the standard objections.

2. Different models can be observed both in the world and in the proposals that have been advanced about how best to promote labor standards. See, e.g., Daniel S. Ehrenberg, "From Intention to Action: An ILO-GATT/WTO Enforce-

ment Regime for International Labor Rights," in *Human Rights, Labor Rights, and International Trade*, eds. Lance A. Compa and Stephen F. Diamond (Philadelphia: University of Pennsylvania Press, 1996); G. B. Nath, "Linking International Labour Standards with Trade: Implications for India," *Indian Journal of Labour Economics* 41, no. 4 (1998): 1005, 1011 (contrasting the structural weakness of the ILO with the WTO's capability for enforcement); Rohini Hensman, "World Trade and Workers' Rights: In Search of an Internationalist Position," *Antipode* 33, no. 3 (2001): 427, 442–446; ICFTU, *Building Workers' Human Rights Into the Global Trading System* (Brussels: ICFTU, 1999), 53 (available online at http://www.icftu.org/www/english/els/escl99BWRGTS.pdf); Pharis J. Harvey, Terry Collingsworth, and Bama Athreya, "Developing Effective Mechanisms for Implementing Labor Rights in the Global Economy," Workers in the Global Economy Project Papers (International Labor Rights Fund, Washington D.C., 1998), sec. III (available online at http://www.laborrights.org/projects/globalecon/ilrf/intro.html); Kimberly Ann Elliott and Richard B. Freeman, *Can Labor Standards Improve Under Globalization?* (Washington D.C.: Institute for International Economics, 2003), 90–92; and Kevin Kolben, "Trade, Monitoring, and the ILO: Working to Improve Conditions in Cambodia's Garment Factories," *Yale Human Rights and Development Law Journal* 7 (2004): 79.

3. We draw here on the terminology developed in Amartya Sen, *The Standard of Living* (Cambridge: Cambridge University Press, 1987).

4. It does not follow from this rejection, of course, that we are indifferent to the losses of those in the focal group who do worse under the new system. We favor measures that minimize these losses.

5. It should be pointed out that Staiger himself resists the description of his argument as an argument for linkage by attempting to distinguish between the economic rationale and the moral or political rationale for maintaining a floor for labor standards. Robert W. Staiger, "A Role for the WTO," in *International Labor Standards*, eds. Kaushik Basu et al. (Malden, Mass.: Blackwell, 2003), 273, 277. However, it is clear that the argument Staiger provides is an argument for linkage as we define it (in Proposition L); Josh Ederington, "Trade and Domestic Policy Linkage in International Agreements," *International Economic Review* 43, no. 4 (2002): 1347, 1361 (using game theory to show that, at least under certain circumstances, linkage can increase the ability to enforce the domestic provisions of an international agreement, in this case higher labor standards).

6. Bagwell and Staiger have presented an alternative way of avoiding such problems, in which countries are required to abide by specific rules when adjusting their labor standards but are not required to promote them to any specific extent. Kyle Bagwell and Robert W. Staiger, "The Simple Economics of Labor Standards and the GATT," in *Social Dimensions of U.S. Trade Policy*, eds. Alan V. Deardorff and Robert M. Stern (Ann Arbor: University of Michigan Press, 2000), 225–226. We discuss

their proposed possible solution in detail below, presenting reasons why some of its elements may be beneficially incorporated into a linkage system.

7. "Race to the bottom" is a widespread but unfortunate name for the more general concern that competitive pressures will undermine efforts to secure basic labor standards. It is unfortunate because it suggests that, absent evidence of *deterioration* of labor standards over time, competitive pressures that undermine efforts to *raise* labor standards are not present. This conclusion would be false, because even if labor standards were everywhere improving, it would not follow that the threat of being undercut by others with lower labor standards was not exerting *downward pressure* on labor standards. Indeed, it is entirely consistent with the fact that much more rapid improvements in labor standards might be obtainable were stronger incentives provided to countries to do so. In such a case, there would be (to use Staiger's phrase) a "regulatory chill" but not an observable race to the bottom. The former concept depends on a counterfactual comparison, while the latter depends on a purely empirical one.

8. Such incentives are already part of the European Union's Generalized System of Preferences. See Tobias Buck, "Brussels to Reward to 'Good' Poor Countries," *Financial Times*, Oct. 21, 2004. It is interesting to note that the linkage proposal of the International Confederation of Free Trade Unions calls for "urgent removal of tariffs and import quotas for least developed countries respecting core labour standards." ICFTU, *Workers' Human Rights*, 23.

9. See also Rob Jenkins, "India and the Trade-and-Labour-Standards Controversy" (paper presented at the seminar "India at the Beginning of the 21st Century," Instituto do Oriente, Lisbon, Mar. 20–23, 2001), 3, 5–7 (available online at http://www.gapresearch.org/governance/The%20Politics%20of%20Trade%20in%20India.pdf), predicting that India, which has opposed linkage, might accept it if wealthy countries abide by Uruguay Round agreements that require them to open their markets in certain cases. The Indian Government Commission on Labour Standards and International Trade issued a report expressing an open-minded position on linkage, especially if appropriate supports were to be offered by developed countries. The chair of the commission, Subramaniam Swamy, argued in a subsequent book that India could be a net gainer should linkage be implemented, in part because of the competitive advantages it would gain relative to countries unlikely to adequately promote labor standards. See Kevin Kolben, "The New Politics of Linkage: India's Opposition to the Workers' Rights Clause," *Indiana Journal of Global Legal Studies* 13, no. 1 (2006).

10. It is far from clear that the motivation behind linkage is in fact protectionism. Krueger attempted to examine this assumption by identifying the constituencies whose representatives supported the Harkin Bill in the U.S. Congress, which proposed the imposition of specific trade sanctions on countries exporting goods produced with child labor. He concluded that self-interested material motives were

not discernible from the empirical profile of these constituencies. Alan Krueger, "Observations on International Labor Standards and Trade," Working Paper no. 362 (National Bureau of Economic Research, Washington D.C., 1996), 13–23. Krueger's argument is cited in Kaushik Basu, "Child Labor: Cause, Consequence, and Cure, with Remarks on International Labor Standards," *Journal of Economic Literature* 37, no. 3 (1999): 1092; and criticized in Jagdish Bhagwati, *In Defense of Globalization* (New York: Oxford University Press, 2004), 244–245. Sandra Polaski argues that where trade treaties have contained a labor clause, it has generally not been misused for protectionist ends. Sandra Polaski, *Trade and Labor Standards: A Strategy for Developing Countries* (Washington D.C.: Carnegie Endowment for International Peace, 2003), 14 (available online at http://www.carnegieendowment.org/pdf/files/Polaski_Trade_English.pdf). A similar finding is presented by Elliott and Freeman, who discuss in detail the existing evidence on such motivations. Elliott and Freeman, *Can Labor Standards Improve?* 84. Critics of linkage often argue as if the mere fact that support for linkage may be due in part to protectionist concerns rules out the possibility that it is desirable. This is false, since it is possible that agents may do the right thing for the wrong reasons or from questionable motivations, just as they may do the wrong thing for the right reasons and from pure motivations. As Alan Krueger, "The Political Economy of Child Labor," in Kaushik Basu et al., eds., *International Labor Standards*, 251, rightly points out, "even if international labor standards were motivated by self-interest, they nonetheless may raise welfare in less developed nations. . . . And the converse is also true: even if international labor standards were motivated by humanitarian concerns they may hurt those they are intended to help in developing countries." Of course, the motivations of agents are certainly relevant in forming predictions about how they will act. It may be quite reasonably feared that if protectionist *motives* drive at least some of those who support linkage, any system of linkage that emerges will likely be *used* for protectionist purposes. However, even agents with largely self-serving motivations can be expected to comply with a system of rules if it provides them with the right incentives to do so. The WTO is built on the premise that situating trade negotiations within a transparent and negotiated system of rules with a binding and impartial dispute settlement mechanism can promote a fairer world trading system, notwithstanding the often self-seeking motivations of the states who participate in the system. Indeed, it seems implausible that any system of international trading rules can be created that could effectively guard *entirely* against such opportunistic misuse.

11. Examples include the National Labor Relations Board in the United States and comparable bodies in other countries, the WTO's Dispute Settlement Body (DSB), existing free trade agreements with labor provisions such as the U.S.-Jordan Free Trade Agreement, the North American Agreement on Labor Cooperation, and the Canada-Chile Free Trade Agreement. See Polaski, *Trade and Labor Standards*, 13–14; Sandra Polaski, "Cambodia Blazes a New Path to Economic Growth and Job

Creation," Carnegie Paper no. 51 (Carnegie Endowment for International Peace, Washington D.C., 2004), 14; Sandra Polaski, "Protecting Labor Rights Through Trade Agreements: An Analytical Guide," *Journal International Law and Policy* 10, no. 1 (2003): 13, 17–20. See also Kolben, "Trade, Monitoring, and the ILO." Ehrenberg, "From Intention to Action," 168, proposes that an "Admissibility Committee" composed of nine members appointed jointly by the ILO and the GATT/WTO and charged with determining whether complaints with respect to the observance of labor standards (specified in terms of eight publicly stated criteria) are admissible for consideration by a linkage enforcement scheme. See also ICFTU, *Workers' Human Rights*, 52–53 (describing how the ILO could report to the WTO on violations of core labor standards); Harvey, Collingsworth, and Athreya, "Implementing Labor Rights," sec. III (proposing that the ILO interact with independent monitors of labor violations).

12. Cf. Rohini Hensman, "World Trade and Workers' Rights: In Search of an Internationalist Position," *Antipode* 33, no. 3 (2001): 433. Indeed, many prominent critics of linkage defend the WTO on similar grounds.

13. It may also be feared that the standard of proof required for establishing that labor standards violations have taken place may be set so low as to make it easy for rich countries to establish claims that labor standards have been violated and difficult for poor countries to deny such claims.

14. This is consistent with the widely discussed concept of the progressive realization of human rights. Existing international treaties do often make allowances for the level of development of countries. Examples include the Kyoto protocol and the TRIPS agreement.

15. Indeed, the Ehrenberg, ICFTU, and Harvey, Collingsworth, and Athreya proposals cited above all insist on such a requirement.

16. Even the WTO DSB, which has not arisen from a truly transparent and participatory process, often makes decisions that are not in the interests of member countries, including the most powerful. See, e.g., Appellate Body of the World Trade Organization, *Panel Report, United States–Transitional Safeguard Measure on Combed Cotton Yarn from Pakistan*, WT/DS192/AB/R (Geneva: WTO, May 31, 2001). For a description of the recent ruling on cotton, which Brazil won against the United States, see "U.S. Loses Cotton Fight with Brazil," *BBC News*, March 3, 2005 (available online at news.bbc.co.uk/2/hi/business/4316671.stm).

17. Cf. Gene M. Grossman and Alan B. Krueger, "Environmental Impacts of a North American Free Trade Agreement," in Peter M. Gerber, *The Mexico-U.S. Free Trade Agreement* (Cambridge, Mass.: MIT Press, 1994), 13, 48. Alan Krueger emphasizes this point, arguing that for this reason it would be difficult for developed countries to exploit labor standards to achieve protectionist ends. Krueger, "International Labor Standards," 12. See also Polaski, *Trade and Labor Standards*, 13 (stating that currently competition for manufacturing occurs only among de-

veloping countries, since textile, apparel, footwear, electronics, etc. are produced almost exclusively in low-wage countries). Basu, "Child Labor," 1114, acknowledges the desirability of collective coordination of standards. Robert Pollin, Justine Burns, and James Heintz, "Global Apparel Production and Sweatshop Labour: Can Raising Retail Prices Finance Living Wages?" *Cambridge Journal of Economics* 28, no. 2 (2004): 153, 156–160, find that increasing the cost of labor, by increasing wages or raising labor standards, does not consistently lead to job losses.

18. See Krueger, "International Labor Standards," 12; cf. Grossman and Krueger, "Environmental Impacts," 48.

19. Jagdish N. Bhagwati and V. K. Ramaswami, "Domestic Distortions, Tariffs, and the Theory of Optimum Subsidy," *Journal of Political Economy* 71, no. 1 (1963): 44–50.

20. See Sanjay G. Reddy, "Pareto-Improving International Labor Standards Agreements: A Simple Model" (working paper, Department of Economics, Barnard College, Columbia University, New York, 2006, available online at http://ssrn.com/abstract=930113).

21. Note that free trade with the wage subsidy and enhanced labor standards and free trade without the wage subsidy or enhanced labor standards are each Pareto superior to autarky (in principle) but that the two free trade alternatives may not be Pareto comparable, because some may do strictly better under the former scheme and others may do strictly better under the latter scheme, depending on the nature and extent of the ex-post taxes and transfers that are implemented. The Pareto ranking of free trade and autarky depend on (1) the existence or absence of a domestic distortion and (2) correction of a domestic distortion at the source or failure to correct the domestic distortion at the source. The ranking is as follows (assuming the existence of efficient tax and transfer instruments and specializing, for simplicity, to the case of production distortions): (1) Without a domestic distortion: free trade is Pareto superior to autarky, because there are gains from trade that can be redistributed in a lump-sum fashion. This is because each unit produced for export satisfies the condition that the world price exceeds the true domestic cost of production; (2) With a domestic distortion: (2.1) If the domestic distortion is corrected at the source, then free trade is Pareto superior to autarky, because there are gains from trade that can be redistributed in a lump-sum fashion. Again, this is because each unit produced for export satisfies the condition that the world price exceeds the true domestic cost of production. (The correction of the domestic distortion at source ensures that the producers' perceived costs are equal to the true domestic costs of production.); (2.2) If the domestic distortion is not corrected at the source, then it is ambiguous whether or not free trade is Pareto superior to autarky, since it is ambiguous whether there are gains from trade. Whether or not there are gains from trade will depend on the nature and extent of the distortion. Consider the following illustrative example: A country produces an exportable commodity (say

oil) with a great deal of attendant pollution per unit produced. This externality is not internalized. (If it were, say through an appropriate Pigouvian tax [case 2.1], then the marginal unit produced would represent its true domestic [social] cost of production. In that case, there would be gains from trade, since oil would be produced for export if and only if the world price were greater than or equal to the true domestic cost of production.) Since the externality is not internalized (case 2.2), oil will be exported as long as the world offer price is greater than or equal to the domestic producer cost. However, since the marginal domestic producer cost is lower than the true marginal domestic cost, there will be a social cost created by these units produced for export. At the margin, the revenue garnered by the sale of these units on the world market will exceed the true domestic cost of their production. Whether there are gains from trade will depend on whether, on average, for the additional units sold due to trade opening the average true domestic cost of their production is higher or lower than the world price. In principle, whether this is so is ambiguous and depends on the level of the world price and the nature and extent of the domestic distortion.

22. Rohini Hensman reports that while "on the whole, the proposal for a workers' rights clause in WTO agreements too has been greeted in a positive spirit by informal sector activists. . . . Once again, this does not mean that all aspects of the proposal are accepted without criticism—for example, the suggestion that it will apply only to export production is seen as a defect—but, rather, that these activists are open to the possibility of using international pressure to secure rights for workers who have little hope of getting them through purely domestic action." Rohini Hensman, "The Impact of Globalisation on Employment in India and Responses from the Formal and Informal Sectors," Working Papers on Asian Labour no. 15 (Amsterdam: CLARA, International Institute of Social History, 2001), 21.

23. Systems of linkage are often, but need not be, justified on the grounds that failure to respect basic labor standards gives an "unfair advantage" to some countries, which advantage must be corrected. Instead, linkage can be justified on the ground that the trading system provides an effective means of altering the incentives faced by countries, creating an environment that better enables and urges them to promote basic labor standards. By justifying linkage in terms of "unfair trade" and referring to countries that do not respect basic standards as "free riders" (IFCTU, *Workers' Human Rights*, 43), proponents of linkage fail to place enough emphasis on a very important class of persons who are harmed by these failures, namely the workers in countries that fail to promote basic labor standards. For this reason, our proposal for linkage (sketched below) differs from others such as Ehrenberg's, whose proposal would allow penalties only against countries whose exports are produced in a way that disrespects basic standards (and only against such exported goods). See, e.g., Ehrenberg, "From Intention to Action," 172–173.

24. This must be true if the labor supply curve is upward sloping or entirely inelastic, as typically assumed.

25. See, e.g., Richard B. Freeman, "Spurts in Union Growth: Defining Moments and Social Processes," Working Paper no. 6012 (National Bureau of Economic Research, Washington D.C., 1997), 10 (available online at http://papers.nber.org/papers/w6012.v5.pdf); Karl Moene and Michael Wallerstein, "Social Democracy as a Development Strategy," in *Globalization and Egalitarian Redistribution*, eds. Pranab Bardhan, Samuel Bowles, and Michael Wallerstein (Princeton, N.J.: Princeton University Press, 2006). Note also that the opposite conclusion could result, for example, if labor unions represent a "labor aristocracy" that successfully demands that public resources be put to purposes other than those that benefit the most disadvantaged.

26. See generally Bhagwati and Ramaswamy, "Domestic Distortions." For discussion, see Arvind Panagariya, "Bhagwati and Ramaswami: Why It *Is* a Classic" (working paper, Department of Economics, University of Maryland, College Park, Nov. 8, 2000), 13.

27. See the appendix to this book.

28. Implicit in this proposition is the application of an appropriate social welfare (or "aggregation") function. An example of an aggregation function to which it clearly applies is that defined by the total wage bill. See, e.g., Martin Rama, "The Consequences of Doubling the Minimum Wage: The Case of Indonesia," Working Paper no. 1643 (World Bank, Washington D.C., 1996, available online at http://ssrn.com/abstract=604935), showing that in Indonesia, a 10 percent increase in average wages, induced by an increase in the minimum wage, was associated with a 2 percent decrease in wage employment, implying a significant increase in the overall wage bill as a result of the minimum wage increase. The seminal detailed empirical research presented by Harrison and Scorse concerning the impact of "antisweatshop" activism on labor market outcomes in Indonesia comes to the conclusion that such activism has had ambiguous results, causing decreases in employment and wages in some sectors and increases in employment and wages elsewhere (including some of the firms targeted by activists). See Ann Harrison and Jason Scorse, "Moving Up or Moving Out? Anti-Sweatshop Activists and Labor Market Outcomes," Working Paper No. 10492 (National Bureau of Economic Research, Washington D.C., 2004), 32–35 (available online at http://www.nber.org/papers/w10492.pdf).

29. See, e.g., Derek Parfit, *Equality or Priority?* (Lawrence: University of Kansas Press, 1995).

30. See, e.g., Kaushik Basu and Pham Hoang Van, "The Economics of Child Labor," American Economic Review 88, no. 3 (1998): 412–413; Basu, "Child Labor," 1115 ("A large-scale withdrawal of child labor can cause adult wages to rise so much that the working class household is better off"). Similarly, under certain conditions, eliminating the right of workers to enter into bonded labor contracts may benefit

such workers, since the availability of such contracts may prevent more beneficial kinds of credit contracts from emerging. See Garance Genicot, "Bonded Labor and Serfdom: A Paradox of Voluntary Choice," *Journal of Development Economics* 67, no. 1 (2002): 101, 119–122.

31. This is true on a subjective preference-based conception of welfare as employed in Basu and Van, "Economics of Child Labor," 36–37. However, the assumption that household welfare can be conceived of without further disaggregation ought to be questioned.

32. An early example of this approach to child labor is presented in Arthur C. Pigou, *The Economics of Welfare*, 4th ed. (London: MacMillan, 1960), 751–753. An exemplary overview of existing approaches of this kind is presented in Drusilla K. Brown, Alan V. Deardorff, and Robert M. Stern, "Child Labor: Theory, Evidence, and Policy," in Kaushik Basu et al., *International Labor Standards*, 225–237.

33. E.g., Mexico's *Progressa* and Brazil's *Bolsa Escola* programs.

34. This could perhaps be recognized by the agent herself under appropriate conditions. To take a rather tired example, although an alcoholic may reveal his preference for beer over beans, it is far from obvious that this preference reflects his best interests. A public policy that hinders the ability of the alcoholic to indulge his preference without restriction may be viewed as enhancing welfare. For discussion of the principles underlying judgments of this type, see, e.g., T. M. Scanlon, "Preference and Urgency," *Journal of Philosophy* 72, no. 19 (1975): 655, 658; Amartya Sen, "Positional Objectivity," *Philosophy and Public Affairs* 22, no. 2 (1993): 126, 134–136. On the outcomes that can arise under imperfect information, see generally Joseph E. Stiglitz, "The Contributions of the Economics of Information to Twentieth Century Economics," *Quarterly Journal of Economics* 115, no. 4 (2000): 1441.

35. The 1996 WTO ministerial meeting, for instance, declared that "the International Labor Organization (ILO) is the competent body to set and deal with these standards, and we affirm our support for its work in promoting them." World Trade Organization, *Ministerial Declaration of 13 December 1996*, WT/MIN(96)/DEC (Geneva: WTO, 1996).

36. There is only one case known to the authors of the ILO having applied penalties to a country due to violation of labor standards: Myanmar in 1996. See Elliott and Freeman, *Can Labor Standards Improve?*, 95.

37. For example, at the 1997 International Labor Conference. The ILO remains relatively toothless even after the strengthening of countries' reporting requirements. See, e.g., Hensman, "World Trade"; Elliott and Freeman, *Can Labor Standards Improve?*, 96–100; ICFTU, "Belarus Is Once Again Censured by the ILO," *ILO Online*, June 14, 2005 (available online at http://www.icftu.org/displaydocument. asp?Index=991221860&Language;=EN), describing the ILO's inability to punish Belarus's violations of trade union rights.

38. See generally Howard Chang, "Carrots, Sticks, and International Externalities," *International Review of Law and Economics* 17, no. 3 (1997): 309.

39. See, e.g., Giancarlo Spagnolo, "Issue Linkage, Delegation, and International Policy Cooperation," Working Paper no. 49.96 (Milan: FEEM, 1999, available online at http://papers.ssrn.com/sol3/papers.cfm?abstract_id=163173).

40. For an argument in this direction with respect to trade and environmental standards, see generally Howard Chang, "An Economic Analysis of Trade Measures to Protect the Global Environment," *Georgetown Law Journal* 83, no. 6 (1995): 2131.

41. For example, it is widely believed that such restrictions played a role in the end of the apartheid regimes in southern Africa (South Africa, Zimbabwe/Rhodesia, and Namibia).

42. See, e.g., S. Prakash Sethi, *Setting Global Standards: Guidelines for Creating Codes of Conduct in Multinational Corporations* (New York: Wiley, 2003); Elliott and Freeman, *Can Labor Standards Improve?*, 27–48; Archon Fung, Dara O'Rourke, and Charles Sabel, "Realizing Labor Standards," in *Can We Put an End to Sweatshops?* (Boston: Beacon Press, 2001), 5–6; Karl Schoenberger, *Levi's Children: Coming to Terms with Human Rights in the Global Marketplace* (New York: Atlantic Press, 2000).

43. For evidence on how codes of conduct fail (often due to competitive pressures) to be fully incorporated into firms' buying practices, see, e.g., Oxfam International, "Trading Away Our Rights: Women Working in Global Supply Chains" (Oxford: Oxfam International, 2004), 38–39 (available online at http://www.oxfam. org.uk/what_we_do/issues/trade/downloads/trading_rights.pdf); Hong Kong Christian Industrial Committee, "How Hasbro, McDonald's, Mattel and Disney Manufacture Their Toys" (Hong Kong: HKCIC, 2001), 29–31 (available online at http://www.cic.org.hk/download/CIC%20Toy%20Report%20Web%20eng.pdf); Kenneth A. Rodman, *Sanctions Beyond Borders: Multinational Corporations and U.S. Economic Statecraft* (Lanham, Md.: Rowman & Littlefield, 2001).

44. Dani Rodrik, "Labor Standards in International Trade," in *Emerging Agenda for Global Trade: High Stakes for Developing Countries*, eds. Robert Z. Lawrence, Dani Rodrik, and John Whalley, Policy Essay no. 20 (Overseas Development Council, Washington D.C., 1996), 61.

45. Tinbergen uses the term "general interest" and refers to a "collective ophelimity function" that represents this general interest "in whatever sense that may be taken" and which is "the object to be maximised." This entity is apparently "a function of a certain number of variables which we shall call the target variables," select numerical values of which are referred to as the targets. The targets are presumed to be chosen so as to maximize the ophelimity function. In contrast, instruments are "variables under the command of the government." Jan Tinbergen, *On the Theory of Economic Policy*, 2nd. ed. (Amsterdam: North-Holland, 1966), 1, 7.

46. Utilitarians, for example, may conceive of this master goal in terms of world welfare and, moreover, specifically understand welfare in terms of subjective preference satisfaction or pleasure. In contrast, Rawlsians evaluate social institutions in terms of the level of social primary goods they engender for their least advantaged participants.

47. See, e.g., Jagdish Bhagwati, "The Question of Linkage," *American Journal of International Law* 96, no. 1 (2002).

48. See, e.g., Bhagwati and Ramaswamy, "Domestic Distortions," 44; Jagdish Bhagwati, V. K. Ramswami, and T. N. Srinivasan, "Domestic Distortions, Tariffs and the Theory of Optimum Subsidy: Some Further Results," *Journal of Political Economy* 77, no. 6 (1969): 1005. Another reason that it may be impossible to attain the level of multiple targets despite the existence of at least as many instruments as targets is the existence of possible causal interdependencies among the targets themselves (as have been, for instance, widely believed to exist between inflation and unemployment). See, e.g., Tinbergen, *Theory of Economic Policy*; Jan Tinbergen, *Economic Policy: Principles and Design*, 4th ed. (Chicago: Rand McNally, 1967).

49. Jan Tinbergen himself strongly supported an integrated international policy to deal jointly with employment and growth objectives. Tinbergen identifies six broad areas in which "tasks should be performed on a world basis, although some may also be subjected to cooperation on a regional basis, under supervision on a world level." Jan Tinbergen, *International Economic Integration*, rev. ed. (Amsterdam: Elsevier, 1954), 145. It is evident that Tinbergen views the areas suitable to be addressed at a centralized (world) level to be determined wholly on empirical grounds. Foremost among these empirical grounds is whether the instruments in question have a "supporting" or a "conflicting" role in the sense that "the use of such an instrument by one country will support the policies of the other countries" or whether its use by one country "conflicts with the objectives of other countries' policies." Ibid., 98–99. The framers of the postwar institutional scheme also considered such integration of objectives quite attractive. For example, the International Trade Organization (ITO) was originally proposed by John Maynard Keynes at the Bretton Woods Conference to further the expansion of world trade as a means to the ends of development, adequate wages, labor standards, and full employment. The Havana Charter, which provided for the creation of the ITO, contained an explicit reference to "Fair Labour Standards" (in Chapter II, Article 7 of the charter) providing for the need to "take fully into account the rights of workers," recognizing that because "unfair labour conditions, particularly in production for export, create difficulties in international trade, each Member shall take whatever action may be appropriate and feasible to eliminate such conditions within its territory" and requiring that the ITO "consult and co-operate with the International Labour Organisation" toward this end. However, the ITO did not come into being because of the failure of the U.S. Senate ultimately to ratify it. For the history of the ITO,

see generally Richard Toye, "Developing Multilateralism: The Havana Charter and the Fight for the International Trade Organization, 1947–48," *International History Review* 25, no. 2 (2003): 253; Daniel Drache, "The Short but Significant Life of the International Trade Organization: Lessons for Our Time," Working Paper no. 62/00 (Centre for the Study of Globalisation and Regionalisation, University of Warwick, Coventry, Nov. 2000); Thomas W. Zeiler, *Free Trade and Free World: The Advent of GATT* (Chapel Hill: University of North Carolina Press, 1999); Howard M. Wachtel, "Labor's Stake in the WTO," *The American Prospect* 9, no. 37 (1998): 34; Mark Levinson, "Global Is as Global Does?" *The Nation*, Dec. 18, 1999; William Diebold Jr., "The End of the ITO," *Essays in International Finance 16* (Princeton, N.J.: International Finance Section, Princeton University, 1952); William Adams Brown, Jr., *The United States and the Restoration of World Trade* (Washington D.C.: Brookings Institution, 1950). On the view of the parties to the ITO that labor standards concerns must play a role in the organization, see Toye, "Developing Multilateralism"; and Drache, "International Trade Organization." For a discussion of the wage-based view of labor standards endorsed in the early stages of GATT negotiations, see Elissa Alben, "GATT and the Fair Wage: A Historical Perspective on the Labor-Trade Link," *Columbia Law Review* 101, no. 6 (2001): 1410.

50. See, e.g., Hensman, "World Trade"; Terry Collingsworth, "International Worker Rights Enforcement," in Compa and Diamond, *Human Rights*.

51. See Spagnolo, "Issue Linkage"; see also Nuno Limão, "Trade Policy, Cross-Border Externalities and Lobbies: Do Linked Agreements Enforce More Cooperative Outcomes?" *Journal of International Economics* 67, no. 1 (2005): 175.

52. Specific subsets of possible strategies are considered in the formal analyses by Spagnolo and the other contributors to this emerging body of literature. See also Nancy Chau and Ravi Kanbur, "The Race to the Bottom, from the Bottom," *Economica* 73, no. 290 (2006): 73 (esp. sec. 4), for a recent example of such a contribution focusing specifically on labor and environmental standards and that attempts to identify conditions under which international agreements on standards may be sustainable.

53. Spagnolo, "Issue Linkage," focuses on the implications of the agents' valuations of different combinations of attainments, whereas Limão, "Trade Policy," focuses on the implications of the causal interconnections between distinct issue areas. According to Spagnolo, there are two kinds of cases to consider. The first is that in which the outcomes are substitutes in the sense that increases in the level of achievement in one outcome dimension are valued less when the level of achievement in the other outcome dimension is higher. The second is that in which the outcomes are complements in the sense that increases in the level of achievement in one outcome dimension are valued more when the level of achievement in the other outcome dimension is higher. When the outcomes are substitutes, then the threat of withdrawal of future cooperation in one issue area alone may be relatively ineffective because cooperation

in the other issue area may secure the rest of the advantages that would have been achieved had there been cooperation in the two issue areas together. When the outcomes are complements, then the threat of withdrawal of cooperation in one issue area alone may be relatively effective, because when cooperation in the second issue area is taking place, then the threat of withdrawal of cooperation entails a significant loss of benefit. Paradoxically, the withdrawal of future cooperation in both issue areas together may not be as effective because the value attached to cooperation in each area diminishes when cooperation in the other issue area does not take place. From the above analysis, it follows that when the issue areas are substitutes, linking them will be advantageous with respect to both of the aspects of enforcement. When the issue areas are complements, whether linking them will be advantageous from the standpoint of enforcement depends on the empirical question of whether the gains from improved allocation of slack enforcement power are greater than the losses from lessened effectiveness of the threat of withdrawal of future cooperation. Therefore, there is no general reason to prefer disaggregated negotiations to linked negotiations from the standpoint of enforcement. For discussion of related issues, see generally Paolo Conconi and Carlo Perroni, "Issue Linkage and Issue Tie-In in Multilateral Negotiations," *Journal of International Economics* 57, no. 2 (2002): 423; Josh Edderington, "Trade and Domestic Policy Linkage in International Agreements," *International Economic Review* 43, no. 4 (2002): 1347.

54. Arvind Panagariya, "Trade-Labour Link: A Post-Seattle Analysis," in *Globalization Under Threat: The Stability of Trade Policy and Multilateral Agreements* (Cheltenham: Edward Elgar, 2001), 101, 104.

55. This narrowly welfarist normative framework is clearly insufficient for capturing the normative significance of labor standards. However, we cannot further address this issue in this section.

56. Other conditions are required, such as the existence of efficient tax and transfer instruments. In the absence of such instruments, there is no guarantee that redistribution of the gains from trade can produce a Pareto improvement.

57. See, e.g., T. N. Srinivasan, "Comment," in Deardorff and Stern, *U.S. Trade Policy*, 236.

58. See Jagdish N. Bhagwati, "Lobbying and Welfare," *Journal of Public Economics* 14, no. 3 (1980): 355; see also Jagdish N. Bhagwati, "Directly Unproductive: Profit-Seeking (DUP) Activities," *Journal of Political Economy* 90, no. 5 (1982): 988; Anne O. Krueger, "The Political Economy of the Rent-Seeking Society," *American Economic Review* 64, no. 3 (1974): 291.

59. There are plausible exceptions to the idea that the conduct of an agent ought to be evaluated independently of others' conduct. For example, there is a long tradition of argument that has emphasized that the obligation of agents to refrain from armament or attack depends on whether they have assurance that other agents abide by corresponding obligations. But cases of this kind appear to involve special

conditions, for example, that those whose well-being is put at risk by the agent's failure to meet the requirement themselves reciprocally put the agent at risk through their failures to abide by this same requirement.

60. Other proposals for linkage have failed to take adequate account of the responsibilities of countries that are the sites of registration, ownership, or management of firms directly or indirectly linked to violations of basic labor standards. A linkage system that fails to broaden its jurisdiction in this way inappropriately focuses on the punishment of developing countries by developed countries. Thus, it will lack legitimacy and effectiveness.

61. There is indeed a wide consensus that this is the case, as the widespread reference in the debate to ILO conventions and other international legal documents specifying international norms makes clear.

62. See, e.g., G. A. Cohen, *History, Labour, and Freedom: Themes from Marx* (Oxford: Oxford University Press, 1989), 209–238; Alan Wertheimer, *Exploitation* (Princeton, N.J.: Princeton University Press, 1999), 207–246.

63. It is common to all rights that they may be asserted without insisting on their absolute priority or unconditionality. This is also recognized in law. Famously, asserting that there is a right to free speech does not establish that people can everywhere and anywhere say what they want. See, e.g., *Schenck v. United States*, 249 U.S. 47 (1919) (holding that the most stringent protection of free speech rights will not protect a man who falsely shouts fire in a theater and causes a panic).

64. See Jagdish Bhagwati, interview by Penny Abeywardena, *Rights News* (Fall 2004): 2–3.

65. See, e.g., Amartya Sen, "Well-Being, Agency and Freedom: The Dewey Lectures 1984," *Journal of Philosophy* 84, no. 2 (1985): 169, on consequentialist theories directly valuing rights fulfillment.

66. See, e.g., Partha Dasgupta and Debraj Ray, "Inequality as a Determinant of Malnutrition and Unemployment: Policy," *Economic Journal* 97, no. 385 (1987): 177; Ross Levine and David Renelt, "A Sensitivity Analysis of Cross-Country Growth Regressions," *American Economic Review* 82, no. 4 (1992): 942; Harvey Leibenstein, *Economic Backwardness and Economic Growth* (London: Chapman and Hall, 1957); Michael J. Piore, "International Labor Standards and Business Strategies," in U.S. Department of Labor, *International Labor Standards and Global Integration: Proceedings of a Symposium* (Washington D.C.: U.S. Department of Labor, 1994), 21; Moene and Wallerstein, "Social Democracy."

67. See, e.g., Dani Rodrik, *The New Global Economy and Developing Countries: Making Openness Work* (Washington D.C.: Overseas Development Council, 1999). It has been argued that governmental enforcement of labor standards has created incentives for technological and organizational innovation and thereby enhanced economic growth in Europe and the United States. See Moene and Wallerstein, "Social Democracy" (studying European cases); Piore, "International Labor Standards"

(studying the nineteenth-century U.S. textile industry); Kenneth D. Boyer, "Deregulation of the Trucking Sector: Specialization, Concentration, Entry, and Financial Distress," *Southern Economic Journal* 59, no. 3 (1993): 481.

68. We apply this concept broadly here, so as potentially to encompass those who may not hold formal citizenship rights, such as legal residents or long-term residents.

69. Rawls' concept of a "decent consultation hierarchy" is a concept of the latter kind. John Rawls, *The Law of Peoples: With "The Idea of Public Reason Revisited"* (Cambridge, Mass.: Harvard University Press, 1999), 71. Whether it is sufficient for regimes to be of this kind or whether regimes must have democratic characteristics in order to guarantee the (internal) moral legitimacy of the linkage scheme that they join is a question we do not directly address here.

70. We leave open the question of whether these necessary conditions for legitimacy are also sufficient.

71. The tripartite model of decision making in the ILO offers a suggestive instance of such a process, which has led to notable consensus of this kind.

72. See John Rawls, *Political Liberalism* (New York: Columbia University Press, 1993); John Gray, *Two Faces of Liberalism* (Cambridge: Polity Press, 2000).

73. See, e.g., Cohen, *History, Labour, and Freedom*.

74. Not all legally binding contracts are morally binding. See David Singh Grewal "Network Power and Globalization," *Ethics & International Affairs* 17, no. 2 (2003): 89, 92–93; see also Cohen, *History, Labour, and Freedom*. We will not address these important concerns at much greater length here, as they seem not to be raised in present discussions of linkage. To the extent they apply to the linkage proposal we make here they would certainly seem also to apply to assessments of whether the entry of countries into the WTO and many other international treaty bodies is unduly coerced.

75. See John Gray, *False Dawn: The Delusions of Global Capitalism* (New York: New Press, 1998), 18.

76. Personal conversation with Kamal Malhotra.

77. For a discussion of the issues of legal interpretation involved, see, e.g., Kyle Bagwell, Petros C. Mavroidis, and Robert W. Staiger, "It's a Question of Market Access," *American Journal of International Law* 96, no. 1 (2002): 56.

78. See Chang, "Economic Analysis"; Chang, "Carrots, Sticks, and International Externalities."

79. See Thomas Robert Malthus, *An Essay on the Principle of Population* (London: J. Johnson, 1798); and David Ricardo, *On the Principles of Political Economy and Taxation* (London: John Murray, 1821), for a highly skeptical view of these prospects, based on the perspective that public supports for the poor would generate perverse effects (of sufficient magnitude to undermine the impact of the supports themselves) on population growth and work effort.

80. See, e.g., Amartya K. Sen, "Rational Fools: A Critique of the Behavioral Foundations of Economic Theory," *Philosophy & Public Affairs* 6, no. 4 (1977): 317; Amartya K. Sen, *On Ethics and Economics* (Malden, Mass.: Blackwell, 1988).

81. See, e.g., Consumer Unity & Trust Society, "Third World Intellectuals and NGOs' Statement Against Linkage," *CUTS International*, Sept. 6, 1999 (available online at http://cuts-international.org/twin-sal.htm).

82. See, e.g., John Rawls, *A Theory of Justice* (Cambridge, Mass.: Belknap Press, 1971).

83. Indeed, it is the norm in international treaties to deem that they have come into force when there have been a sufficient number of signatories or ratifications.

84. We recognize that additional approaches may also exist.

85. This suggests that proponents of trade liberalization who are critical of its current pace should favor linkage. In the present political climate, it is far from obvious that adopting linkage will bring about a *lesser* degree of trade liberalization than would otherwise take place. See, e.g., Polaski, "Cambodia."

86. There is considerable evidence of such competitive pressures among developing countries, most recently as a result of the end of the Multi Fiber Arrangement. Unsurprisingly in this context, there is, contrary to popular impression, considerable evidence of support for linkage by developing country labor unions. See, e.g., Gerard Griffin, Chris Nyland, and Anne O'Rourke, "Trade Unions and the Social Clause: A North South Union Divide?" Working Paper no. 81 (Melbourne: National Key Center in Industrial Relations, Monash University, 2002). There is archival evidence that strong support for the labor standards provisions in the proposed postwar ITO was provided at the postwar Havana Conference by representatives of developing countries (in particular, Cuba and India). The authors were alerted to this evidence through conversations with Mark Levinson.

87. The literature on efficiency wages suggests that there may be productivity gains to be achieved as a result of higher wages, although whether this will result from general, as opposed to firm-specific or industry-specific, wage increases depends on the specific mechanism by which it is assumed that wages enhance productivity. Collective action problems among employers can lead to the failure to realize these gains in the absence of determined coordination (as emphasized, for instance, in the literature on the nutrition-productivity relationship).

88. The possible collective action problem among employers may otherwise prevent productivity-enhancing investments in the labor force.

89. Of course, on the other side, there is the risk to firms that linkage will reduce the ability of firms to threaten workers in developed countries with relocation as a means of gaining concessions. Such relocation threats may be a determinant of profits in industries in which rent sharing takes place.

90. See, e.g., Elizabeth Becker, "Low Cost and Sweatshop-Free," *New York Times*, May 12, 2005.

7. SKETCH OF ONE POSSIBLE LINKAGE SYSTEM

1. It is hardly difficult to find flaws in these institutions.

2. See General Conference of the International Labour Organization, 86th sess., *ILO Declaration on Fundamental Principles and Rights at Work* (Geneva: International Labour Organization, June 1998, available online at http://www.ilo.org/public/english/standards/relm/ilc/ilc86/com-dtxt.htm), providing for periodic self-reporting by countries, reviews of those reports by experts, and the provision of technical assistance in response to needs identified in these reports.

8. CONCLUSION

1. Pascal Lamy, the present director general of the WTO, has noted that there is at present an "imbalance of our international legal order" and has argued that it is therefore desirable to develop an understanding of WTO law as complementing and supporting other international legal orders that focus on nontrade concerns, as well as to strengthen these other legal orders. See Pascal Lamy, "The Place and Role of the WTO (WTO Law) in the International Legal Order" (Address before the European Society of International Law, Sorbonne, Paris, May 19, 2006, available online at http://www.wto.org/english/news_e/sppl_e/sppl26_e.htm). Our proposal appears not to be at odds with an emerging interpretation of WTO jurisprudence.

APPENDIX. EMPIRICAL EVIDENCE ON THE LIKELY EFFECTS OF IMPROVEMENTS IN LABOR STANDARDS

1. We use the phrase "labor-intensive products" to denote goods that could be the subject of export-oriented production in labor-abundant countries because their production in all countries involves the relatively intensive use of labor as compared to other factors of production. There are of course technical problems involved in presenting this definition, which following the custom we sidestep.

2. The question may quite reasonably be raised as to why a good is produced at all in developed countries if there are large cost disadvantages associated with production of the good in developed countries. One answer may be that the figures compared refer to variable costs. Developed-country production of labor-intensive goods, which would otherwise be uneconomical, may occur due to the existence of prior investments in plant and fixed capital. Developed-country production may also take place due to other advantages it may have, for instance, proximity to markets (making it possible, for instance, to meet "just-in-time" production demands). See Frederick H. Abernathy, John T. Dunlop, Janice H. Ham-

mond, and David Weil, *A Stitch in Time: Lean Retailing and the Transformation of Manufacturing* (New York: Oxford University Press, 1999), 269. Finally, there may be less developed-country production of the *same* goods that are produced in developing countries than is at first suggested by the generally available data, which covers highly aggregative categories of goods. Specific goods even within labor-intensive production (especially those requiring higher skills and specialized knowledge to produce) may still be most economical to produce in developed countries, whereas other goods may be wholly uneconomical to produce in developed countries at prevailing wage rates. Although the mass production of T-shirts is quite likely to take place in a developing country, the production of an expensive dress shirt in a small batch that follows the pattern of a fashion designer in a metropolitan capital is far less likely to be undertaken in a developing country.

3. UN Industrial Development Organization, *Industrial Statistics Database at the Three-Digit Level of ISIC (INDSTAT3)*, CD-Rom, rev. 2 (Vienna: UNIDO, 2004).

4. See the authors' Summary of Data on the Share of Direct Labor Costs in the Total Costs of Surveyed Manufacturing Enterprises (by industry and income level of country), available online at http://www.alternatefutures.org.

5. An Excel spreadsheet containing the arithmetical model is available online at http://www.alternatefutures.org.

6. Which assumptions are appropriate is far from obvious. There is some reason to believe that in developing countries, the stages of production antecedent to the final one may be more labor intensive, but also that they may employ workers at lower wages. The net impact on the share of labor costs in total costs is ambiguous.

7. Of course, in practice the good may not be economical to produce in the North. In that case, this ratio is best interpreted as that which *would* prevail if the good were to be produced in the North (at the prevailing factor prices, using cost-minimizing techniques).

8. This ratio is known for specific goods and countries. In 1997, the unit cost to retailers of a casual men's shirt produced in the United States was estimated at $7.58, and the unit cost to retailers of a casual men's shirt produced in Mexico was estimated at $4.45. Unit costs of producing clothing items in other developing countries have been deemed comparable to those in Mexico. See Abernathy et al., *Stitch in Time*, 223–242; see also Pollin, Burns, and Heintz, "Global Apparel Production." In 2001, the unit cost to retailers ("unit price realization") of a men's shirt was $4.21 in Bangladesh and $4.02 in China. See Gopal Joshi, "Overview of Competitiveness, Productivity, and Job Quality in the South Asian Garment Industry," in *Garment Industry in South Asia: Rags or Riches?*, ed. Gopal Joshi (New Delhi: ILO, 2002), 8. In 2003, the average export price for trousers, underwear, woven shirts, and knit shirts was $1.84 in China, $7.63 in the United States, and

$4.42 in other exporting countries. See National Council of Textile Organisations, "Analysis Shows Chinese Apparel Prices 76% Below U.S. Prices and 58% Below Rest of World's Prices" (Dec. 15, 2004, available online at http://www.ncto.org/newsroom/pr200414.asp). In December 2004, with the assistance of the UNITE union, the authors interviewed New York manufacturers of girls' specialty dresses engaged in global subcontracting of garment production. We were told that costs of production in Mexico are roughly one-third of those in the United States and costs of production in China and Sri Lanka are roughly one-fifth of those in the United States. The assumption of a ratio of unit costs of about two seems, in light of these reports, to be wholly reasonable.

9. See, e.g., George Wehrfritz and Alexandra Seno, "Succeeding at Sewing," *Newsweek*, Jan. 10, 2005 ("According to A. T. Kearney, labor for a shirt made in Bangladesh runs just $1.52, compared with $2.28 in China, but after factoring in materials and transportation, the total cost of the Chinese shirt is $11.15—almost a dollar cheaper"). Labor costs in the garment industry are lower in Bangladesh than in China but overall production costs are lower in China than in Bangladesh: Keith Bradsher, "Bangladesh Survives to Export Again: Competition Means Learning to Offer More Than Just Low Wages," *New York Times*, Dec. 14, 2004. The relative unimportance of labor costs as compared to other considerations that play a role in the decision to source garments in one developing country rather than another is forcefully emphasized in a recent guide for garment industry buyers. See David Birnbaum, *Birnbaum's Global Guide to Winning the Great Garment War* (Hong Kong: Third Horizon Press, 2000).

10. See Pollin, Burns, and Heintz, "Global Apparel Production," table 7.

11. Dehejia and Samy, "Trade and Labour Standards," 32.

12. Jai S. Mah, "Core Labour Standards and Export Performance in Developing Countries," *World Economy* 20, no. 6 (1997): 773.

13. Vivek H. Dehejia and Yiagadessen Samy, "Trade and Labour Standards—Theory, New Empirical Evidence, and Policy Implications," CESifo Working Paper no. 830 (Munich: CESifo, 2002), 15; see Dani Rodrik, "Labor Standards in International Trade," in *Emerging Agenda for Global Trade: High Stakes for Developing Countries*, eds. Robert Z. Lawrence, Dani Rodrik, and John Whalley, Policy Essay no. 20 (Washington D.C.: Overseas Development Council, 1996), 52–59.

14. Dehejia and Samy "Trade and Labour Standards," 21.

15. Ibid., 23.

16. Ibid., 31. Emphasis added.

17. See generally Ajit Singh and Ann Zammit, "Labor Standards and the 'Race to the Bottom': Rethinking Globalization and Workers' Rights from Developmental and Solidaristic Perspectives," *Oxford Review of Economic Policy* 20, no. 1 (2004).

18. See ibid., 94.

COMMENTARY BY KYLE BAGWELL: ECONOMIC THEORY, WTO RULES,
AND LINKAGE

1. I originally provided my comments to the authors in response to an earlier draft of their work, entitled "Just Linkage: International Trade and Labor Standards." I have updated those comments here slightly in order to improve conformity with the authors' revised draft. I thank the authors for the opportunity to comment on their work. I also thank Petros C. Mavroidis and Robert W. Staiger for many helpful discussions.

2. Kyle Bagwell and Robert W. Staiger, "The Simple Economics of Labor Standards and the GATT," in *Social Dimensions of U.S. Trade Policy*, eds. Alan V. Deardorff and Robert M. Stern (Ann Arbor: University of Michigan Press, 2000), 195–231; Kyle Bagwell and Robert W. Staiger, "Domestic Policies, National Sovereignty and International Economic Institutions," *Quarterly Journal of Economics* 116, no. 2 (2001): 519–562; Kyle Bagwell and Robert W. Staiger, "The WTO as a Mechanism for Securing Market Access Property Rights: Implications for Global Labor and Environmental Issues," *Journal of Economic Perspectives* 15, no. 3 (2001): 69–88; Kyle Bagwell and Robert W. Staiger, *The Economics of the World Trading System* (Cambridge, Mass.: MIT Press, 2002); and Kyle Bagwell, Petros C. Mavroidis, and Robert W. Staiger, "It's a Question of Market Access," *American Journal of International Law* 96, no. 1 (2002): 56–76.

3. Barry and Reddy are clearly sympathetic to this answer. For example, on page 55, they stress that "there is no guarantee that the aggregation function used by the government appropriately reflects the subjective preferences of the population it represents."

4. The discussion here follows Kyle Bagwell and Robert W. Staiger, "An Economic Theory of GATT," *American Economic Review* 89, no. 1 (1999): 215–248; and Bagwell and Staiger, *World Trading System*.

5. In a two-good setting, a country's "terms of trade" is the price of its export good divided by the price of its import good, with both prices evaluated on world markets.

6. I discuss nonpecuniary externalities such as humanitarian concerns below.

7. The theoretical foundation for this conclusion is located in Bagwell and Staiger, "Labor Standards"; and Bagwell and Staiger, "Domestic Policies."

8. See Gea M. Lee, "Trade Agreements with Domestic Policies as Disguised Protection," *Journal of International Economics* 71, no. 1 (2007): 241–259, for further development of such a within-country linkage.

9. Bagwell, Mavroidis, and Staiger, "Market Access."

10. Ibid.

11. As Bagwell, Mavroidis, and Staiger (ibid.) discuss, it is also possible to contemplate the use of an NVC by a country when a second country reduces its labor standards in an export industry and thereby decreases the former country's access to the market in a third (importing) country.

12. Ibid., 68.

13. By contrast, for the product at hand, the governments of other exporting countries enjoy a terms-of-trade gain. See also note 11 above.

14. For further discussion of problematic features of the WTO treatment of subsidies, see Kyle Bagwell and Robert W. Staiger, "Will International Rules on Subsidies Disrupt the World Trading System?" *American Economic Review* 96, no. 3 (2006): 877–895.

15. The Subsidies and Countervailing Measures (SCM) Agreement of the WTO provisionally permitted certain exceptions for subsidies that "promote adaptation of existing facilities to new environmental requirements imposed by law and/or regulations which result in greater constraints and financial burden on firms . . . " (footnote omitted, SCM Agreement 8.2 (c)). These exceptions are no longer in effect, however. One possibility would be to build from this language and modify the SCM Agreement to permit certain exceptions for subsidies that accompany new labor standards requirements.

16. As I discuss below, such programs are even more attractive when labor standards choices entail nonpecuniary externalities.

17. It is reasonable to expect that many governments may enjoy nonpecuniary benefits following such an increase in labor standards. The attendant possibility of free riding suggests that such negotiations may work best if conducted at a multilateral level.

18. Howard F. Chang, "Carrots, Sticks, and International Externalities," *International Review of Law and Economics* 17, no. 3 (1997): 309–324.

19. Bagwell, Mavroidis, and Staiger, "Market Access."

20. For further discussion, see Paola Conconi and Carlo Perroni, "Issue Linkage and Issue Tie-In in International Negotiations," *Journal of International Economics* 57, no. 2 (2002): 423–447; Josh Ederington, "International Coordination of Trade and Domestic Policies," *American Economic Review* 91, no. 5 (2001): 1580–1593; Nuno Limão, "Trade Policy, Cross-Border Externalities, and Lobbies: Do Linked Agreements Enforce More Cooperative Outcomes?" *Journal of International Economics* 67, no. 1 (2005): 175–199; and Giancarlo Spagnolo, "Issue Linkage, Credible Delegation, and Policy Cooperation," Discussion Paper no. 2778 (London: Centre for Economic Policy Research, 2001). I am pleased to see that the authors' revised draft now includes an extensive and thoughtful discussion of this literature.

21. Bagwell, Mavroidis, and Staiger, "Market Access."

COMMENTARY BY ROHINI HENSMAN:
FINE-TUNING THE LINKAGE PROPOSAL

1. Robert J. Flanagan, "Labor Standards and International Competitive Advantage," in *International Labor Standards: Globalization, Trade, and Public Policy*, eds. Robert J. Flanagan and William B. Gould IV (Palo Alto, Calif.: Stanford University Press, 2004), 26.

2. Frances William, "WTO Rejects Textile Quota Reprieve," *Business Standard*, April 30, 2004; and K. G. Narendranath, "US, EU Jittery as Deadline for Freeing of Textiles Nears," *Economic Times*, February 16, 2004.

3. Edward Alden, "US White-Collar Job Losses Touch a Raw Nerve," *Business Standard*, January 29, 2004.

4. Celia Mather, "Unions Face Up to Contract/Agency Labour," *International Union Rights* 12, no. 1 (2005): 22.

5. General Conference of the International Labour Organization, 90th sess., *Resolution Concerning Decent Work and the Informal Economy* (Geneva: International Labor Organization, 2002).

6. Philip Alston, "'Core Labour Standards' and the Transformation of the International Labour Rights Regime," *European Journal of International Law* 15, no. 3 (2004): 457–521.

7. General Conference of the International Labour Organization, 86th sess., *ILO Declaration on Fundamental Principles and Rights at Work* (Geneva: International Labor Organization, 1998).

8. Global Business Policy Council, *FDI Confidence Audit: India* (Alexandria, Va.: A. T. Kearney, 2001).

9. Kala Vijayraghavan, "If You Can't Beat Chinese Imports, Source from Them," *Economic Times*, November 30, 2000.

10. Kimberly Ann Elliott and Richard B. Freeman, *Can Labor Standards Improve Under Globalization?* (Washington D.C.: Institute for International Economics, 2003), 90–91.

11. Iftikhar Ahmed, "Getting Rid of Child Labour," *Economic and Political Weekly* 34, no. 27 (1999): 1820.

12. Neera Burra, "Rights Versus Needs: Is It in the 'Best Interest of the Child'?" in *Child Labour and the Right to Education in South Asia: Needs Versus Rights?*, eds. Naila Kabeer, Geetha Nambissan, and Ramya Subramanian (New Delhi: Sage Publications, 2003), 73–94.

13. Rohini Hensman, *Globalisation and the Changing Regime of Workers' Rights: Formal and Informal Workers in Bombay in the Context of a Globalising Economy* (Amsterdam: Academisch Proefschrift, Universiteit van Amsterdam, 2006), 127.

14. Ibid., 156.

15. Doug Miller, "Preparing for the Long Haul: Negotiating International Framework Agreements in the Global Textile, Garment, and Footwear Sector," *Global Social Policy* 4, no. 2 (2004): 215–239; Alice Kwan and Stephen Frost, "'Made in China': Rules and Regulations Versus Corporate Codes of Conduct in the Toy Sector," in *Corporate Responsibility and Labour Rights: Codes of Conduct in the Global Economy*, eds. Rhys Jenkins, Ruth Pearson, and Gill Seyfang (London: Earthscan, 2002), 124–134; Dara O'Rourke, "Monitoring the Monitors: A Critique of Corporate Third-Party Labour Monitoring," in Jenkins, Pearson, and Seyfang, eds., *Corporate Responsibility*, 196–208; and many others.

COMMENTARY BY ROBERT E. GOODIN: THE ETHICS OF POLITICAL LINKAGE

1. Daniel C. Thomas, *The Helsinki Effect: International Norms, Human Rights, and the Demise of Communism* (Princeton, N.J.: Princeton University Press, 2001).

2. *Nollan v. California Coastal Com.*, 483 S. Ct. 825 (1987).

3. I have offered my own views on this theory elsewhere. See Robert E. Goodin, "The Political Realism of Free Movement," in *Free Movement: Ethical Issues in the Transnational Migration of People and Money*, eds. Brian Barry and Robert E. Goodin (University Park, Penn.: Penn State University Press, 1992).

4. Lon Fuller, *The Morality of Law* (New Haven, Conn.: Yale University Press, 1964).

5. *Western Union Tel. Co. v. Kansas*, 216 S. Ct. 1 (1910).

6. Hugo Grotius, *The Law of War and Peace*, ed. F. W. Kelsey, trans. J. B. Scott (Dobbs Ferry, N.Y.: Oceana, 1964), III.iv.10; Thomas Hobbes, *Leviathan* (1651), chap. 20; and John Locke, *Second Treatise of Government*, paragraphs 23, 85.

7. Emmerich de Vattel, *The Law of Nations; Or, the Principles of Natural Law*, ed. Joseph Chitty, trans. Charles C. Fenwick (1863; Dobbs Ferry, N.Y.: Oceana, 1964), sec. 100; and Henry Sidgwick, *Elements of Politics* (London: Macmillan, 1891), 235. Cf. Richard A. Epstein, "Unconstitutional Conditions, State Power, and the Limits of Consent," *Harvard Law Review* 102, no. 1 (1988): 7.

8. In law as well as morals, this is best interpreted as "the purpose for which we think we should allow those powers to be exercised in the present": that, rather than as a reference to the original intentions of the original legislators who enacted the power-conferring statute in the first place.

9. I defend this way of interpreting the "impermissible conditions" doctrine, and offer many more examples along these lines, in Robert E. Goodin, "Support with Strings: Workfare as an 'Impermissible Condition,'" *Journal of Applied Philosophy* 21, no. 3 (2004): 297–308. Although not uncontentious, this interpretation has been explicitly endorsed by the U.S. Supreme Court (*Nollan*, 483 S. Ct. 825).

10. See Alan Story, "Property in International Law: Need Cuba Compensate U.S. Titleholders for Nationalizing Their Property?" *Journal of Political Philosophy* 6, no. 3 (1998): 306–333, for a powerfully put skeptical view.

11. Cuban Liberty and Democratic Solidarity (LIBERTAD) Act of 1996 (Helms-Burton Act), U.S. Code 22 (1996), §§ 6021 et seq., sec. 3.

REPLY TO COMMENTATORS

1. For simplicity, we focus here on partial equilibrium effects alone, i.e., on the direct impact of labor standards improvements and countervailing policies on producers in specific industries.

2. See comment by Kyle Bagwell in this volume.

3. See comment by Kyle Bagwell in this volume.

4. See comment by Kyle Bagwell in this volume.

5. See, however, Sanjay G. Reddy, "Pareto Improving International Labor Standards Agreements: A Simple Model," (working paper, Dept. of Economics, Barnard college, Columbia University, New York: 2007, available online at http://papers.ssrn.com/sol3/papers.cfm?abstract_id = 930113).

6. See comment by Kyle Bagwell in this volume.

7. Some theorists think of human rights as a type of legal rights, and thus as conferring legal rather than ethical claims on persons. It is certainly true that human rights are enshrined in legal instruments, and that honoring human rights claims will require the development of legal rights, some of which will be defined as human rights, but it does not follow from this that human rights are legal rights. Indeed, nearly all human rights advocates would affirm that human rights were often violated prior to the development of formal legal human rights instruments. For an extended discussion, see Amartya Sen, "Elements of a Theory of Human Rights," *Philosophy and Public Affairs* 32, no. 4 (2004): 315–356.

8. For an extended discussion of the idea of claims on institutions, see Thomas Pogge, "The International Significance of Human Rights," *The Journal of Ethics* 4, no. 1 (2000): 45–69.

9. There is thus an important sense in which even these standards would not be "categorical" in the sense affirmed by Hensman, even though we would agree that certain practices (e.g., employing slave labor) are categorically unacceptable, ethically speaking.

10. Some may deny, of course, that there are any reasons other than relative effectiveness relevant in assessing linkage or any other institutional arrangement, but this would seem to be a minority view.

11. A view of this type is presented by Rohini Hensman in her comment in this volume.

12. See Joel Feinberg, "The Expressive Function of Punishment," *Monist* 49 (1965): 397–423.

13. This example is from Goodin, but he does not himself endorse such an argument.

14. See Robert E. Goodin, "Support with Strings: Workfare as an 'Impermissible Condition,'" *Journal of Applied Philosophy* 21, no. 3 (2004): 301.

15. A different *historical* version of the germaneness test could be formulated, according to which an agent cannot permissibly use a power for any purposes other than those for which it actually *has been* conferred, whatever the best reasons for granting it that power may now be (or indeed may have been at the time at which it was conferred). As Goodin points out, the question of how legislative purposes should be conceived and interpreted is notoriously controversial, making the historical version of the germaneness test quite difficult to apply in practice. However, even if it were shown that linkage between trade and labor standards failed to meet this historical germaneness test, this would not provide a decisive reason against our proposal, since it is intended to convince others of the reasons that they *now* have to confer certain powers on countries and other agencies. One can endorse linkage even if it fails the historical germaneness test on the ground that the promotion of labor standards is germane to the purposes for which the power to shape trade policies ought to be accorded to governments.

16. We use "privilege" here in its Hohfeldian sense: A has a moral privilege to φ if and only if A has no moral duty not to φ.

17. Other relevant examples are discussed in Goodin, "Support with Strings," 297–308.

18. Michael Walzer, *Spheres of Justice: A Defense of Pluralism and Equality* (New York: Basic Books, 1983), 23. See also 100–103.

19. Such concerns are emphasized in Leif Wenar, "Property Rights and the Resource Curse," unpublished manuscript on file with authors.

20. For an extended argument concerning the instrumental importance of associational rights, see Risa L. Lieberwitz, "Linking Trade and Labor Standards: Prioritizing the Right of Association," *Cornell International Law Journal* 39, no. 3 (2006): 641–654.